Complete Cheerleading

Justin Carrier

Donna McKay

HUMAN
KINETICS

Library of Congress Cataloging-in-Publication Data

Carrier, Justin, 1977-
  Complete cheerleading / Justin Carrier, Donna McKay.
    p. cm.
  Includes index.
  ISBN 0-7360-5739-0 (soft cover)
  1. Cheerleading. I. McKay, Donna, 1955- II. Title.
  LB3635.C37 2006
  791.6'4--dc22

2005019556

ISBN: 0-7360-5739-0

The Web addresses cited in this text were current as of October 2005, unless otherwise noted.

Acquisitions Editor: Jana Hunter; **Developmental Editor:** Kase Johnstun; **Assistant Editor:** Cory Weber; **Copyeditor:** John Wentworth; **Proofreader:** PagePerfect Editorial Services; **Indexer:** Betty Frizzéll; **Graphic Designer:** Nancy Rasmus; **Graphic Artist:** Tara Welsch; **Photo Manager:** Dan Wendt; **Cover Designer:** Keith Blomberg; **Photographer (cover):** © RubberBall Productions; **Photographer (interior):** Page v, two photos on left © Human Kinetics, photo on right by Paul Hoge; all other photos by Jesse Scofield, unless otherwise noted; **Printer:** Versa Press

Human Kinetics books are available at special discounts for bulk purchase. Special editions or book excerpts can also be created to specification. For details, contact the Special Sales Manager at Human Kinetics.

Printed in the United States of America   10   9   8   7   6   5   4   3   2   1

Human Kinetics
Web site: www.HumanKinetics.com

United States: Human Kinetics
P.O. Box 5076
Champaign, IL 61825-5076
800-747-4457
e-mail: humank@hkusa.com

Canada: Human Kinetics
475 Devonshire Road Unit 100
Windsor, ON N8Y 2L5
800-465-7301 (in Canada only)
e-mail: orders@hkcanada.com

Europe: Human Kinetics
107 Bradford Road
Stanningley
Leeds LS28 6AT, United Kingdom
+44 (0) 113 255 5665
e-mail: hk@hkeurope.com

Australia: Human Kinetics
57A Price Avenue
Lower Mitcham, South Australia 5062
08 8277 1555
e-mail: liaw@hkaustralia.com

New Zealand: Human Kinetics
Division of Sports Distributors NZ Ltd.
P.O. Box 300 226 Albany
North Shore City
Auckland
0064 9 448 1207
e-mail: info@humankinetics.co.nz

Complete
Cheerleading

contents

acknowledgments

I sincerely appreciate, both professionally and personally, all of the important people that have made the execution of this project possible.

First of all, I would like to thank my mother for her unwavering love. Your personality and passion have shaped me into the very person I am today.

To my brothers for their constant support of any project I take on. Your respect and approval of what I do drives many of my decisions.

To Moki, my rock of a best friend. Your constancy in my life has given me the confidence I need to tackle some of life's biggest obstacles.

To Joe O'Toole—constant dedication and commitment to detail are attributes I learned from you. Your knowledge is invaluable.

To Heather Jones and The Colony High School Cheerleaders—thank you for your time and skills in creating the photos for this book.

To both the AACCA and USASF for their continued leadership in the cheerleading world. The instructional angles of these organizations are incredibly thorough, and they are leaders in cheerleading education.

To everyone at the NCA for giving me an avenue to succeed. The opportunities that this company has given me are endless, and I know how lucky I am to work in such a unique industry with such special people. Specifically, to Buffy, for molding me, helping me to produce my best, and paving the way for my professional future.

To Donna McKay for making this project twice as memorable and for keeping my timelines on track.

A special thanks to anyone involved in this unique activity called "cheerleading." Whether on the sideline or at a competition, cheerleading has provided more friendships, memories, and milestones than I will ever know what to do with.

—*Justin Carrier*

The writing of this book would not have been possible without the influence and impact of many special people in my life.

First and foremost, I'd like to thank my parents, Bob and Mary Zinkula, for all of their sacrifices, high expectations, and support. By your firm, yet loving guidance, you have instilled in me strong family values and a keen work ethic.

To my incredible husband, John, for his patience, encouragement, and love of adventure. You make me unbelievably happy!

To my sisters and brothers, Diane, Tom, Sandy, Ken, Jerry, Sharon, JoAnn, and Mark, for always being there when I've needed them, pushing me to do my best, and making sure to keep me humble.

To my nieces and nephews for bringing humor and light to my life, and especially to my goddaughters, Gracie, Courtney, and Erin.

To Jana Hunter and Kase Johnstun for their wonderful expertise, valuable advice, and generous assistance.

To Jen Kroening and Troy Rood for their generous technical advice.

To Justin Carrier, my co-author, a special thanks for his invaluable collaboration and enthusiasm.

Finally, to *all* of the friends, colleagues, teachers, and cheerleaders with whom I've had contact over the years. You have all been valuable and essential to my life, and you are not forgotten.

—*Donna McKay*

one

Voice Control

Photo by Paul Hoge

What excitement! The game is on, and the crowd is roaring! The band is blasting, the announcer is broadcasting, the referees' whistles are blowing, and the players are yelling to fire each other up. Amidst all this chaos, the cheerleaders are shouting, trying to lead a chant. Is it any wonder that cheerleaders have problems not only with voice projection but also with voice protection?

Cheerleaders are an important asset to any athletic program. They support the school's athletic teams, lead school spirit, and get fans involved in athletic competitions. To lead effectively and gain a crowd's support, cheerleaders need to convey their expectations in a way that fans will notice and understand. This can present a challenge for cheerleaders because it's often difficult to project over all of the noise present at a game.

The way in which cheerleaders shout while leading cheers and chants can make a big difference not only in getting the crowd to participate but also in protecting the cheerleaders' voices. When cheerleaders get excited, their voices get higher and they speak faster, which can make it difficult for fans to cheer along with the cheerleaders. Such cheering can also cause vocal strain and damage to the vocal cords. Once they've had proper instruction and understand how to cheer correctly and safely, cheerleaders can improve and protect their cheer voices. Maintaining vocal health is important because strong cheerleader voices are crucial for leading fans effectively.

Elements of Voice Control

The four main areas of voice control are articulation, expression, pitch (tone), and projection (volume). Understanding each of these elements can help cheerleaders protect their voices when cheering. Each of these elements is important for cheerleaders' vocal health and plays a key role in helping fans follow the cheerleaders' directions.

Articulation refers to the enunciation of words cheerleaders use when cheering. For fans to participate in cheers, they have to understand what the cheerleaders are saying, so it's essential for cheerleaders to emphasize and enunciate each word. Slowing down cheers and chants makes it easier to articulate them. Of course, cheerleaders don't want to slow down cheers and chants too much or they will sound boring, but fans can more easily understand and participate when cheers and chants aren't rushed. Cheerleaders also need to make sure they aren't barking their words because barking makes chants and cheers sound choppy. Articulating cheers and chants can help cheerleaders hit sharper motions because it's easier to hit motions on specific syllables or words rather than on words running together. For example, cheerleaders can lead the chant, "F-I-G-H-T, Fight Mustangs Fight," and hit a motion for each letter or word. Articulating the letters and words of this chant with vocal emphasis makes it much easier to physically hit motions with emphasis, too.

Expression is how cheerleaders say the words as they cheer. Cheerleaders express by using inflection and modulation. When using inflection, cheerleaders accent words to draw attention to them and build crowd enthusiasm. Cheerleaders should always stress syllables or words in each line or phrase of a cheer or chant. For example, when shouting, "Go! Fight! Win!" all three words are emphasized because each word is important for fan response. When shouting, "Go, Panthers, Go!" both "Go" words should be emphasized. The first word gains the crowd's attention, and the last word finishes the cheer with enthusiasm. It's more enthusiastic to begin and end strong than to drop the last word or syllable. Inflection helps the crowd know which words are important, especially when cheerleaders want fans to participate in an answer-back chant.

Another way to gain and keep a crowd's attention is to modulate, or vary, voices so words are shouted with interest. This means cheerleaders should have enthusiasm in their voices when shouting out cheers so they sound as if they really mean what they're saying. Cheerleaders often cheer in monotone voices, especially when they're familiar with the material. Monotone voices are boring and seldom elicit fan participation. However, cheerleaders must not modulate their voices too much or they end up singing the cheer. When using singsong voices, cheerleaders sound as if they're telling a story instead of leading a cheer. Using vocal expression when cheering attracts the crowd's attention and encourages fans to cheer along.

Pitch (or tone) is the quality of the sound of the voice (also called the timbre). Low-pitched voices are best, but cheerleaders should take care not to shout unnaturally low. Voices need to sound natural and unaffected. Cheerleaders who cheer with unusually high voices sound squeaky, strained, and annoying. Cheerleaders' voices tend to get higher as they get more excited, so they must work to maintain conscious control of the voice. Many times fans try to mimic how the cheerleaders are cheering. But usually fans' voices are not warmed up, so they're not able to (or wouldn't want to) shout with high, shrill voices. Fans might then become discouraged and not cheer at all. A high, shrill pitch can also strain a cheerleader's voice.

Projection (or volume) refers to the ability to send out the voice with intensity (loudness). Cheerleaders' voices need to be loud, and this can be achieved through deep breathing from the diaphragm. To project, cheerleaders draw in large amounts of air and then shout out their words at full volume. When projecting, it's best to use a low-pitched, normal speaking voice, which allows a louder projection and helps a voice to carry. An easy way to increase volume is to make sure *all* cheerleaders are projecting loudly. Cheerleaders can't gain crowd support if the fans can't hear the cheers.

Using megaphones helps project cheerleaders' voices.

Voice Preparation

Most cheerleaders are careful to warm up their muscles before cheering, but they often neglect to warm up their voices. Voices have more volume and project better when warmed up. A proper warm-up also helps voices last longer.

An important way to prepare the voice for cheering is to drink plenty of water, which keeps the vocal areas hydrated and allows the vocal cords to vibrate. When the vocal area remains moist, there's less strain, and vocal cords vibrate easier. It takes about 20 minutes for water to get to the membranes in the larynx, so cheerleaders should drink liquids before the start of a game as well as throughout the game. They shouldn't wait until they're thirsty but should remain hydrated at all times. Cheerleaders need to drink water before, during (at time-outs and halftime), and after cheering.

Cheerleaders also need to focus on how to use their voices correctly when they cheer. Many people think of cheering as screaming, which is harmful to the vocal cords. Rather than screaming or shrieking, cheerleaders should be thinking of projecting. Part of this is learning how to support their voices with their breathing. Cheer volume shouldn't come from the throat but from the air supporting the voice, which means using the diaphragm to increase volume. The louder cheerleaders cheer, the more they need to focus their sound into their faces. It sounds strange, but cheerleaders should feel their cheeks slightly vibrate when they raise the volume of their voices. For practice, ask cheerleaders to yell the word "go" from their diaphragms and to focus on feeling the vibration in their cheeks. Next, ask them to yell the word "go" from their throats and to note the lack of vibration. Cheerleaders should be able to hear how much fuller their voices sound when they use their diaphragms to cheer.

Suggestions for Protecting the Voice

Along with using the suggestions already discussed, cheerleaders can protect their voices in other ways. Here are some useful tips to follow:

1. Warm up and cool down the voice when cheering.

2. Inhale deeply to get lots of air, and then cheer while exhaling.

3. Use a low-pitched, natural voice.

4. Relax the neck and facial muscles to cheer naturally and allow more air to enter the lungs. To relax these muscles, fake a yawn that stretches out the neck and face.

5. Use signs to help fans see the words you want them to yell.

6. Use a megaphone to project your voice during cheers.

7. Avoid cheering when your voice is hoarse—you'll just strain your voice even more.

8. Don't cheer when you're sick because you're more likely to strain your vocal cords.

9. When speaking, use soft, light voices and avoid whispering to protect the voice.

10. Drink lots of water to keep vocal areas hydrated.

11. Avoid caffeinated beverages (they cause dehydration).

12. Avoid milk products if they coat the throat and produce phlegm. (Some people don't have problems with milk products and find the extra coating helpful.)

Concerns About the Voice

Cheerleaders need to be aware of signs of vocal abuse. If the voice feels tired after a day or night of cheering, it needs a rest. Unfortunately, the vocal cords don't have nerve endings, so we don't know when they're being abused. If cheerleaders continue to abuse their voices when their vocal cords are tired, they can do long-term damage to the voice. As stated earlier, the absolute best thing cheerleaders can do for their voices is to drink plenty of water.

Cheerleaders should be concerned if they experience continual hoarseness or soreness in the throat or if the voice is lost altogether. A scratchy or hoarse voice often means the vocal folds are swollen, which can be aggravated by a lack of sleep. In such a case, the cheerleader should get eight hours of sleep a night and avoid loud talking or shouting until the swelling decreases. If a cheerleader still has hoarseness or scratchiness for more than two weeks after resting the voice, a doctor should be consulted. Of course, if a lump is felt in the throat or neck, a doctor should be seen immediately.

Exercises for Breathing and Voice Warm-Up

Several breathing and warm-up exercises are useful when working on voice technique and control. These exercises are most valuable at the beginning of a season so that proper technique can be practiced from the start. It's hard to break bad vocal habits once they develop.

Proper vocal technique begins with breathing exercises. Along with water intake, proper breathing is one of the most critical factors in developing a healthy voice. Cheerleaders can develop voice stamina simply by learning how to breathe correctly. Cheerleaders should learn breathing exercises during practice so that they're ready to use them during games.

BREATHING EXERCISE 1

Purpose: To practice using the diaphragm to increase voice volume. Many people raise their chests or shoulders when they take big breaths, but this isn't correct. The only part of the body that should move is the abdomen. Once you have isolated your diaphragm, practice projecting words as you exhale.

Procedure

1. Lie with your back flat on the floor and knees bent.
2. Place one hand on your abdomen and one on your chest (figure 1.1).
3. Breathe in through your nose, pushing your abdomen out but keeping your chest still. Focus on your deep breathing.
4. When exhaling, pull your abdomen in, keeping your chest still.
5. Once you have isolated your diaphragm, practice projecting words commonly used in cheers.

Figure 1.1 Breathing exercise 1.

BREATHING EXERCISE 2

Purpose: To learn correct breathing.

Procedure

1. Lie with your back on the floor and arms at your sides.
2. Raise your tongue up slightly toward the back of your throat and breathe in through your mouth (it should sound loud). You should feel your lungs filling up, beginning in your lower back.

3. The abdomen should rise, but no other body part needs to move in order to breathe properly.
4. Exhale with a "shh" sound.
5. Repeat four times.

BREATHING EXERCISE 3

Purpose: To practice taking in deep breaths, as cheerleaders do when they're cheering.

Procedure

1. Pant in and out quickly through the nose (think of a dog sniffing something).
2. Your belly should be moving rapidly, but there should be no other movement. Put your hands on your belly to feel how much it's moving.

Points: If you feel light-headed, stop doing this exercise.

BREATHING EXERCISE 4

Purpose: To help isolate the diaphragm for correct breathing.

Procedure

This exercise needs to be done with low breathing, which means only the belly should move, not the chest or shoulders.

1. Quickly take in a full breath through the mouth.
2. Relax as you exhale.
3. Repeat several times.
4. Take in a slow, relaxed breath and exhale quickly (punch out breath).

Points: Cheerleaders need to allow time to get their voices warmed up. If they have been talking an average amount during the day, they probably don't need to spend much time warming up their voices. But they should not wake up from a nap and start cheering. Warm-up exercises can help prepare voices for cheering at games. Although it's easy to forget, it's also a good idea to do these same exercises after cheering to cool the voice down.

WARM-UP EXERCISE 1

One way to warm up a voice is simply to make a low noise, like a hum. Cheerleaders should focus their voices to get their foreheads and noses to vibrate.

Purpose: To warm up the voice in preparation for cheering.

Procedure

1. Keep lips closed but loose.
2. Hum at a pitch that's slightly higher than your normal speaking pitch.
3. Complete eight counts of humming at medium speed followed by eight counts of breathing.
4. Repeat the exercise four times.

WARM-UP EXERCISE 2

After completing the first warm-up exercise, cheerleaders can move on to this one that involves making two sounds at different pitches.

Purpose: To warm up the voice in preparation for cheering.

Procedure

1. Keep lips closed but loose.
2. Hum at a pitch that's lower than your speaking voice; then open to an "ah" on a pitch that's higher than your speaking voice.
3. Go back and forth between the two sounds four times.
4. Repeat the exercise, but this time sound "ah" on the low pitch and hum on the higher pitch.
5. Repeat the entire sequence.

WARM-UP EXERCISE 3

This warm-up exercise involves making lip trills that sound like a siren. Lip trills are made by buzzing the lips together.

Purpose: To warm up the voice in preparation for cheering.

Procedure

1. Begin by making a low trilling sound by buzzing lips together.
2. Start low and slowly go up high, higher, highest, and back down in one breath. The slower you trill up and down, the better.
3. Repeat this exercise four times.

WARM-UP EXERCISE 4

In this exercise, air is inhaled and exhaled quite quickly while emitting a sound. The focus is on the tone, which should be loud and clear without straining the throat. This is the same technique cheerleaders use when cheering.

Purpose: To warm up the voice in preparation for cheering.

Procedure

1. Take in a normal (low and deep) breath and punch out the word "hey." Push out the air quickly as if reacting to being punched in the belly.
2. Repeat several times.

Points: Cheerleaders might be able to gain more volume just by changing their cheering pitch. They can experiment to find a pitch in which they're maximizing the volume without straining the voice and throat. It really doesn't matter which exercises cheerleaders use to warm up as long as they increase volume and intensity gradually while hitting both the high and low ends of their vocal ranges.

Voice Drills

Voice drills focus on the correct way to articulate, express, and inflect cheer words to incite maximum crowd participation. Voices need to be synchronized so that a squad is cheering as one. Words are shouted, not barked or sung, by amplifying the voice. Cheerleaders need to know the key words to emphasize, such as the school name, colors, and mascot; each line should finish with a strong "up" inflection. When inflection is "down," crowds lose the important words, and the cheer ends anticlimactically.

It helps for cheerleaders to hear how to shout out cheers and chants correctly so they understand what to do. As with the breathing and warm-up exercises, a coach or more experienced cheerleader can demonstrate for newer or younger cheerleaders. When performing these drills, cheerleaders should practice tone of voice as well.

ARTICULATION AND EXPRESSION DRILL

Purpose: To practice enunciating words while cheering with articulation and expression.

Procedure

1. Sit in a circle facing each other.
2. Shout out the words to a chant or cheer. Everyone shouts each word.
3. Practice enunciating words and projecting naturally from the diaphragm.
4. A coach or experienced cheerleader should stop and restart the drill if words are not articulated or projected with expression.

Points: The cheer or chant can be broken into parts with cheerleaders practicing the first part, then starting over and adding the next part.

INFLECTION DRILL

Purpose: To practice placing the proper inflection on cheer or chant words to increase crowd involvement.

Procedure

1. Sit in a circle facing each other.
2. Focus on accenting the first and last or most important word of each line of a cheer or chant.
3. Cheering should be natural and from the diaphragm.
4. A coach or experienced cheerleader should stop and restart the drill if words are not inflected correctly.

Points: The cheer or chant can be broken into parts with cheerleaders practicing the first part, then starting over and adding on the next part.

Summary

The voice plays an important part in a cheerleader's role as crowd leader. By remembering the elements of voice control—articulation, expression, pitch, and projection—cheerleaders can lead fans more effectively. With proper breathing and vocal preparation, cheerleaders can cheer loudly and safely. So enjoy the excitement and noise of the game! Use the diaphragm, inhale deeply, and shout your cheers out! "We are the best! We are M-C-H-S!"

two

Motion Technique

© Human Kinetics

Who wouldn't want to find an easy way to make any squad look great? Motions are one of the easiest skills for cheerleaders to perfect, but they are often overlooked in favor of more difficult skills, such as stunts. Cheerleaders with strong motion technique (the components that make up each individual movement) can improve the look of any cheer, chant, dance, jump, or stunt.

Motions are used continually to lead the crowd and emphasize words for crowd response. When performing motions it's always important to execute with poise, smiles, and spirit. With confidence and strong motions, cheerleaders gain the respect of the fans, who are then more likely to respond. A bonus of sound motion technique is the "wow" factor it brings to any skill. Solid, clean motions are always impressive!

Motions are important not only when cheering in front of a crowd; they're also crucial during tryouts and competitions. Judges look for cheerleaders with sharp motions at the correct levels. Because motions are used in every area of cheerleading, it's important to spend time practicing them.

Teaching Elements of Motion Technique

Motion technique involves three main components: placement, pathway, and precision.

Placement defines the correct location of a motion. Each motion has a definite position or level. When hitting motions, arms should be tightened through the elbows and shoulders relaxed. Motions should hit slightly forward so that arms can be seen out of the corner of the eyes.

Pathway indicates the transition between motions—moving from one motion to the next. To look uniform, all cheerleaders need to hit motions in the same way. Because it's hard to get swinging motions together, the most direct route between motions is usually the most uniform. For example, to move from a right bow and arrow to a left bow and arrow, the most direct route is to move straight across the body rather than swinging the motion down, around, and back up.

Precision refers to the sharpness of motions. To look precise, cheerleaders need to "hit" their motions on a word or count. Hand positions also need to be precise. Wrists should remain straight and level. Thumbs should wrap over the knuckles. All fists should face the same direction.

Individual motions are actually made up of hand, arm, and body positions, although most people simply refer to the arm positions as motions. There are any number of motions that can be executed simply by varying hand, arm, and body positions. For example, fists can be held in buckets (hand position) in a T motion (arm position) with legs in a cheer stance (body position). Changing any one of these positions to a new hand, arm, or body position results in a new motion. Each motion still contains all the elements of motion technique, and it's the motion technique that makes these motions look sharp.

Hand Positions

Hand position refers to what the hand should look like during a cheerleading skill. All cheerleaders will have the same hand positions when hitting motions so that skills look uniform and clean. The most basic hand positions are bucket,

candlestick, blade, jazz hands, clap, and clasp (figures 2.1–2.6). Bucket, clap, and clasp are the most commonly used hand positions when cheerleaders are performing chants and cheers; these can be used interchangeably.

Figure 2.1   Bucket.

Figure 2.2   Candlestick.

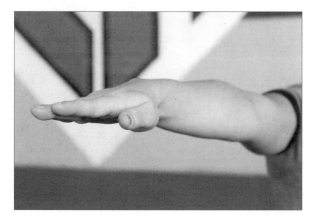

Figure 2.3   Blade.

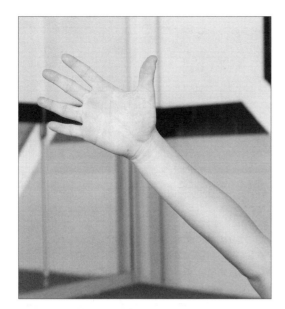

Figure 2.4 Jazz Hands.

Arm Positions

Arm positions add emphasis during cheers, chants, jumps, and dances. They are an important visual used to catch the eyes of the crowd. It's essential that arm positions are accurate and strong so that squads look identical and no one stands out. New motions can be developed by combining two arm positions, such as one arm in a high V and the other in a low V, which forms a diagonal. Any arm motion can be used at any time, but the most common motion used to gain a crowd response is the punch motion. The most basic arm positions are the high V, low V, T motion, half T, touchdown, low touchdown, bow and arrow, muscle man, overhead clasp, dagger, box, punch, L motion, diagonal, K motion, and checkmark (figures 2.7–2.22).

Figure 2.5 Clap.

Figure 2.7 High V.

Figure 2.6 Clasp.

Figure 2.8 Low V.

Figure 2.9 T Motion.

Figure 2.10 Half T.

Figure 2.11 Touchdown.

Figure 2.12 Low Touchdown.

Figure 2.13 Bow and Arrow.

Figure 2.14 Muscle Man.

Figure 2.15   Overhead Clasp.

Figure 2.16   Dagger.

Figure 2.17   Box.

Figure 2.18   Punch.

Figure 2.19   L Motion.

Figure 2.20   Diagonal.

Figure 2.21   K Motion.

Figure 2.22   Checkmark.

Figure 2.23   Beginning stance.

Figure 2.24   Cheer stance.

Body Positions

Motions can be performed in many body positions. Body positions are used to change the look of a cheer, chant, or dance. For example, when part of a squad shifts to a lower body position while the rest of a squad remains in a higher body position, levels are created. The most commonly used body positions are the beginning stance, cheer stance, lunge, squat, and kneel (figures 2.23–2.28). When leading chants at games, the cheer stance is the most common body position. The cheer stance, plus all other body positions, can be used interchangeably in cheers and dances.

Figure 2.25 Side lunge.

Figure 2.26 Front lunge.

Figure 2.27 Squat.

Figure 2.28 Kneel.

Fine-Tuning Motion Technique

All cheerleaders want to improve, and motion technique is one area that can be perfected with determination. Proper motion technique can be developed in several ways and worked on individually, with partners, or in groups. Improved motion technique can be achieved by practicing easier motions and progressing to more difficult ones, reviewing motions in a cheer or chant, checking motions in lines, practicing motions in front of a mirror, or reviewing videotaped motions. Drills aimed at improving motion technique are also helpful.

The most efficient way to work on motion technique is to perfect easier motions before moving onto more advanced ones. Begin working on basic motions such as high V, low V, touchdown, low touchdown, T, clasp, and clap. Use the elements of motion technique (placement, pathway, and precision) to improve these basic motions. Once the basic motions are mastered, move on to more intermediate motions such as punch, half T, overhead clasp, tabletop, and box. Again, perfect these motions before advancing to the difficult motions such as L, diagonal, bow and arrow, muscle man, K, and checkmark.

REVIEW MOTIONS IN A CHEER OR CHANT

Cheerleaders perform cheers or chants to a natural break (pause or end of word sequence). Motion technique is critiqued for this section. If necessary, the section is repeated until motions are improved. The cheer or chant is then continued to the next natural break. Motion technique in this section is critiqued and the section repeated until motions are improved enough to move on. When the cheer or chant has been critiqued for each section, the entire cheer or chant is performed from start to finish.

CHECK MOTIONS IN LINES

Cheerleaders form lines with three or four cheerleaders behind the first cheerleader in each line. If all cheerleaders have the same placement or levels, only the front cheerleader's motions should be seen. If there's a large discrepancy in cheerleaders' heights, the horizontal motions of some cheerleaders might be visible. This is okay as long as their motions are parallel with the other cheerleaders, which would indicate that their motions are level. Check motion levels from the front—high V, low V, diagonals, side lunge, L, muscle man, T, and so on. Adjust motion levels so that individual cheerleaders can't be seen from the front. Also check motion levels from the side, such as punch, touchdown, overhead clasp, and front lunge. Motion levels should line up; no one should have motions more forward or backward than the others.

PRACTICE MOTIONS IN FRONT OF A MIRROR

Cheerleaders can perfect their motion technique by practicing in front of mirrors (preferably) or windows (if mirrors aren't available). Cheerleaders can use cheers, chants, or motion technique drills to practice and improve motion technique. Sometimes it's easier for cheerleaders to actually see their own motions and make corrections rather than have someone else correct them. If mirrors aren't available, try using the front of a trophy case or another window. It can also help for cheerleaders to have pictures of correct motions to help them critique themselves at home.

VIDEOTAPE MOTIONS

Videotaping motions is another way in which cheerleaders can see their own motions—including placement, pathway, and precision—and critique them individually. Motions are easy to critique because the tape can be rewound and reviewed for different specifics each time. Cheerleaders can watch videotapes with the coach or on their own. It's usually helpful for the coach to point out areas requiring improvement before cheerleaders take videotapes home.

Critiquing Motions

When critiquing motions, coaches need to ensure that all cheerleaders are performing motions in the same way. This is important because motions should all look alike when being performed by a squad. It helps for a coach or cheerleading partner to correct motion technique as cheerleaders practice the motions. One of the best ways for cheerleaders to correct motions is to have them hit a motion, hold it while they get critiqued, then hit the motion again. Coaches or partners can also physically correct motions by actually straightening wrists, placing motions at the proper levels, and making other changes. Use the following checklist to assess motion technique.

Are motion levels accurate?

- Correct motions that are too high or too low (check from front).
- Correct motions that are too forward or backward (check from side). If hitting motions are backward, have cheerleaders practice with backs against a wall so the motions can't be hit behind the body.

Is the same pathway used from one motion to the next? (You should choose and demonstrate a pathway for all to follow.)

- Arms should usually travel the shortest route to the next motion.
- Arms can break from one motion to the next instead of going straight to the new motion. Example: low touchdown breaks to tabletop to touchdown (rather than low touchdown straight up to touchdown). This is fine as long as all cheerleaders are consistent.
- Swinging motions are hard to synchronize and can look sloppy.

Are motions hit on the correct word, beat, or count?

- All motions hit at the beginning of a word, beat, or count should be consistent.

- Watch for anticipated motions (moving before word, beat, or count).
- Watch for late motions (hitting at end or after word, beat, or count).

Are wrists level?

- Wrists should not be cocked (flexed) or turned.
- Tighten elbows instead of wrists. Excessive tension causes bent wrists.
- Physically straighten wrists.

Are fists and blades facing the correct direction?

- All fists are buckets or daggers or candlesticks.
- Palms of hands on blades should be facing the same direction (usually down).

Are fists formed correctly?

- Thumbs should be wrapped outside of fists and should not be sticking up.
- Fists should be closed tightly so that no one is able to see through them (that is, no doughnut holes).

Is posture correct?

- Shoulders should be back and relaxed.
- Head and chest should be high.
- Belly should be pulled in.

Are shoulders and hips square to the front?

- Upper body and hips should not be turned to the side (including lunges).

Are facial expressions spirited but natural?

- Practice smiles while performing motions.

Developing Creative Motion Sequences

Most squads hit motions in synchronization. A basic variation is hitting motions in opposition from each other. For example, the front line hits a high V as the back row hits a low V. Another basic variation is to use motion cotangents that move from front to back or side to side. This means that the front line hits a motion, then the second line hits it, and so on (or vice versa).

You can make motion sequences more creative by moving from inside to outside or outside to inside. To move inside to outside, a group is divided into five sections. The middle section hits a motion, then the two sections between the middle and outside sections hit the motion. Finally, the outside sections hit the motion (the sequence is reversed for moving outside to inside).

Photo by Paul Hoge

Strong motions help cheerleaders lead a crowd's response.

Another creative way to use motions for visual effects is through the use of ripples. Ripples occur when cheerleaders use motions to create a wave-like visual. Usually a cheerleader (or group) begins a motion, and the next cheerleader (or group) begins the same motion at the same time as the first one is ending. The ripple continues down the line until all individual cheerleaders (or groups) have hit the motion. Many times a squad will then reverse the ripple and return the other way.

Add-ons and level changes can also add creativity to motion technique. Add-ons occur when cheerleaders begin with one motion, then others join in as they hit the next motion, and still others join in on the next motion. Motions performed with cheerleaders at different levels are also visually pleasing. All cheerleaders might be standing, and then the front row might kneel for the next sequence.

Using motions in imaginative ways can draw attention to a squad's cheer, chant, or dance. It's also much more interesting for a crowd or audience to watch creative motion sequences with level changes.

Motion Drills

Cheerleaders and coaches can use drills to improve motion technique. Coaches should choose drills that best meet motion improvement needs and practice schedules. It's a good idea to vary the motion drills used at practice not only to focus on different areas of motion technique, but also to keep cheerleader interest high. The drills listed below offer a variety of options for both partner and group situations.

INDIVIDUAL MOTION DRILL

Purpose: To help cheerleaders focus on performing each motion properly. Use this drill early in the season to teach correct motion placement and precision.

Procedure

1. Cheerleaders are in a cheer stance with arms down at their sides.

2. Coach counts "5, 6, 7, 8, hit!"
3. Cheerleaders freeze that motion.
4. Coach or partner corrects motion, cheerleaders shake it out, and hit it again.
5. Move to the next motion.

Points: Don't move to the next motion until the first motion is perfected.

ADD-ON MOTION DRILL

Purpose: To help cheerleaders focus on performing each motion properly. Use this drill to clean up a cheer or chant by focusing on all components of motion technique.

Procedure

1. Cheerleaders are in a cheer stance with arms down at their sides.
2. Coach counts "5, 6, 7, 8, hit!"

3. Cheerleaders freeze that motion.

4. Coach or partner corrects motion, cheerleaders shake it out, and hit it again.

5. Once motion is perfected, hit it, and move to the next motion.

Points: Each time a motion is perfected, cheerleaders start at the beginning and hit all previous motions up to the new motion, which is then critiqued. Cheerleaders learn to hit motions in a sequence, and all cheerleaders are sharpening the motions in a cheer at the same time.

MOTION TECHNIQUE DRILL

Purpose: To practice the skill of hitting prearranged motions on each count in a group. This drill allows for a quick practice of all commonly used motions while allowing coaches to detect incorrect motion levels and timing.

Procedure

1. Cheerleaders are in a cheer stance with arms down at their sides.

2. Coach begins counting "5, 6, 7, 8, 1."

3. Cheerleaders hit first motion on 1, second motion on 2, and so on.

4. Go through all 16 motions to two 8 counts—don't stop between 8 counts.

5. After the first run through, stop each motion and critique.

6. Perform the drill again all the way through.

Points: Following is an example of a 16-count motion technique drill. Use this drill at the beginning of a season to improve motion technique. Return to the drill when motion technique needs to be practiced.

1. High V	9. Left diagonal
2. Low V	10. Right diagonal
3. Touchdown	11. Left L
4. Half T	12. Right L
5. T motion	13. Muscle man
6. Right punch	14. Clasp
7. Left K	15. Clap
8. Right K	16. Hands at sides

PARTNER REVIEW DRILL

Purpose: To give cheerleaders further practice at performing motions. Through the use of feedback, each cheerleader becomes aware of proper motion technique and corrections needed.

Procedure

1. Cheerleaders pair up and determine who will perform first and who will review. Performing cheerleaders are in a cheer stance.

2. Using the Motion Technique Drill, call out each motion (5, 6, 7, 8, high V).

3. The performing cheerleader hits the motion, and the reviewer gives feedback.

4. Repeat for all motions.

5. Partners switch positions and repeat the drill.

Points: The reviewer's feedback should be positive and constructive. A bonus to this drill is that the reviewing cheerleaders also learn by critiquing.

MOTIONS TO MUSIC DRILL

Purpose: To practice motions to music for variety.

Procedure

1. Pick an upbeat, popular song with a good beat.

2. Using the Motion Technique Drill described earlier, have the squad hit motions to the beats of music.

3. Cheerleaders can repeat the Motion Technique Drill sequence a set number of times or until the song is finished.

Points: For fun variations, add body positions, dance moves, level changes, and ripples. This is a good drill to help cheerleaders practice hitting motions during dances or pom routines, which are situations in which motions tend to be sloppy.

Summary

Using strategies from this chapter, cheerleaders can enhance their motion technique. Motion technique is one of the easiest skills to refine and, with practice, motions will improve. Remember that practice does not make perfect. Perfect practice makes perfect! Motions should be executed in practice the same way they will be performed—with perfection. Through continuous training of proper motion technique, hitting motions sharply and correctly becomes second nature, allowing cheerleaders to concentrate on other skills. Strong motion technique affects the overall impact of *every* cheerleading skill.

three

Jump Technique

Jump, everybody! Jump, everybody! Jump! How exciting it is to watch cheerleaders jump with enthusiasm at dramatic times during a game. Jumps draw attention not only to great plays but also to the cheerleaders themselves, so it's necessary to execute them with perfection. Of course, this holds true for games and at tryouts and competitions. To facilitate improvement, cheerleaders should perform jumps with proper technique and timing at every practice. Jumps are a skill that can always be improved. Attaining perfection is hard work, but a squad's high, hyperextended, synchronized jumps will be noticed and add to the thrill of the game and the effect of a routine.

Jump Conditioning

It takes stamina, strength, and flexibility to improve jumping skills—for that matter, stamina, strength, and flexibility improve *every* area of a cheerleading routine. Endurance training prevents fatigue during jumping, cheering, dancing, and performing. Strength training enhances stunts, jumps, motions, and dances. Flexibility training allows for hyperextended jumps and stretches during stunts, and it also reduces the risk of injury.

- Jumping with continuous energy requires stamina. Jump performance suffers and injuries occur when cheerleaders are tired. There are many ways to work on endurance training and jump technique at the same time. One approach is to perform consecutive tuck jumps to increase stamina and blood flow to the muscles. This allows muscles to warm up before practicing more difficult jumps. Executing a variety of jumps at every practice, completing at least 50 total jumps, is another strategy. Cheerleaders can execute each jump 5 to 10 times, perform stamina jumps, and do jumps in combinations (such as right-side hurdler, toe touch, and left-side hurdler). Stamina is also improved through strength training.

- Strength training, along with increasing stamina, is necessary for gaining height on jumps and for reducing the risk of injury. Strength training should focus on hip flexors, hamstrings, quadriceps, inner thighs, ankles, abdominals, and shoulders. Squats, lunges, and cleans are a few of the lifts that will increase strength for jumps. Strong abdominal muscles help lift the legs for higher jumps, so crunches are necessary, too. A knowledgeable coach or teacher can help cheerleaders set up an appropriate weight program, so take advantage of these experts.

- Flexibility is a key to injury prevention and increased jump flexibility. Stretching, as part of a proper warm-up, should be completed before jumping. It's necessary to completely stretch out the hamstrings, groin, quadriceps, and lower back muscles. Once a muscle is pulled it will continue to hamper a cheerleader until it has time to rest and heal, which is very hard to accommodate during a busy season. The best time to increase flexibility through multiple stretches is at the end of practice. Flexibility from stretching improves proper leg lift, increases leg height, and reduces the chance of injuries during jumps. For these reasons, enough time should be given for proper stretching before and after jumping at practices, games, and performances.

Elements of Jump Technique

It's important for coaches and cheerleaders to be familiar with the elements in each jump. Every jump should include an approach, lift, execution, and landing. These elements combine to form a jump from start to finish. Knowledge of these elements makes it easier to critique and improve jumps. By breaking down jumps and critiquing each part, cheerleaders can improve jumps both individually and collectively as a squad.

- The approach is the first stage of a jump. Stand with legs together and arms down at the sides of the body. To begin the jump, lift the arms into a high V (figure 3.1). As the knees bend, swing the arms down in front of the body, and push off through the balls of the feet by rolling through from heel to toe. This method is called the whip approach and is the most common approach used when jumping. For a squad to look uniform and maintain the same timing, all squad members need to use the same approach.

- The lift occurs after a cheerleader leaves the ground. Lifting from the abdominals helps get the torso higher. Pull the head, chest, and shoulders up and keep the back straight. Strong arm motions help lift the body by continuing around and hitting at shoulder level or above. When arms hit below shoulder level, maximum

Figure 3.1 Approach.

Figure 3.2 Lift.

lift cannot be attained. Arm motions during the lift should be clean and sharp, similar to normal motion technique. Timing of arms and legs is essential for obtaining maximum height during lift. For this jump the legs should be kept straight (figure 3.2).

• Execution is hitting a jump at its peak or maximum height. Keep the head and chest high. Whip the feet up to the hands for a higher jump. Rotate the hips up and back to help lift the legs higher. Using the abdominal muscles, the legs are extended. Arms should hit a sharp, strong high V or T motion. Toes are pointed (figure 3.3).

• A proper landing involves whipping legs and feet together to end with a small rebound. Bend knees slightly when landing to absorb the weight (knees should not bend past a 90-degree angle). Snap arms and legs down at the same time. Legs and feet are together (not apart), with the arms at the sides of the body. Feet land at the same time, softly and silently (like a cat) on the balls of the feet and then rolling to the heels. Jumps end with a clean finish (figure 3.4).

Figure 3.3 Execution.

Figure 3.4   Landing.

Teaching Jumps

Because there are jumps for all levels—beginning, intermediate, and advanced—*any* cheerleader can jump. It's best to begin with perfecting easier jumps (tuck and spread eagle) before moving on to harder jumps (front hurdler, pike, and around the world), which in turn should be perfected before tackling combination and stamina jumps. It helps cheerleaders to understand jump technique when they see jumps demonstrated correctly or at least see pictures of the jumps. It also helps to have cheerleaders sit on the floor to feel the correct leg form for the double hook jump (also known as the sit jump) and the side-hurdler jump before they actually jump into the air. Even if jumps are only at a beginning level, they are still essential to effective cheerleading.

Jumps are distinguished from one another during the execution phase. At the height of the jump, a skill is demonstrated. For example, the execution phase of a toe touch is different from that of a pike. However, every jump has the same fundamentals: head and chest up, back straight, toes pointed, legs lifted up to hands, and feet snapped together during landing.

When jumps are practiced in succession, there is usually a prep between jumps—that is, a small bounce between each jump. Jumps performed without preps are called stamina jumps. These are advanced jumps that require strength and endurance. Jump combinations are another way to work on jumps. These jumps are usually done in groups of two or three. For example, one combination could be a pike followed by a front hurdler. Another could be a right-side hurdler, a toe touch, and a left-side hurdler. Combination jumps add variety to cheers and routines while providing endurance training for cheerleaders. You can increase crowd interest by adding diversity at games and performances by using a variety of jumps.

When jumping, remember that form is always more important than height. It's better for jumps to be lower and look clean than to be higher and awkward. Strong motions with correct arm levels make jumps look clean. If cheerleaders don't have jump height, they can always make their arm motions sharp and point their toes for great looking jumps. The following jumps are in order from easiest to hardest (figures 3.5–3.13).

Figure 3.5   Tuck.

Figure 3.6 Spread Eagle.

Figure 3.7 Double Hook.

Figure 3.8 Herkie.

Figure 3.9 Toe Touch.

Figure 3.10   Side Hurdler.

Figure 3.11   Front Hurdler.

Figure 3.12   Pike

Figure 3.13   Double Nine.

Fine-Tuning Form

So, how can a cheerleader develop great jumps? Practice, practice, practice. At times, cheerleaders will become frustrated when they can't hit a jump just right, but they need to persevere.

Proper jump execution, like motion technique, can be developed in several ways and worked on individually, with partners, or in groups. Developing jumps begins by practicing easier jumps before progressing to more difficult ones. For example, doing easy tuck jumps is a good warm-up to attempting other jumps. To improve, cheerleaders should work on each jump with correct form 5 to 10 times at each practice session, executing a total of 40 to 50 jumps. Timing is a significant part of jump technique as well, especially when performing stamina and combination jump sequences. Timing can be improved with proper training. Practicing jumps by hitting each jump element on a specific count or syllable helps to improve timing and also enhances synchronization of squad jumps.

Jump Quality

The quality of a squad's jumps says a great deal about the squad's skill level as a whole. When critiquing jumps, a coach should be specific with suggestions without critiquing every element of every jump. It's easier to focus on one element at a time, such as keeping the head and chest up. The next practice focus can be on another element, such as keeping toes pointed. Cheerleaders need specific feedback on what to change and how to change it. Be aware of the following when fine-tuning jumps:

- Bend all the way through the leg and push or spring off from the toes.
- Don't take small prep jumps or extra bounces or shift weight up and down on the balls of the feet.
- Spring up and off the surface instead of pushing weight down into it.
- Keep wrists level, not bent.
- Get good height by lifting the torso, not just the legs.
- Lift legs and feet up to hands (not vice versa).
- Keep head and chest up and back straight.
- Sit into jumps.
- Keep toes pointed.
- Keep arms at shoulder level or higher.
- Keep legs straight (especially during execution and landing).
- Use clean arm motions (placement, pathway, and precision).
- Land on toes with feet and legs together.
- Include spirited facial expressions.

A good way to work on jumps is in circles or lines with others critiquing. As with motions, practicing in front of a mirror (or reviewing videotaped jumps) helps cheerleaders see what they need to improve on while practicing alone. Drills aimed at improving jump execution and timing can be useful. Jumps such as the herkie, double hook, side hurdler, front hurdler, and double nine need to be practiced so either leg can be used in each position. Cheerleaders need to be able to jump with either leg for uniformity when incorporating a variety of jumps into a cheer or routine. Finally, when practicing for jump improvement, remember to smile!

PRACTICE JUMPS IN PROGRESSION FROM EASIEST TO MOST DIFFICULT   To learn proper jumping skills, begin practicing the easiest jumps first. Cheerleaders will be able to concentrate on the jump elements—approach, lift, execution, and landing—when the jumps are easy to perform. Simple jumps will also help increase coordination and confidence. The easiest jumps are the spread eagle, double hook, and herkie. Toe touches are usually the most popular jump, so after learning the easy jumps, move to the toe touch. Once the elements of a jump have been mastered, you can add new jumps to each practice until all jumps have been covered.

JUMP CIRCLES   Cheerleaders stand in a circle facing each other. The first cheerleader does a jump; then, going around the circle, each cheerleader does the same jump. When everyone has finished, the first cheerleader does another jump, and this jump is then repeated around the circle. The coach or others in the circle critique each jump. Keep circles small so each cheerleader gets more time to practice.

JUMP LINES   An easy way to perfect jumps is to put three or four cheerleaders in each line. The cheerleader at the head of each line turns and critiques the next one in line. That cheerleader then completes five jumps or a jump combination while the first cheerleader critiques. The critiquing cheerleader goes to the end of the line, and the cheerleader who just jumped goes to the critiquing position. The next cheerleader in line performs the same five jumps or jump combination and gets critiqued, and so on until the first cheerleader is at the head of the line again. At this point she executes a new jump, and the process is repeated. To help perfect rhythm and timing, have cheerleaders at the front of each line perform jumps to eight counts. Coaches can also be walking in front of the lines helping to critique.

PRACTICE JUMPS IN FRONT OF A MIRROR   It's always beneficial for cheerleaders to see themselves jump. Other people can critique, but until cheerleaders see their own jumps, it can be hard for them to understand what needs to be changed. This exercise also helps perfect jump timing. If mirrors are not available, use big windows or trophy case windows.

PRACTICE WITH PARTNERS   One cheerleader performs a set of five jumps while a partner critiques. The partner does the same set of jumps while the first cheerleader critiques. The first cheerleader then completes the next set of five jumps. Partners alternate jumps and critiquing until all jumps are covered.

PRACTICE WITH THE ENTIRE SQUAD   In a cheer formation, the entire squad performs jumps together to eight-counts. Clasp on 1, 2. Hit high

V on 3, 4. Jump on 5, 6. End jump and clean on 7, 8. When the entire squad jumps together, it's more apparent which cheerleaders are off on timing, motions, and height. With many cheerleaders participating at once, performing jumps in a cheer formation makes it easier to check that they're using the same approach and have the same jump timing and identical arm levels. Arm levels are higher than leg levels, so it's more noticeable when levels are off. Misplaced arm motions by some squad members make squad jumps look off or out of sync, so it's necessary for the entire squad to hit sharp, accurate motions during jump execution.

CHEER INCORPORATION   When working on a jump in a cheer, practice the jump to the words of the cheer. This technique helps perfect timing of jumps in cheers right away so that jumps won't have to be changed later. It also helps cheerleaders attain uniform jump execution.

VIDEOTAPE JUMPS   Videotaping is a great way to critique jumps. Videotaping allows cheerleaders to see and critique their own jumps. They can see toes that aren't pointed, feet not landing together, and other performance flaws. A videotape can be replayed to evaluate detailed parts of each jump.

Jumps add excitement during games.

Correcting Common Jump Errors

When critiquing, use different phrases to promote jump improvement. Saying only, "Point your toes" might be too vague. Using more specific cues helps get desired results. Here are some common jump errors with ideas and prompts for correction:

Squad Timing Is Off

Prompts

Bend knees and push off balls of feet.

Land on count 6.

Hit high V on count 1.

Practice Ideas

All squad members use the same approach.

All squad members have same height on lift (jumps are different heights).

All squad members hit each element of jump on same count or syllable.

All squad members hit motions in their proper locations (placement).

Flexed Feet

Prompts

Push heels through top of the foot.

Push through feet and toes.

Point toes to floor.

Point ankles.

Extend ankles.

Point shoelaces to front.

Lead jump with toes.

Land on balls of feet.

Touch the ground with pointed toes on landing.

Practice Ideas

Hold objects in hands during jump to avoid reaching for toes.

Landing With Feet Apart or With Bent Knees

Prompts

Snap legs up *and* down.

Whip legs.

Squeeze legs together.

Squeeze gluteus to help pull legs together.

Pull down from ankles.

Lift, then hit jump (hitting jump too soon, hitting jump on lift).

Use arms to bring legs up and snap arms down with legs.

Practice Ideas

Increase jump height with jump drills.

Lower the jump to land with feet together and gradually increase jump height.

Leaning Over

Prompts

Keep chin up.

Keep back straight.

Keep head up.

Lift chest up.

Keep shoulders over hips.

Practice Ideas

Hold objects in hands during jump to avoid reaching for toes.

Imagine hooks holding shoulders up to avoid leaning over.

While standing, bend at the waist and lift leg; then stand straight and lift leg (cheerleaders see that legs can lift higher when back is straight).

Low Jumps

Prompts

Use arms to help lift (strong approach and lift).

Lift arms to T motion or higher.

Push balls of feet off ground during lift.

Jump off the ground as if it's a spring-board.

Pop through legs on approach.

Lift up through chest and torso.

Lift from the abdominals.

Sit into the jump (to rotate hips back).

Extend through the whole leg.

Lift legs and feet up to hands and arms.

Practice Ideas

Increase flexibility by stretching.

Strengthen leg muscles by using jump drills and lifting weights.

Jump Conditioning Drills

Jump drills are a great way to perfect jump technique by increasing cardiovascular conditioning, strength, flexibility, and form. This section comprises conditioning drills that will improve jump skills and technique. Many are also designed to aid in cardiovascular conditioning and to increase muscle strength and flexibility.

These drills can be performed as a group, with partners, or by using circuit training. For circuit training, the coach can choose four or five stations to meet a squad's jumping needs. At each station, hang a sign with the name of the drill to be performed. For example, station 1 could be Altitude Jumps. Station 2 might be Forearm Lifts. Place the signs at different places in the practice area and have cheerleaders rotate from station to station. Using stations is an organized way for a group of drills to be performed quickly.

During practice, decide which jump skills need to be improved and choose drills for those areas. Critiquing should occur during drills so that cheerleaders can be sure they're doing the drills correctly and get suggestions for improvement. Jump drills can be completed in groups or with partners. If cheerleaders are serious about improving their jump technique, these jump drills can be used year-round as part of individual workouts.

FOREARM LIFT

Purpose: To increase height and proper form for hyperextended pointed toe touches.

Procedure

1. A partner supports the cheerleader who is jumping by holding her arms in a right angle position.

2. As the cheerleader jumps, the partner

pushes against the jumper's arms to keep her shoulders up.

3. The jumper should concentrate on keeping her head and chest up (figure 3.14).

Points: This exercise is effective to use with advanced jumps.

Figure 3.14   Forearm Lift.

FRONT HURDLER KICKS

Purpose: To improve flexibility and leg speed.

Procedure

1. Begin with arms in a touchdown motion.

2. Kick one leg forward while keeping the supporting leg straight. Toes should be pointed during the kick.

3. Whip the kicks both up and down in a controlled manner. The force of the kick should be the same on the way up and down (figure 3.15).

4. Perform five times, and then switch to the other leg.

5. Work up to 10 kicks for each leg.

Points: Cheerleaders should kick legs as close to their face as possible while keeping correct form.

Figure 3.15   Front Hurdler Kicks.

HAND ON BACK

Purpose: To improve height on toe touches.

Procedure

1. A partner stands behind a cheerleader with a hand on her back.

2. Performing a toe-touch jump, the cheerleader jumps as high as possible.

3. The partner's hand on her back helps the cheerleader keep balance and not fall backward during the jump.

4. Perform 10 jumps.

Points: Cheerleaders will experience more confidence to jump high when they're not worried about falling.

HIP ROLL DRILL

Purpose: To improve hip roll for the toe touch.

Procedure

1. Partner stands behind cheerleader with hands on the cheerleader's hips.

2. Partner puts thumbs on cheerleader's lower back.

3. Partner's fingers wrap around hips to front.

4. Partner forces cheerleader's hips up during jumps by pushing in with thumbs (figure 3.16).

5. Perform 10 to 15 jumps.

Points: Partners should be ready to catch in case cheerleader falls back.

Figure 3.16   Hip Roll Drill.

LEG KICKS

Purpose: To improve leg speed on the jump.

Procedure

1. Begin with legs together and arms in a T motion.
2. Kick one leg to the side, behind arm, while keeping the supporting leg straight. The leg should be straight and the toes pointed during the kick.
3. Whip the kicks both up and down in a controlled manner. The force of the kick should be the same on the way up and down (figure 3.17).
4. Perform 10 times, and then switch legs.

Points: The purpose of this drill is to kick the leg as high as possible while keeping correct form. Keep abdominals tight, back straight, and chest up.

Figure 3.17 Leg Kicks.

ALTITUDE JUMPS

Purpose: To increase leg strength and jump height.

Procedure

1. Stand in front of a chair that's 24 or 36 inches tall.

2. Keeping legs and feet together, jump up onto the chair.
3. Immediately jump to the ground and then back up again (figure 3.18).
4. Perform 10 times. Repeat for two or three sets.
5. When this drill becomes too easy, try jumping up onto chairs without using the arms (keep them overhead).

Points: Bend knees slightly when landing on the ground to absorb impact. As an alternative, boxes of varying heights can be placed in a line. Jump up on the first box, down on the other side, up on the second box, and so on.

Figure 3.18 Altitude Jumps.

CALF BUSTERS

Purpose: To increase ankle strength.

Procedure

1. Stand with feet together and legs locked.
2. Lift heels off the ground with weight on balls of feet.
3. Bounce up and down without touching heels to ground or bending knees (figure 3.19).
4. Begin with 50 bounces and work up.

Points: Be sure to stretch out calf muscles before attempting this drill.

Figure 3.19   Calf Busters.

CALF RAISES

Purpose: To improve flexibility of ankles for jumps.

Procedure

1. Stand on a chair or bleachers with both heels hanging over the edge. Face partner and hold onto her hands for support.
2. Drop heels down as far as possible to stretch.
3. Lift up to the balls of the feet.
4. At the top, squeeze out an extra stretch up (figure 3.20).

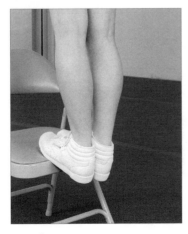

Figure 3.20   Calf Raises.

5. Perform in groups of 5 (up to 15 total), switching off with partner.

Points: Work up to 15 calf raises in a row.

CARDIO JUMP LINES

Purpose: To increase stamina.

Procedure

1. Cheerleaders are in jump lines.
2. While the first cheerleader in line does five jumps, the other cheerleaders in line run in place.
3. The first cheerleader runs to the end of the line when finished, and the second cheerleader jumps while others in line run.
4. The drill ends when every cheerleader in line has performed all jumps.

Points: This drill works all jumps while conditioning the squad.

GRAVITY STRETCHING

Purpose: To improve flexibility of the inner thighs for toe touches.

Procedure

1. Lie on back on the floor.
2. Lift legs up and apart so that gravity can pull legs toward floor.
3. Hold for a slow count of 20 (figure 3.21).
4. Repeat at least three times.

Points: Avoid bouncing, which can cause pulled muscles. Let gravity pull legs toward floor.

Figure 3.21   Gravity Stretching.

HIP FLEXOR STRETCH

Purpose: To increase abdominal and hip flexor strength.

Procedure

1. Sit on the floor in a straddle position.
2. Place hands on ground in front of the body between the knees.
3. Lift right leg one to two inches off the ground, hold for five seconds, and return leg to ground.
4. Lift left leg one to two inches off the ground and hold for five seconds.
5. Return to the right leg and repeat.
6. Alternate legs until each leg has held the lift for 15 seconds.
7. Don't let heels touch the ground.
8. Keep legs straight with knees locked; knees rotate slightly back during lifts.
9. Back remains straight and toes pointed (figure 3.22).
10. Repeat the drill lifting both legs at once for a total of 15 seconds.
11. Work up to 15 leg lifts in a row without alternating between lifts.

Points: To keep back straight, sit against a wall when lifting legs. If five seconds is too long, begin with three seconds and repeat the lift five times for each leg, followed by both legs.

Figure 3.22 Hip Flexor Stretch.

LEG THROWS

Purpose: To increase abdominal strength.

Procedure

1. One cheerleader lies on her back on the floor.
2. The cheerleader throwing legs stands near the head of the cheerleader on the floor (one foot on either side of her head).
3. The cheerleader on the floor grabs the thrower's ankles.
4. The cheerleader on the floor brings her legs up to the thrower.
5. The thrower flings legs toward floor as the cheerleader on the floor tightens her abdominal muscles to control legs (don't let legs hit the ground).
6. The cheerleader brings legs back up to starting position quickly but with control (figure 3.23).

Points: Legs can also be tossed side to side. Be sure cheerleader controls leg throw to prevent muscle strain.

Figure 3.23 Leg Throws.

LOWER BACK LIFT

Purpose: To increase flexibility and stamina.

Procedure

1. Jumper stands behind partner; partner bends at waist with hands on sides.
2. Jumper places hands on partner's lower back.
3. Jumps are executed in a series, one right after the other.

Points: This drill should be done after warming up and stretching.

PLYOMETRICS WITH BOXES

Purpose: To increase leg strength and jump height.

Procedure

1. Place boxes of varying heights (6 inches, 12 inches, 18 inches) about 8 inches apart.
2. With feet and knees together and facing a box, pull knees up to chest and jump over the first box.
3. Land on balls of feet and roll back to heels.
4. Jump over all boxes in the line (figure 3.24).
5. Perform this drill two to three times.

Figure 3.24 Plyometrics With Boxes.

Points: Be sure cheerleaders are jumping with correct form, with knees and feet together. Body stays in a straight line and doesn't turn sideways. To increase difficulty, have cheerleaders land on toes, pull knees up to chest quickly, and jump over the next box without rolling back to heels. Rest legs by doing this drill on alternate days.

PLYOMETRICS WITHOUT BOXES

Purpose: To increase leg strength and jump height.

Procedure

1. With hands in the air, jump as high as possible without bending legs.
2. Cushion landing by bending knees (no farther than a 90-degree angle).
3. Keep jumps slow and controlled by jumping to counts. Jump on the number (down one, down two, down three, down four, down five).
4. Perform 15 jumps in groups of five.
5. Repeat with right and left leg alternating five jumps on each leg up to 15 jumps total on each leg.
6. Work up to 15 jumps in a row for right, left, and both legs.

Points: Be sure cheerleaders jump with correct form, with knees and feet together. The body stays in a straight line and doesn't turn sideways. Cheerleaders should jump off the ground by contracting the calf muscles. Rest legs by doing this drill on alternate days.

RUNNER'S LUNGE

Purpose: To increase hip and leg flexibility.

Procedure

1. Step forward into a low lunge position.
2. Place both hands on the floor on either side of the forward foot.
3. Push chest toward floor and hold stretch (figure 3.25).
4. Repeat with the other leg and hip.

Figure 3.25   Runner's Lunge.

Points: The knee of the bent leg should not go past the ankle. It should stay directly above the ankle or slightly behind it.

SITTING TOE TOUCHES

Purpose: To strengthen hip flexors and abdominals to improve toe touches.

Procedure

1. Sit in a tuck position with knees to chest and feet off the ground.
2. Arms are in a tabletop position.
3. Hit arms and legs out in a toe touch (bring legs up to arms). Keep chest up.
4. Return to starting position.
5. Perform three toe touches in a row.
6. Repeat five times.
7. Work up to 15 continuous toe touches.

Points: Count out toe touches to keep them continuous. When strength increases perform 30 toe touches in a row for added improvement.

SPREAD EAGLE STAMINA BUILDERS

Purpose: To increase strength, build stamina, and perfect landing jumps with feet together.

Procedure

1. Perform spread eagle jumps simultaneously with hands at waist (no prep between jumps).
2. Keep hips tight and knees facing forward during jumps.

3. Snap legs up and down (figure 3.26).
4. Do at least 10 jumps and work up to 20 jumps.

Points: This drill helps cheerleaders use their inner thighs to improve jumps. The drill can also be used to help flyers stay tight in stunts.

Figure 3.26   Spread Eagle Stamina Builders.

STAMINA TUCKS

Purpose: To create stamina and gain strength.

Procedure

1. Perform five tucks without preps between each jump.
2. Do 3 sets, working up 10 tucks for each set.

Points: Focus on getting height while executing tucks with correct form.

STANDING WALL JUMPS

Purpose: To increase leg strength and jump height.

Procedure

1. Pick a spot on the wall and keep eyes fixed on the spot.

2. Stand in front of the spot with feet together.

3. While jumping, try to touch the spot with alternating hands.

4. Jump continuously and try to touch the spot on each jump (figure 3.27).

5. Perform 10 jumps 5 times.

Points: Keep legs together during jumps by tightening legs and glutes.

Figure 3.27 Standing Wall Jumps.

STRADDLE LEG LIFTS

Purpose: To increase abdominal and hip flexor strength and improve hyperextension of toe touch.

Procedure

1. Sit on the floor in a straddle position.

2. Place hands on ground in front of and close to body.

3. Lift legs up and down 10 times. Don't touch floor with legs during lifts.

4. Keep legs straight with knees locked.

5. Back stays straight and toes pointed.

6. Rotate hips back and under during lifts.

7. Legs should increase in height during lifts.

8. Perform for three sets of ten lifts.

Points: To prevent leaning back when lifting legs, sit with back against a wall. Knees rotate slightly back during lifts.

V-UPS

Purpose: To strengthen abdominal muscles.

Procedure

1. Lie with back flat on the floor.

2. Arms and legs are extended; toes are pointed.

3. Tighten abdominals and leg and back muscles and lift quickly to an abdominal crunch position with arms in a T motion, legs in a straddle position, and back straight.

4. Keep toes pointed throughout the lift.

5. Return to starting position

6. Repeat for three sets of 5 working up to three sets of 15.

Points: Lift motion should be quick but controlled. If V-Ups are too hard, begin with crunches. Lie on the floor with knees bent and arms crossed over chest. Use abdominal muscles to lift the head, neck, and shoulders off the ground (about three inches). Return to beginning position and repeat.

Summary

Jumps are a critical part of cheerleading and a good indication of a squad's ability. It takes work for jumps to develop, but with dedicated training, jumps will improve over time. Strength, flexibility, and endurance are crucial to jump development because these three components help improve jump technique and execution. By using drills and strategies from this chapter, cheerleaders will develop strong, eye-catching jumps to impress fans and judges.

four

Tumbling

If incorporated correctly and used at the right time, tumbling can be a real attention getter and crowd pleaser. Tumbling is very dynamic and a great way to shake a crowd up quickly at a game.

In the earlier days of cheerleading, few cheerleaders on a squad possessed any tumbling skills. Today's most athletic and competitive cheerleading teams have a full squad of tumblers and gymnasts. In this chapter we'll review basic tumbling skills and progressions. Note that learning these skills requires extensive individual instruction and leadership. No one should ever attempt gymnastics or tumbling skills armed only with instructions from a book.

Squads often have several tumblers— or, in some cases, the entire squad—performing the same tumbling skills, so it's important for each cheerleader to learn the same basic technique. This allows skills to be performed identically and simultaneously. When a team goes to choreograph a cheer or chant for a pep rally or performance, identical technique in tumbling strengthens the uniformity of the presentation.

Even for older teams, it's very possible for a squad to learn many new and exciting tumbling skills. Of course, such learning takes time and a consistent effort from everyone involved. The quality of what a team performs is far more important than the level of difficulty they attempt. One thing that makes a squad dynamic and exciting to watch is when skills are performed so precisely that they seem effortless. Any inconsistency in proper form or positioning detracts from the overall level of a team's performance.

In contrast to the principle many cheerleaders abide by, when tumbling it's not good enough for a cheerleader to land on her feet. Technique, progression, and safety are of utmost concern.

Hands-On Spotting for Tumbling

Basically, two types of spotting methods are employed when a squad is learning a new tumbling skill. One method is called "hands-on spotting," and the other method uses a spotting belt. Which method works best depends on the circumstances. For our purposes, we'll discuss only the hands-on method, which is the most commonly used and the one best suited for the skills we'll describe.

In the hands-on method, the spotter who is spotting a tumbling skill should stand somewhere between the takeoff point (the point from which the cheerleader leaves the ground) and the landing point. Although this is a great rule of thumb, a spotter also needs to be ready to travel in any direction to assist the tumbler. When learning new skills, tumblers can be inconsistent and unpredictable.

In the hands-on method, a coach can physically manipulate the situation and ensure a cheerleader's safe execution of a skill. The coach can manipulate the tumbler's body by putting pressure and force on the skills and assisting in a safe landing. As mentioned, although the hands-on method is the most common in spotting for tumbling, it requires extensive training and expertise to execute effectively. Even the most focused and attentive spotter needs to be alert and continue to practice these skills to remain effective.

Hands-on spotting is an evolving process because the level of participation from the spotter can vary significantly for each individual. Ideally, when a tumbler begins a new skill progression, the spotter will be very close to the tumbler. As the tumbler becomes more confident with the skill, the spotter can begin to back off and allow the tumbler to throw more and more of the skill without assistance. A tumbler's learning process can be tedious for the spotter because the movements of the tumbler are quite repetitious, but repetition is the key to skill development. As a tumbler's skill proficiency increases, spotters can

determine the parts of the skill that still require hands-on manipulation. At this point, a spotter's job becomes less participatory; he or she steps in only when assistance is necessary.

A Spotter's Dos and Don'ts in Tumbling

1. *Do* be certain that cheerleaders are ready and experienced enough to attempt a particular skill. Tumbling can be scary for newcomers; make sure they have the background necessary.

   Don't rush a cheerleader into trying something she isn't ready for just for the sake of adding that skill to a routine.

2. *Do* learn how to spot for even the easiest of skills. Like stunting, tumbling is progressive; techniques mastered at earlier levels will get spotters through some harder skills.

   Don't focus only on how to spot more difficult passes because these are the "only ones my cheerleaders will ever work on."

3. *Do* sit down with the cheerleader you are about to spot to go over technique, safety patterns, and to develop trust. Communication between tumbler and spotter is key to a positive working relationship in tumbling.

   Don't rush an athlete into trying a skill without first developing a solid working relationship.

4. *Do* be sure that both you and the tumbler are in proper position and that the environment is conducive to concentration. Cheerleaders should practice tumbling on a flat, matted surface.

   Don't set yourself up for failure by teaching in an unsafe environment. Make sure radios are turned down, telephones are not distracting, and that everyone is taking the session seriously.

5. *Do* appreciate and understand the full scope of the skill being spotted.

   Don't ignore critical aspects that can create an unsafe environment or hinder the cheerleader from improving safely.

6. *Do* make sure the margin of safety is always in the tumbler's favor when trying a new tumbling skill.

   Don't misgauge a tumbler's readiness. For example, use mats as long as necessary to make an athlete feel secure.

7. *Do* read each cheerleader individually to understand her strong and weak areas.

   Don't assume all cheerleaders learn the same way and at the same pace; don't ignore their uniqueness.

8. *Do* be prepared for the unexpected.

   Don't get into a spotting "rut" in which you begin to spot on autopilot and ignore individual circumstances.

9. *Do* make the cheerleader's head and neck your number one priority when spotting.

   Don't compromise your spotting technique just to keep yourself out of harm's way.

10. *Do* know and respect your limitations.

    Don't put an individual's health at risk because of your own ignorance or lack of ability.

When tumbling, cheerleaders have their own set of dos and don'ts. Tumbling is such an individual activity that each cheerleader must also follow a personal set of guidelines, implement the safety precautions for each attempted skill, and ultimately be responsible for his or her own well-being. A coach is responsible for training cheerleaders in tumbling, but the cheerleaders themselves must be accountable in regards to their own safety.

A Cheerleader's Dos and Don'ts in Tumbling

1. *Do* demonstrate the ability to do basic, lead-up skills with good form and without assistance before progressing to the next skill.

   Don't jump into a new tumbling pass with no background or experience. This could cause injury.

2. *Do* understand the mechanics and risks of each skill before you try it.

   Don't wait until after you've tried a skill for the first time to ask or be told how the skill is meant to be executed.

3. *Do* ask questions about tumbling technique when you have them.

   Don't be afraid of annoying your spotter. Be safe rather than sorry.

4. *Do* mentally picture a tumbling trick before you attempt it.

   Don't force yourself into a situation in which you're not comfortable.

5. *Do* have a qualified spotter with you when tumbling.

   Don't attempt new skills alone or without proper supervision.

6. *Do* consider each progression with caution.

   Don't underestimate the complexity of a skill when you see others are executing it with ease. People progress at different rates.

7. *Do* attempt newer and more difficult skills earlier in practice when your body is not tired. Fatigue can set in quickly while tumbling.

   Don't use new skills for conditioning.

8. *Do* communicate to your spotter or coach when you're not feeling well.

   Don't try to impress your coach by attempting a new trick when your body is not 100 percent.

9. *Do* warm up properly before beginning to tumble.

   Don't get impatient and practice in an unsafe manner.

10. *Do* give 100 percent when you decide to attempt a skill.

    Don't give up in the middle of a trick because you're nervous or have changed your mind. Stopping in the middle can be dangerous.

Standing Tumbling Skills Used in Cheerleading

Standing tumbling skills include any skill that starts from a standing position. When performing tumbling skills from a standing position, cheerleaders do not have the advantage of traveling momentum behind them as they do when performing running tumbling skills (see next section); therefore, these skills typically require a true mastery of technique. The following are a handful of standing tumbling skills that cheerleaders should strive to master.

Forward Roll

Tumbler: Squat down, place hands on the ground about shoulder-width apart, tuck head in (with chin down), and roll onto upper back (see figure). Rotate onto feet, continuing to a standing position.

Spotter: Place hands on the tumbler's waist and help guide her through each phase of the movement.

Backward Roll

Tumbler: Squat down with hands positioned next to the ears (palms up), tuck head in (with chin down), and roll backward while placing the weight of your body on your hands (not your head) as shown in the figure. Continue on through a squat to a standing position.

Spotter: Place hands on the tumbler's waist and help guide her through each phase of the movement.

As a prerequisite to the cartwheel, the cheerleader should have mastered a handstand. A cartwheel includes moving sideways through a straddled handstand.

Tumbler: With feet in a staggered position and hands placed sequentially in front of and in line with the body, drive the lead leg over the head (see figure). As you move through the straddled handstand position, the weight of your body shifts from the hands to the feet in the same sequential fashion (hand, hand, foot, foot).

Spotter: Place hands on the tumbler's waist and help lift her through each movement.

Front Handspring

Tumbler: Perform a skip-step hurdle forward into and through a handstand, pushing back with the lead leg while driving the back leg over the head and landing in an upright position.

Spotter: As the tumbler places her hands on the mat, place an arm on her waist and a hand on her closest arm (this controls rotation). Maintain contact with the tumbler until the skill is completed.

Back Handspring

Tumbler: From a standing position, move into a sitting position (back and chest upright, arms side by side, and knees directly over ankles—as if sitting in a chair). Jump backward into a handstand position. Follow with a quick downward snap of the legs to finish in a standing position.

Spotter: With a hand on the lower back of the tumbler, help support her as she jumps backward into a handstand position (see figure a). Place your other hand at the back of her legs to assist the handstand (see figure b) and the follow-through on the landing (see figure c).

a   b

c

Tumbler: Put two or more back handsprings together in a continuous movement. Don't neglect the important sitting position that is crucial to the execution of the back handspring.

Spotter: Move quickly with the tumbler, maintaining contact throughout the execution of the back handsprings. You might need to support more and more weight as each handspring becomes weaker than the one before. With one hand, keep constant contact with the tumbler's lower back to give lifting support. With the other hand, assist the legs as they come over the top for the snap-down. Be prepared to move quickly sideways and parallel to the movement of the tumbler.

Standing Back Tuck

The standing back tuck is an advanced tumbling pass that many advanced teams require their cheerleaders to master to make the squad.

Tumbler: From a standing position, jump up, throwing arms up and over the head and pulling knees to the arms. While pulling with the stomach and arms, visually locate the landing point (see figure). Open up toward the end of the jump to land on the feet with chest up.

Spotter: Place one hand at the back of the tumbler's waist to assist in the lift. Once the tumbler lifts up, use your other hand to pull her knees over and assist in the rotation. Spotting the landing is crucial because many tumblers won't know exactly when to open up and place their feet on the ground. Be ready for the tumbler to open up too early or not complete the rotation. Landing is usually spotted at the waist.

Running Tumbling Skills Used in Cheerleading

Running tumbling skills include any skill that is initiated from a running entrance. The forward momentum the cheerleader gains from running will aid in the successful execution of these tumbling skills. The following are a handful of examples of running tumbling skills that cheerleaders should strive to master.

Round-Off

Tumbler: A round-off is a forward-facing cartwheel. From a standing position, do a quarter-turn, transferring body weight to your hands (see figure), then bring your legs together in a handstand position. Follow by snapping down your legs and finishing with another quarter-turn so that you end up facing the opposite way from which you began.

Spotter: Place hands on the tumbler's waist to provide lifting assistance, especially during the handstand phase.

Round-Off Back Handspring

Tumbler: A round-off back handspring is executed by performing a round-off followed immediately by a back handspring. Follow the instructions for each of these skills as described previously. Don't attempt this combination of skills until you have mastered each skill on its own. You might find the back handspring is easier to execute with the aid of the momentum from the round-off.

Spotter: As the tumbler's feet snap down out of the round-off, place a hand on her back as she "sits" for the back handspring and lift against her until she lands safely on the floor.

Multiple Round-Off Back Handsprings

Tumbler: This is a combination of a round-off with at least two back handsprings connected in continuous movement. Follow the instructions for these skills as previously described. Don't attempt this skill until you have mastered the standing back handspring.

Spotter: As the tumbler's feet snap down out of the round-off, place a hand on her back and spot each succeeding back handspring, keeping the tumbler from sitting too closely to the ground. Be prepared for a pause or an unorthodox entry into the second back handspring when this skill is first attempted.

Round-Off Back Handspring Back Tuck

Tumbler: Before attempting this skill, warm up with a series of successful round-off back handspring rebounds to ensure that your back handspring has enough power to warrant finishing in a back tuck. When performing a round-off back handspring back tuck, as you rebound from your back handspring, lift with your shoulders, pulling your knees to your hands. Open up toward the end of the rotation to visually locate your landing, then land safely on your feet, with chest up.

Spotter: As the tumbler's feet snap down out of her back handspring, place a hand on her back and continue to lift, helping the rotation of the back tuck.

Spotting Tips: Spotters should be aware of two possibilities when spotting tumblers for the round-off back handspring back tuck: (1) The tumbler might rush the skill and not get enough height to safely execute her rotation. The spotter must then vigorously lift the tumbler's back to give her enough height; (2) The tumbler might be uncomfortable in the air and stop her rotation while upside down. The spotter must move quickly to complete the tumbler's rotation process for her.

Round-Off Back Handspring Layout

Tumbler: This skill is basically the round-off back handspring back tuck in a layout position (body extended). Don't attempt this skill until you can perform a round-off back handspring back tuck with power and ease. As you execute your rotation, extend your body, squeezing your abdominals and pointing your toes; bring your body up to and in line with your arms. Take care not to arch your body and throw your head back before you finish your rotation.

Spotter: Lift the tumbler's back during the initiation of the layout. As she begins to rotate, place your other hand on her leg to help complete the pass (see figure). Underrotation is very common when learning a layout (as with any new rotating skill), so pay special attention to the landing phase of the pass. Another common problem for tumblers early in the learning process is continuously piking down because they lack confidence in their ability to finish the rotation.

Round-Off Back Handspring Full Twist

Tumbler: Be sure you have mastered all the skills previously described before attempting a round-off back handspring full twist. This skill is the same as the round-off back handspring layout except that you add a full twist during your rotation. During the layout phase of the tumbling pass, reach over your shoulder while squeezing your hips and shoulders (see figure). Once you complete the twist (while flipping), open up to a landing. When practicing your twist, think of the hands on a clock—your full twist should start at 10 o'clock and finish at 2 o'clock.

Spotter: You need to be trained specifically for this skill. You must be able to hold a majority of the tumbler's weight as she first learns to perform a full twist. Assisting in the landing is crucial because most injuries during full twists occur at the landing.

Incorporating Tumbling into Cheerleading

Whether tumbling should be incorporated into a cheer or routine is usually up to the coach. Many cheerleading teams can't tumble at all and don't require their members to learn how. Although most competitive teams include tumbling, there has been a recent trend for teams to compete in divisions in which tumbling is not scored or mandated. Whatever the case, a team should add tumbling into a cheer, chant, or routine only if the skills are safe and complement the routine as a whole.

Considerations for Adding Tumbling to a Routine

1. As always, safety is the top priority. If some of your cheerleaders aren't ready for tumbling, don't push them too fast.

2. Whenever a new skill is added, it should enhance and not detract from the cheer or chant.

3. The technique used must be consistent, sharp, clean, and identical so that the rhythm is not altered.

4. The cheers being called out are important (they're the main reason the cheerleaders are there), so the voices of your cheerleaders must be loud, no matter what.

5. When setting formations, consider how much space the tumbling skills will require for safe transition to the next part of the routine.

Summary

Tumbling continues to be an exciting and challenging aspect of cheerleading, and both cheerleaders and coaches need to continue to make safety their number one priority. Practicing in a safe environment and performing with confidence will ultimately enhance the squad's experience.

Stunt Safety and Spotting

For both cheerleaders and fans, probably the most appealing and enjoyable part of cheerleading is stunting. Crowds in stadiums watch stunts in amazement; viewers at home observe with eyes glued to the television. It seems amazing that people can hold other people above their heads!

In preparing to stunt, cheerleaders should be in top physical shape. Mental strength is also important. Cheerleaders must believe they are capable of any stunting skill they attempt and maintain a positive attitude as they start their learning sessions.

Hours and hours of practice and execution go into creating a strong stunting team—but before cheerleaders start to execute new stunts, the issue of safety must be addressed. Stunting is the most rewarding aspect of cheerleading but is also the most dangerous and must be treated accordingly. Nearly every stunt requires spotters. Spotting is a basic skill that must be mastered before a squad attempts to stunt.

Preparing to Stunt

Before a team's first practice or game, many factors need to be addressed. Coaches and cheerleaders need to be educated on spotting and safety before a cheerleader ever leaves the ground. While preparation might seem elementary to an experienced squad, it is always a vital part of successful stunting. Preparing for any new stunt (from basic to advanced) goes hand-in-hand with spotting and safety.

Location

An important consideration before working on stunts is *where* the stunting is going to occur. When choosing a location, consider floor surface, ceiling height, surroundings, readiness for an emergency, and sufficient space for all team members.

FLOOR SURFACE   To prevent feet from sliding, make sure your floor surface is even and dry. If you're inside, the floor should be checked regularly for moisture. Keep rags handy for drying any spots that become damp. If you're outside, make sure the grass has no moisture and no divots. Always check grassy areas thoroughly for possible hazards. Hidden holes or bumps can be perilous. Take every measure to stunt on a surface that is dry and even.

When inside, choose a sturdy but giving surface, such as a foam mat. Learning brand new stunts on a hard gym floor is risky. You want a surface strong enough to hold cheerleaders as they maneuver through different stunts but soft enough to give a little during landings.

As cheerleaders become experienced and practiced at stunts and pyramids, floor surface becomes less of a priority. Still, whenever possible, choose a dry and even surface with at least a little give. *Never* stunt on concrete!

CEILING HEIGHT   Consider the height of the stunts your squad will be attempting. If your cheerleaders are beginners or intermediates, ceiling height is less of a consideration. However, when cheerleaders start throwing advanced or elite skills and basket tosses, ceiling height becomes a primary concern. If you

have a detailed list of stunts at the beginning of practice, double-check the list in light of ceiling restrictions before attempting stunts.

SURROUNDINGS   Practice in an area in which cheerleaders can focus without being distracted. Many cheerleading squads run practice next to the basketball team's practice. This environment simulates a true cheering environment, but practice needs to be a time for cheerleaders to concentrate on improving their skills. They are often performing skills not yet mastered, so they need a high level of focus and discipline. Aside from obvious distractions such as flying basketballs, the mere presence of significant peers might divert the attention of your cheerleaders.

READINESS FOR AN EMERGENCY   Hold your practices in an area easily identified by a physical address or landmark. Should an emergency occur, you want to be able to specify your location quickly. Always plan for the worst-case scenario. Choose a place from which you can give emergency personnel clear instructions on where and how to find you.

SUFFICIENT SPACE FOR ALL TEAM MEMBERS   Make sure to take into account the size of your team and the size of the area in which you're running your stunt practice. If floor space allows only one or two stunts to be practiced at a time, and you have five stunt groups, you better look for a different practice area. Stunting takes a lot of space. You also want to allow room between groups so that cheerleaders can focus on the task at hand without distractions.

Clothing

Tell your squad to avoid loose or baggy clothing when stunting. Often, when spotters spot a stunt, the clothing is the first part of the partner they can grab. Loose clothing might interfere with a spotter's ability to get a good grasp. Cheerleaders should also avoid wearing pants or anything on their legs. Typically, human skin allows for much better traction than warm-ups or other pants. Ankles should be clear so back spotters can get a good grip on the stunters' legs.

No jewelry should be worn when stunting. Most cheerleading injuries involve cheerleaders who wear jewelry while stunting. Jewelry is a risk not just for the cheerleader wearing it but for all squad members involved in the stunt. Most safety-governing bodies have issued rules forbidding jewelry during performances and competitions. Jewelry is a risk at any level. The no-jewelry rule cannot be emphasized enough as cheerleading strives to be considered with the same respect as other jewelry-intolerant sporting groups.

Cheerleaders should not wear sunglasses. When possible, choose a practice spot in which glare from the sun is not a factor. But even when practicing in a sunny area, cheerleaders should avoid wearing sunglasses. An unexpected movement might knock the glasses an inch in any direction, compromising visibility.

Shoes must be worn at all times. Shoes create much better traction on the ground than do socks or bare feet. As a base, it's difficult to stabilize a stunt in bare feet, causing a safety hazard. As a partner, a shoe allows for a much flatter surface (the bottom of the shoe) for bases to brace when building. Although performing without shoes can make cheerleaders feel lighter and more nimble, the hazards of stunting in bare feet outweigh the benefits.

Accountability

The first principle of safety is that every member of a cheerleading squad must be accountable for the safety of each other member. Most accidents occur because teammates assume that other teammates are taking responsibility. This is especially true when teams are trying new skills.

How to Spot

A few general guidelines on spotting can help ensure a safe practice environment. Cheerleaders over the years have learned to adhere to an important rule of thumb—if you can reach it, touch it! If you can touch it, grab it! A spotter's number one goal is to bring the partner down to the ground as slowly and safely as possible. Top consideration is given to the head, neck,

Even when you assign six spotters to surround a stunt group, safety isn't always ensured. Sometimes all six spotters assume the other five will make the save if need be. Every member must be on his or her toes, ready to help a partner when necessary. Reinforce proper attention to safety. If a breakdown in accountability occurs, you might have all members of the squad do 50 push-ups, 200 sit-ups, or 2 laps around the stadium track. These consequences shouldn't be looked at as penalties but as positive motivators to keep safety a priority.

Attitude

As in every other area of life, a positive attitude is important in cheerleading. If a cheerleader thinks, "we're *never* going to hit this stunt," chances are that cheerleader will be correct. Be realistic, yes, but always remain positive. Stunting requires a great deal of mental preparation that should not be undermined by a negative attitude or lack of motivation.

Warm-Up

The warm-up is discussed in chapter 15 as a necessary component of all practices. In any situation, mild to moderate cardiorespiratory exercise, such as jogging in place or taking a lap around the gym, before stretching allows for muscles to warm up, which creates a more functional stretch. When warming up specifically for stunts, you need to have particular muscle groups stretched and ready to go. Cheerleaders use their entire body in most stunts, but the quadriceps, triceps, and shoulder muscles should be particularly well rested and then well stretched before stunting.

and spinal cord. The law of gravity has taught us that the further something falls, the more momentum it picks up. A spotter's responsibility is to slow a falling partner down early, before it becomes impossible to control her landing. Thus, good spotting sometimes requires reaching for a falling partner with the fingertips, ensuring that contact is made well before she hits the ground. That said, a spotter should usually try to pull the partner into their body to help stop the fall. Many times, arms and legs are not strong enough to stop a fall, but using a body for support can make a big difference in softening the landing.

Clear verbal communication is necessary when spotting stunts, especially new stunts. Simple, predefined terms such as "down," "back," and "clap" can help bases, partners, and spotters communicate at a moment's notice. "Down" typically means bring the stunt down quickly before it falls over. "Back" usually means the stunt is falling backward, so spotters should quickly assist on the backside of the stunt. "Clap" is used to remind the partner to clap her arms above her head to avoid taking out the bases as she comes down.

Many teams still use the sea-of-hands formation. A sea of hands is when all members of the squad not actively involved in a stunt put their hands up into the air in order to spot the partner. As mentioned earlier, a problem in this approach arises when spotters assume the spotter standing next to them will take ownership of the spotting in case something happens. Because many people are involved in the sea of hands formation, it's more likely for spotters to become lax and assume someone else will cover for them. Spotters must commit their total attention to the safety of the partners. If one person relaxes, an accident might occur.

Four-Corner Spotting

Four-corner spotting creates accountability among spotters and is more reliable than the less effective sea of hands. Using the four corners, you assign each of four spotters a corner of a stunt. As each spotter stands in attention, he or she is assigned responsibility for two sides and one corner of the stunt. In effect, each corner has one designated spotter, and each side has two spotters (figure 5.1). This formation gives spotters a definite responsibility and ownership of their territory. A sea of hands provides more warm bodies, but the four-corner formation provides more focus. Four-corner spotting is typically used

Figure 5.1   Four-corner spotting.

in the earlier stages of learning new stunts and stressed less as members of the squad become familiar and comfortable with their roles.

Fine-Tuning Form

It is paramount that cheerleaders and coaches be physically and mentally prepared for the task of spotting a stunt. Being alert and aware that mistakes can occur during a stunt keeps spotters cautious and responsible when working with their teammates. Spotting the same stunt numerous times during practice is important because the repetition enables cheerleaders to quickly recognize potential problems before it's too late.

Safety-Governing Bodies

When attempting new skills, athletes and coaches should be familiar with the safety associations that govern their area, league, district, or organization. The NFHS (National Federation of State High Schools) offers a comprehensive set of guidelines. Most cheerleading camp and competition companies (including the National Cheerleaders Association) have rules for the sideline and competitive atmosphere that reflect the NFHS's position on safety.

The AACCA (American Association of Cheerleading Coaches and Advisors) is an organization that was formed in 1987 as a response to the increasing concern about cheerleading safety standards and the lack of coaches' education. Its purpose is the development of safety standards for cheerleading and for educating coaches through conferences, the AACCA Cheerleading Safety Manual, and safety credentialing. The AACCA partners with the NFHS, the NCAA, and the USASF (United States All Star Federation) to promote cheerleading safety in secondary schools, colleges, and the all-star community. They can be found on-line at www.aacca.org.

The USASF governs the all-star cheerleading world. They provide educational classes, a credentialing system for coaches and athletes, and competition standards that strive to protect the future of the all-star community. For up-to-date information on USASF safety standards, visit their website at www.usasf.net.

Spotting Drills

To make safe catches quickly, cheerleaders must be able to react *immediately*. The decision of a spotter on which hand to put out or for a partner to know where to place her arms while falling might be the difference in whether a fall is safe or dangerous. The drills that follow should be run for stunt groups to practice their roles in a falling situation.

BEAR HUG DRILL

Purpose: To train bases to be active spotters and reach for the partner rather than waiting to catch her.

Procedure

1. A partner stands on a chair or box.
2. Two spotters position in front of the chair.
3. The partner practices falling while the spotters practice bear-hugging the partner safely to the ground (figure 5.2).

Points: Spotters tend to get lazy during this exercise. A coach or supervisor should discuss the importance of consistency in this drill to persuade the squad of its importance.

Figure 5.2 Bear Hug Drill.

PARTNER FALLING DRILLS

Purpose: To train partners to keep arms locked above the head during a fall.

Procedure

1. A partner stands on a chair or box.

2. Four spotters surround the chair or box.

3. The partner practices falling in different directions. When falling to the sides or front, she locks out her arms and clasps her hands above her head. When falling backward, she puts her arms in a T formation to give the back spotters a place to scoop her up. The partner remains in lockout or T position until both feet are safely on the ground and bases and spotters have stepped away from the stunt (figure 5.3).

Points: Cheerleaders should not confuse the T formation in this drill with hitting a T motion in a cradle (see cradle stunt in chapter 6). This is a common misconception. Also, as happens in the Bear Hug Drill, participants in this drill tend to get lazy. A coach or supervisor needs to reinforce the principles of safety during this drill.

Figure 5.3   Partner Falling Drills.

Summary

With the correct tools and knowledge, getting prepared to stunt can be a fun team-building activity. Teamwork is an essential part of cheerleading and a critical factor in creating a safe environment for stunting. Straying from the principles expressed in this chapter creates the opportunity for danger in an activity that should be inspiring and entertaining. Spotting and safety must always come first in any cheer program.

six

Basic Stunt Technique

© RubberBall Productions

Many times cheerleaders want to rush through basic stunts to get to flashier, more advanced stunts. But coaches and cheerleaders need to realize that basic stunts are the building blocks for all future stunts. If cheerleaders don't learn correct safety and stunting techniques at the basic level, they will likely have problems perfecting more difficult stunts at the intermediate and advanced levels.

Typically, squads most likely to use basic stunts are new or inexperienced. That said, however, every year squads of all ability levels should begin their season with step-up drills and checking off stunts in progression up to their level. If this is done, coaches can be assured that veteran cheerleaders are physically able and mentally prepared to perform advanced stunts safely. By reviewing fundamentals, cheerleaders are reminded of basic techniques required in all stunting.

It's also extremely important for cheerleaders to remain aware of safety issues when stunting. Cheerleaders need to be reminded that they can only stunt with proper supervision and on safe surfaces. Stunts should be performed perfectly 10 out of 10 times before cheerleaders progress to the next stunt in the progression. When performing stunts correctly, cheerleaders create a memory of movement. That is, they reach a point at which they can automatically stunt properly without needing to focus on basics such as "step, lock, tighten" and other fundamentals.

Stunt Positions and Responsibilities

A stunt group is comprised of three basic positions: a base, a partner (or flyer), and a spotter. Usually, two (or more) cheerleaders form a base, but some stunts are performed with a single base. Sometimes stunts have a back spotter as well as a front spotter for additional stability. Each person in a stunt needs to know his or her responsibilities plus proper building technique for the stunt to be performed safely and correctly. With every person in a stunt doing his or her part, stunts are built more safely, and trust is formed among teammates. Bases and spotters must not be afraid to catch, and partners should not be afraid of heights.

BASE   The base consists of the cheerleaders (or single cheerleader in single-based stunts) who are holding up the partner. The base's responsibilities include supporting the partner by providing a solid foundation of support. Bases are the primary catchers during stunt dismounts. Bases are always in contact with the performing surface and must be ready to adjust their grip or stance as well as be ready to move to keep a stunt solid. Bases should lock legs and arms at the same time during a lift. Precise timing among the base cheerleaders and the partner makes stunts cleaner, more impressive to watch, and easier to perform. Stunting is also easier if the two bases in a stunt are similar in height and strength. Here are some guidelines for proper base technique:

- Chest and head are up; back is straight.
- Legs are stationary and set shoulder-width apart in a double-lunge position. Feet are angled slightly outward.
- Arms are close to the body with hands placed in a cupped position by the bellybutton during preparation and lift.
- Legs are used during lift (sponge down and up).
- Bases are close together throughout stunt (no farther apart than partner's shoulders).
- Eyes are on partner.
- Arms are locked when extended.
- Knees are bent to cushion dismount.
- The catch is high.

PARTNER   The partner is the cheerleader on top of a stunt supported by the base. The partner's responsibility is to climb lightly. For a stunt to be its strongest, the partner needs to stay tight throughout the stunt, including the dismount. Correct timing and weight transfer during stunts allow bases and partners to hit stunts effectively. To lift herself into the stunt, the partner needs to push off the base's shoulders. Stunts are easier if the partner is strong, with good body awareness and control. Here are some guidelines for proper partner technique:

- Arms are used during stunt building.
- Step, lock, and tighten legs.
- Feet are close together when climbing into a stunt (to avoid pushing bases apart).
- Pull up and stay tight; raise up through the shoulders. Keep hips up.
- Shoulders, hips, knees, and ankles are in line.
- Eyes look up.

SPOTTER   A spotter's main responsibility is to protect the head, neck, and spine of the partner. Spotters are in contact with the performing surface and assist the bases and partners during stunts by providing extra stability and support. Many times, the spotter controls the timing of the stunt by counting during stunt building and dismounting. Spotters must be attentive, keeping hands and arms extended up toward the partner to help prevent injuries. A spotter's torso cannot be under the stunt or else the partner might fall right over the spotter's head. A spotter's hands cannot grab the sole of the partner or the hands of the bases under the partner's foot.

Not all stunts need spotters—they are only required for stunts in which the bases' arms extend above the head (exceptions to this rule are listed for individual stunts)—but spotters should help with most stunts until the stunts are mastered. Stunts are easier to perform if spotters are tall and quick thinking. Here are some guidelines for proper spotter technique:

- Maintain constant attention on the stunt.
- Stay alert.

- Keep eyes on partner.
- Position to catch the stunt if it falls.
- Help control the stunt.
- Keep hands on partner, if possible.
- Keep partner's feet close together.

Stunt Communication

Timing is important for synchronization of movement among bases, partners, and spotters. When correct timing is used, the strength of all stunt participants is coordinated to more easily build the stunt, whereas incorrect timing is a major cause of stunt mishaps. Squads should use the same counts when building and dismounting stunts. Most squads use the counts "one, two, down, up" to keep consistency in timing, which leads to safer stunting. Only one person (usually the back spotter) should be talking during stunts and communicating the counts for the stunt group.

Before a partner leaves the ground, all involved cheerleaders need to know what to do to build a stunt and how to dismount from it. It helps for stunt groups to count out the stunt on the ground with the partner putting hands instead of feet in the bases' hands during this count practice. Stunts are only put up in the air once everyone is clear on counts and responsibilities. Once a stunt is built, the spotter controls the dismount—unless the partner feels the need to come down. In this case, the partner calls "down," and the bases quickly dismount the partner together. This kind of dismount is used only in situations in which the partner feels the stunt is not safe. Ideally, the spotter would be aware of the situation and call the stunt "down" before the partner.

Perfection Before Progression

One of the most common phrases in cheerleading is "perfection before progression," which refers to the necessity of getting a skill down right before moving on to the next skill. After watching the stunts of other teams at summer camp, games, or competitions, cheerleaders are often anxious to try the stunts themselves. For safety reasons it's very important for cheerleaders to progress naturally to those skills rather than jumping into them.

There is a natural progression in building stunts that should be followed closely. Most skills in cheerleading, basic through advanced, are based on fundamentals. When cheerleaders attempt skills that go beyond these fundamentals, they don't have a fair shot to master the skills.

Perfection before progression ensures that a team has mastered the necessary technique before moving on. For example, a squad should never try a straight-up extension before they have mastered the extension prep. The techniques in an extension prep are almost identical to those involved in an extension. If a team decides to go straight to the extension, they *might* be able to muscle the stunt to the correct position. But failing to master the skills necessary to begin with will make future progression much more difficult. The rule for progressing is that cheerleaders should be able to perform a skill 10 out of 10 times before moving on to the next skill.

Basic Grips

Five kinds of grip are common in basic stunts: thigh stand, handshake, four fingers forward, extension prep, and shoulder stand. Which grip to use depends on the position of the partner and base(s) in the stunts. Stunt and dismount examples are given after a summary of each type of grip.

THIGH STAND   The inside arm of the base is wrapped around the partner's leg above the knee with the hand in a fist. The outside hand of the base grabs under the partner's toe (figure 6.1). This grip is used for all variations of thigh stands.

HANDSHAKE   The base and partner join hands as if they're shaking hands (figure 6.2). This grip is used for shoulder sits, shoulder stands, chairs, suspended splits, and some dismounts.

Figure 6.1   Thigh stand.

Figure 6.2   Handshake.

FOUR FINGERS FORWARD   The outside hand of the base is in a handshake position with the partner. The base uses his or her other arm to support the partner's upper arm, with fingers facing forward and thumb facing back, to help control the landing (figure 6.3). This grip is used for suspended splits and step-off dismounts.

EXTENSION PREP   The base supports the partner's foot at chest level by holding the partner's foot at the heel and toe. This grip is used for double-based thigh stand hitches and stunts at the extension prep level.

SHOULDER STAND   As the partner stands on the base's shoulders, the base grabs the partner's calves right below the knee. The base pulls down and slightly inward on the partner's calves to stabilize the stunt. The base's elbows stay forward to keep the stunt tight (figure 6.4). This grip is used for shoulder stands.

Figure 6.3   Four fingers forward.

Figure 6.4   Shoulder stand.

Dismounts

Dismounts have progressions just as stunts do. The easiest and safest dismount for beginners is the step off, in which the bases and spotter maintain continual contact with the partner until she is safely on the ground. The shove-wrap dismount is the next step. A partner learns to control her body while dismounting from a stunt. The bases and spotters assist the partner at the waist. The highest-level dismount for beginning squads is the cradle. In a cradle, the bases sponge, toss the partner into the air, and catch her in their arms. Cheerleaders can use bleachers or sturdy chairs to practice dismounts and catches before building an actual stunt. The partner stands on the bleacher or chair and dismounts to bases using proper technique.

Once dismounts are mastered from bleachers or chairs, cheerleaders can start practicing their dismounts from actual stunts.

As we mentioned earlier, the most common counts for dismounts are "one, two, down, up," so that everyone knows when the stunt is coming down and timing stays consistent. Cheerleaders sponge on the "down" count for both building and dismounting stunts. The "up" count is used by stunt groups to push up the partner into a stunt or dismount the partner from a stunt. Some squads choose to use "one, two, shove, wrap" for the shove-wrap dismount. Again, the main point is that everyone knows the counts and their responsibilities before the stunt is built.

Bases: Bases hold the partner's hands in a four-fingers-forward grip to control the landing (see figure).

Partner: Partner holds the outside hands of the bases while stepping off the stunt. Partner should bend knees slightly to absorb weight on landing.

Spotter: Spotter assists the dismount by holding partner at the waist.

Common Problems	Corrections
Partner falls forward or to the side.	Bases need to keep the partner steady and push up under her arms. Spotter lifts slightly at the partner's waist. The partner helps dismount by absorbing her own weight when stepping down.

Bases: Bases use arms to assist the partner's landing by catching her at the waist. On "shove," bases sponge slightly, push the partner's feet together, and let them drop. On "wrap," bases step in toward the partner and wrap their arms around and above her waist. Bases should place their heads behind the partner's back to avoid being hit by her elbows. To reduce the impact of landing, the bases lift up as the partner reaches the ground.

Partner: Partner's hands are straight overhead in a touchdown position; hands can be clasped together. She must be sure to keep her arms up and tight so she doesn't strike the bases with her arms. The partner stays tight with legs together and her back straight (see figure).

Spotter: Spotter uses arms to assist the partner's landing by catching her at the waist. The spotter calls the dismount by saying "one, two, shove, wrap." The spotter can help the bases push the partner's feet together as well as slow down and control the speed of the dismount by pushing slightly upward.

Common Problems	Corrections
Partner falls forward.	The base needs to catch high and wrap arms above the partner's waist to control the momentum of her upper body. The spotter needs to slow down the dismount.
The partner falls to one side.	The partner needs to hold her body tight and keep her chest up. She should bend her knees to absorb her weight and help catch herself when reaching the floor or ground.

Cradle

Bases: In a cradle, bases and spotter catch the partner. The bases drive up through the legs and arms to push partner into the air. The bases keep hands and arms extended up in the air by following through when tossing the partner up. This allows the bases to catch the partner high and absorb her weight through the legs during the catch. The bases catch the partner with one hand under her legs and the other hand behind her upper back and then hugs her into the cradle. Bases should keep their backs straight and stay close together during the cradle.

Partner: The partner stays tight during the sponge (don't bend legs), whips arms up into a touchdown position, and rides the toss. She lifts her legs and pikes her lower body during the descent into the cradle, keeping her head and chest up. She keeps her feet and legs together with feet at eye level and toes pointed. Arms are in a T position (see figure). During the cradle, she wraps her arms around the bases' shoulders.

Spotter: The spotter also catches high and scoops under the partner's arms to protect her head, neck, and spine.

Common Problems	Corrections
The partner is kneed in the back.	The bases and spotter are not keeping hands and arms extended following the toss. They need to begin catching above their head and shoulder level. The bases and spotter must slow the partner down and catch her at chest level.
The partner's head and back are caught low to the ground.	The partner needs to catch around the bases' shoulders. The base cheerleaders need to stay close together and not back out. The bases and spotter need to keep hands up and catch high.
Bases' heads are hitting each other.	The two bases are leaning over and catching with their backs and not their legs, which might mean they are too far apart from one another. Bases might be catching the partner too low. They need to keep their hands and arms up during the toss and begin slowing the partner down to catch her at chest level.
The partner's feet are hitting the ground.	The partner needs to tighten her abdominal muscles and hold her feet up in a pike position. Bases need to make sure they each have one arm catching the partner's legs under the upper calves.

Basic Stunt Technique

The basic stunts described in this chapter are listed in progression from easiest to more difficult. Cheerleaders and coaches shouldn't skip a stunt to progress at a faster rate. Each stunt has techniques that are used in subsequent stunts, so mastering these techniques makes the more difficult stunts easier to perform. Many of these stunts don't require a spotter, but spotters should be used until stunts are mastered. It can help to spread experienced cheerleaders throughout the stunt groups to help the less experienced cheerleaders progress more quickly. As we mentioned earlier, you should always use the same counts when building and dismounting from stunts. By learning and mastering correct techniques for basic stunting, cheerleaders will be able to master higher-level stunts more quickly and efficiently.

Step-Up

Bases: No bases in this drill.

Partner: Facing a bleacher or chair, step up with one foot, lock out leg, place other foot on bleacher or chair, lock, and tighten as arms hit a high V position. Partners may also step, lock, and tighten to pull other leg into a liberty or stretch position (see figure). Step down and repeat.

Spotter: Support partner at waist for balance as she is stepping up and down.

Points: You can use bleachers, steps, or benches for this drill.

Common Problem	Correction
Partner is not locking out legs.	Stress "step, lock, tighten" technique; partner should squeeze gluteus, lock knees, and pull up through her upper body.

Bases: Step into a deep lunge position (in either direction) to form a pocket at hip joint, with hips and shoulders facing forward. Thigh on bent leg is parallel to floor, knee doesn't go past toes, and back leg is straight and locked. On set counts, wrap arm and hand around knee (thigh-stand grip) as partner steps into the pocket. Pull down and in toward body to stabilize the stunt. When partner lifts other leg, grab leg as close to the ankle as possible and lift to an L position with arm extended. For dismount, guide partner's leg to front and assist at waist as partner steps or hops to floor.

Partner: Stand behind base. On set counts, push on base's shoulders while stepping into pocket with outside leg (right leg in right pocket or left leg in left pocket, depending on the lunge direction). Lock leg and tighten. Weight should be toward the center of the base to keep balanced. When balanced, lift other leg behind base's head to an L position (parallel to ground) for base to grab. Toe is pointed and arms are in a high V position (see figure). For dismount, bring leg in L position around to front and step off base to floor.

Spotter: *Not required but may be used until stunt is mastered.* Assist partner at waist during climb and support during stunt. Spotter may move to the side and grab partner's waist during dismount.

Points: This is a good stunt to help partners practice the step, lock, and tighten technique. Base needs to keep head and chest up during stunt. Both spotter and base should keep hips and shoulders facing forward.

Common Problems	Corrections
The partner falls forward.	The partner needs to lock out her climbing leg to control hips and balance. Her hips should be in line with her shoulders, knee, and ankle. The base needs to keep partner's climbing leg steady and support tightly above the knee. The spotter assists the partner by lifting straight up.
Bases have improper lunge and no pocket.	Bases need to keep head and chest up and legs apart in a deep lunge. Thigh of bent leg should be parallel to the ground to form a pocket.

Single-Based Thigh Stand Variations

Bases: Step into a deep lunge position, in either direction, as in the L stand. On set counts, grip under the partner's toe with outside hand as partner steps into the pocket. Wrap around knee with inside arm (thigh-stand grip). For dismount, assist at waist as partner steps or hops to the floor.

Partner: On set counts, step into base's pocket with inside leg, lock leg, and tighten. Weight should be toward the center of the base to keep balanced. Lift other leg into either a lib or heel stretch position. For the liberty variation, arms are in a high V (see figure a). For the heel stretch variation, one hand holds leg and other arm is in a high V (see figure b). For dismount, step off base to floor.

Spotter: *Not required but may be used until stunt is mastered.* Assist partner at waist during climb and support during stunt.

Points: Both base and spotter need to keep hips and shoulders facing forward. Use counts to build stunt.

a

b

Bases: Step into a deep lunge position to form a pocket at hip joint with hips and shoulders facing forward. Thigh on bent leg is parallel to the ground, knee doesn't go past toes, and back leg is straight and locked. On set counts, grip under partner's toe with outside hand and wrap above knee with inside arm (thigh-stand grip) as partner steps into the pocket. For dismount, use outside hand to grab partner's hand in a handshake grip, sponge, and assist as partner jumps to the floor. Inside hand supports partner under the arm with four-fingers-forward grip.

Partner: On set counts, step or hop into one base's pocket and lock. Step other foot into second base's pocket and lock. Tighten and raise arms to a high V position (see figure). For dismount, grab outside hands of bases, bend knees slightly, and jump off.

Spotter: *Not required but may be used until stunt is mastered.* Hold partner's waist and assist straight up into stunt, stabilize during stunt, and assist to floor on dismount.

Points: The feet of the bases' bent legs should overlap next to each other.

(continued)

Common Problems	Corrections
The partner is climbing with bent legs.	She needs to lock out her climbing leg before stepping up with her second leg.
The partner is looking down or dropping her shoulders.	Instruct her to focus eyes up on a spot while climbing and pull up through her chest. She should step, lock, and tighten to pull up her chest, shoulders, and head.
The partner falls forward.	She needs to lock out her climbing leg to control her hips and push her weight straight down onto the bases. Her hips should be in line over her ankles and knees. Bases need to support partner's legs above her knees and hold other hand under partner's toes. Spotter assists partner by lifting straight up.
Bases have improper lunge and no pocket.	Bases need to keep heads and chests up and legs apart in a deep lunge. Thighs of bent legs should be parallel to the ground to form pockets.

Double-Based Thigh Stand Hitch Variation

Bases: First base is in a deep lunge position to form a pocket at hip joint with hips and shoulders facing forward. Thigh on bent leg is parallel to the ground, knee doesn't go past toe, and back leg is straight and locked. On set counts, grip under partner's toe with outside hand and wrap above knee with inside arm (thigh-stand grip) as partner steps into pocket. Second base stands facing first base; bases are shoulder-width apart. When partner steps into pocket and locks leg, second base grabs partner's other foot, raises foot to chin (extension prep level), and pivots out to face the front. Hands are holding partner's toe and foot in an extension prep grip (see figure). Dismount is similar to the dismount for the single-based L stand. First base should use outside hand to grab partner's hand in a handshake grip, sponge, and assist as she jumps to floor. Inside hand supports partner under arm with four-fingers-forward grip. Second base should sponge, release partner's foot, and be ready to assist at partner's waist.

Partner: On set counts, step into first base's pocket, lock, and tighten. Lift second leg and bend knee so leg is in a hitch position as second base grabs foot. Arms hit a high V position. For dismount, grab outside hand of first base, bend knees slightly, and jump off.

Spotter: *Not required but may be used until stunt is mastered.* Hold partner's waist and assist straight up into stunt, stabilize during stunt, and assist to ground on dismount.

Shoulder Sit

Bases: Step into a deep lunge position (in either direction) to form a pocket at hip joint with hips and shoulders facing forward. Thigh on bent leg is parallel to the ground, knee doesn't go past toes, and back leg is straight and locked. On set counts, wrap arm around knee (thigh-stand grip) as partner steps into the pocket. Stand as partner brings other leg around shoulders to sit. Wrap hands around partner's thighs and pull down. For dismount, reach under partner's thighs to grab one hand at a time in a handshake grip. Sponge, shrug shoulders, and straighten arms as legs extend to pop partner off back. Maintain contact until partner is safely on floor or mat.

Partner: Stand behind base. On set counts, push on base's shoulders while stepping into pocket with outside leg (use leg as a walk up into the stunt). Lock leg and tighten. When balanced, swing other leg around base's shoulders, slip leg up to shoulder, and sit down. Feet are wrapped behind base's back (see figure). For dismount, hold hands with base in a handshake grip between legs, straighten legs, lock arms, and stay tight. Slip off the back of the stunt while maintaining hand-to-hand contact with base.

Spotter: *Not required but may be used until stunt is mastered.* Hold onto partner's waist and assist her to base's shoulders. For dismount, support partner at waist and guide to the floor or mat.

Points: Building a shoulder sit from an L-stand stunt is easy. The leg forming the L position is swung around the base's shoulder as base stands.

(continued)

Common Problem	Correction
The stunt falls backward.	The base should keep upper-body weight slightly forward. The partner needs to step, lock, and be balanced before swinging her leg in a controlled manner over the base's shoulder. Timing between the base and partner must be synchronized when the base stands up from the lunge position.

Single-Based Shoulder Stand

Bases: Stand in a double lunge with hips and shoulders facing forward. Reach overhead with arms and grab partner's hands in a handshake grip. On set counts, push up and extend arms as partner steps with foot onto first shoulder. Stand up as partner steps with other foot onto seconds shoulder. Release one hand at a time to grab partner's calves (shoulder-stand grip). Pull down and in on calves to stabilize stunt with elbows pointing forward. For dismount, grab partner's hands in a handshake grip. Support partner as she steps off to floor. Press against partner's hands to slow dismount.

Partner: Stand behind base, reach up, and grab base's hands in a handshake grip. On set counts, push against base's hands, step into pocket, and lock leg. With other foot, step onto base's shoulder, close to the neck. Continue pushing against base's hands while stepping up to other shoulder with first foot. Lock both legs, release hands one at a time, stand, and tighten. Hit a high V motion (see figure). For dismount, bend at waist and grab base's hands in a handshake grip; step off stunt while base helps support weight.

Spotter: *Not required but may be used until stunt is mastered.* Support at waist during climb into stunt and then hold thighs or calves during the stunt. Move to the side and grab waist during dismount.

Points: Base should keep legs shoulder-width apart for balance.

Common Problems	Corrections
The partner falls back.	Partner needs to step, lock, and tighten while keeping her weight straight above the base. Her shoulders, hips, knees, and ankles should be in a straight line. Base pulls down and in on the partner's calves. Base keeps elbows facing forward.
The partner can't get both feet up on base's shoulders.	Both the partner and base must push against each other's hands to get partner up on the shoulders. Timing is important. The base needs to stand when the partner's foot leaves the pocket while continuing to push against the partner's hands. The partner should use momentum to climb onto shoulders and not stop between steps.

Russian Lift

Bases: Step into a double lunge position, keeping head up and back straight. Reach up to grab under partner's arms with bent arms. On set counts, sponge and pop arms and legs to stand upright with legs and arms locked. For dismount, bend knees and arms to lower partner to floor or mat.

Partner: Stand behind base and step into base's pockets. Rest knees on base's sides for balance. Hit a T position with arms and lean slightly forward with bent knees so base can grab under arms. As base pops up, grab ankles or calves in a toe-touch position and lock out arms. For dismount, release ankles, support weight on base's shoulders, and ease to floor or mat (see figure).

Spotter: *Not required but may be used until stunt is mastered.* Assist partner at waist during lift. Let go when stunt is balanced. For dismount, grab waist of partner and assist to floor.

Points: For variation, the Russian lift can be transitioned to a double-based straddle lift (page 76) in which two bases grab the partner's ankles and upper thighs. The partner is held at shoulder level. If bases extend arms, a spotter is needed behind the stunt.

Common Problem	Correction
The stunt falls backward.	The base should keep weight forward on knees in double lunge position before standing up. The partner leans slightly forward over base. Correct timing between the base and partner helps maintain balance on lift. The spotter grips partner's waist firmly to help balance the stunt.

Bases: Stand close to partner, squat down, and place one hand in middle of partner's seat. Grab ankle of partner's hitched (bent) leg. On set counts, step forward, sponge, and push up under partner's seat as partner jumps up. Push straight up with locked arm under seat. Hand on partner's ankle pushes upward for balance and support. For dismount, sponge and lightly drop partner forward off stunt; grab waist to slow her dismount to floor or mat.

Partner: Stand in front of base on one leg with other leg hitched (bent in a lib position). Grab hands of spotter in front (handshake grip). On set counts, sponge straight leg, jump up and slightly back while straightening hitched leg and bending the other. At the same time, extend arms and push against spotter's hands. Sit on base's hand with weight slightly back. Shoulders line up over hips. Rest bent leg against base's forearm for balance. When balanced, hit high V position with arms (see figure). For dismount, keep chest up as base drops stunt to floor; bend knees to absorb landing.

Spotter: Stand in front of and close to partner and clasp hands in handshake grip. Sponge, extend arms, and push up against spotter's hands. Grab partner's waist during dismount.

Points: Another way to get into a chair is a calf pop, in which the spotter stands with back to the stunt in a forward lunge position and hands extended overhead. The partner grabs the spotter's hands in a handshake grip and steps on the spotter's back calf. The spotter and partner sponge, and spotter pops partner up. Timing is important. Base technique is the same as described above.

Common Problems	Corrections
The partner can't get up into the chair.	The base needs to lock out the arm under partner's seat. The base's arm should be straight up over the shoulder to control balance of partner's weight. The partner must push off spotter's hands and jump high to help the base lift. The partner and spotter should lock arms when the partner is being pushed up into the stunt.
The partner falls forward.	The partner needs to sit straight up with shoulders back to shift her weight slightly backward. This weight shift helps compensate the weight of the partner's legs in front of the base.

Double-Based Straddle Lift

Bases: Stand shoulder-width apart facing each other. When partner lifts right leg, base on right side grabs under partner's thigh and ankle or midcalf. On set counts, sponge and lift partner's leg to shoulder or chest height (you can begin in a double lunge position if you need more force to drive partner up into stunt). As partner is lifted, second base grabs partner's other leg under thigh and ankle and lifts leg to shoulder. During partner lift, both bases step out with outside leg to face front at a slight angle. For dismount, walk partner's legs together and lower her to floor.

Partner: Lift right leg so base can grab it. On set counts, sponge and jump up, lifting other leg for second base to catch. Sit in a straddle position with arms in a high V (see figure). For dismount, bring legs together as bases walk legs to center; jump lightly to the floor or mat.

Spotter: *Not required but may be used until stunt is mastered.* Hold partner's waist. Sponge on counts with base and partner, and drive partner up. Support partner at waist during stunt and dismount.

Points: Bases can also extend the straddle lift above their heads by straightening and locking out their arms, but a back spotter would be required for this stunt. If the spotter steps under the stunt to support the partner's seat, he or she becomes the third base. This means a second spotter needs to be behind the stunt in case it falls backward. Another way to build this stunt is for both bases to squat down with hands on partner's thighs and ankles or midcalves. On set counts, bases sponge and drive up with their legs as the partner jumps to the straddle position. The spotter assists at the waist.

Common Problems	Corrections
The partner is not getting enough lift up to the straddle position.	Try using an extra spotter in the front. The partner holds front spotter's hands in a handshake grip and pushes off to get lift.
Bases are not strong enough to lift and hold up partner.	The back spotter can become a third base to lift and hold under the partner's seat. If the spotter becomes a base, a separate spotter is needed behind the stunt.

Bases: Use the same technique as in the double-based thigh stand (page 69). Once partner is in thigh stand (figure a), grab partner's ankle and upper thigh. On set counts, sponge and lift partner to straddle position. For dismount, walk legs together and lower partner to floor or mat.

Partner: Use the same technique as in the double-based thigh stand. On set counts, sponge legs (figure b) and lift out to straddle bases, staying tight. Sit in a straddle position with arms in a high V (figure c). For dismount, bring legs together as bases walk legs to center; jump lightly to the floor.

Spotter: *Not required but may be used until stunt is mastered.* Hold partner's waist. Sponge on counts with base and partner, and drive partner up. Support partner at waist during stunt and dismount.

Points: Bases can also extend the straddle lift above their heads by straightening their arms, but a back spotter is required for this stunt. For a variation, the straddle lift can be brought down to a thigh stand. Bases sponge, step to a lunge position, and place partner's feet in pockets for thigh stand. Partner pulls hips under shoulders and brings feet together for bases to grab. Spotter supports partner's waist.

a

b

c

Double-Based Suspended Splits

Bases: Both bases face front on either side of partner. Inside hand uses four-fingers-forward grip on partner's upper arm; outside hand grips partner's hand in a handshake grip with arm locked. On set counts, sponge and push up through partner's shoulder. One base will grab partner's leg with inside hand, turn, and place leg on inside shoulder. Front base should grab partner's leg above the ankle and turn to face away from the stunt. Back base should grab partner's leg near the knee or thigh and turn to face the stunt. Continue holding partner's hands throughout the stunt. For dismount, sponge, push partner's legs to center, and assist landing with four-fingers-forward grip.

Partner: On set counts, sponge, jump up while pushing down on bases' hands, and lift legs to split position on bases' shoulders. Keep head and chest up and back straight. Continue holding bases' hands throughout stunt. For dismount, bring legs together and jump lightly to the floor.

Spotter: *Not required but may be used until stunt is mastered.* Assist partner at waist during lift and dismount.

Points: A triple-based suspended splits can be performed using a front base. The front base holds the hands of the partner, while the side bases hold her ankles and upper thighs. If dropping to suspended splits from an extended position, four bases need to slow the partner's momentum by supporting under the legs and thighs—or three bases may slow the momentum and the fourth base holds the partner's hands. The partner must maintain hand-to-hand and body contact with a base during suspended splits.

Common Problem	Correction
The partner isn't getting enough lift up to the split position.	Correct timing is important. Be sure all participants are sponging and extending at the same time. For extra help, use an additional base in front. The front base has his or her back to the stunt and hands above head. Front base grabs partner's hands in a handshake grip. On set counts, all three bases sponge and push the partner up. Partner pushes through the front base's arms during the lift.

Bases: Two side bases face each other shoulder-width apart. Squat down and place one hand on partner's upper calf and one on partner's middle back. Back base stands and places hands on partner's upper back. On set counts, sponge, and push partner straight up overhead. Lock out arms. For dismount, sponge, push partner into air, and catch high for a cradle dismount. Side bases catch under partner's back and legs. Back base catches under partner's arms.

Partner: Stand with back to bases. On set counts, sponge, jump up and back, and keep body tight. Arms may be at sides or in a T position (see figure). Keep head in line with body and chin tucked (don't drop head back out of alignment with body). For dismount, keep body tight as bases sponge. On pop, hit a pike position with lower body for a cradle dismount. Grab around side bases' shoulders with arms.

Spotter: No spotter is required.

Points: This stunt is performed at a side angle to the crowd. A double-based deadman lift, using only side bases, requires a spotter at the head and shoulders.

Common Problem	Correction
The bases can't stabilize the stunt.	The bases need to use their legs to forcefully drive the partner up and lock out arms at the top. The partner must stay tight. If she's loose, it's hard for the bases to hold up the stunt.

Hang Drill

Bases: Stand in double lunge position facing each other. Keep chest and head up and back straight.

Partner: Place hands on bases' shoulders. On set counts, jump up and push through arms and shoulders, keeping arms straight and locked out. Hold body up in a hang position with knees bent (as if putting feet in bases' hands) for 10 seconds (see figure).

Spotter: Hold partner at waist.

Points: This drill is performed before attempting an extension prep. The partner must be able to hold her own body weight. She needs to be to be able to push off the bases' shoulders during stunts so that very little weight is placed in the bases' hands.

Common Problem	Correction
The partner can't hold herself up.	Partner should jump high enough to obtain the necessary leverage to hold herself up. She needs to lock out her arms and must be strong enough to hold up her body weight. She may need to lift weights to build strength.

Summary

Learning and practicing correct techniques for basic stunting allows squads to perform higher-level stunts more easily, efficiently, and safely. Every person involved in a stunt must know his or her role in regard to proper technique and responsibility throughout the stunt sequence, including the dismount. Once the basic stunts are mastered, cheerleaders are ready to move on to intermediate stunts. Remember—perfec-tion before progression! For safety and liability purposes, cheerleaders should never progress to higher-level stunts until they have perfected the lead-up stunts. Cheerleaders can always choose among basic level stunts for variety and crowd-pleasing visual effects to impress the fans. As cheerleaders gain confidence, their stunting skills will improve, and they'll find more advanced stunts easier to achieve.

seven

Intermediate Stunts

© Photosport

Intermediate stunts are for teams on which many members have had stunting experience. Generally speaking, these stunts stop at shoulder height. Any stunt group attempting intermediate stunts should have previously mastered basic stunts (chapter 6). In some cases, advanced teams might perform intermediate stunts as well. This is because intermediate stunts are often easier than advanced stunts, and after exceptionally long games or performances—when cheerleaders are tiring—intermediate stunts are safer to build. As with any new stunt, proper technique should be used when learning intermediate stunts, and safety is a top priority.

Extension Prep to Cradle

Bases: Bases are in double-lunge formations, facing each other. First base grabs under partner's foot. On sponge, second base grabs under the other foot. Driving through the legs, bases lift. When catching the dismount, bases dip with legs and extend arms as they drive through legs. Bases catch partner high and absorb weight into legs. They then bring partner to the ground.

Partner: Place first foot into first base's hands. With weight on the bases' shoulders, sponge second foot into secondary base's hand. Push off the shoulder and straighten legs for lift (see figure). During dismount, stay tight through the dip, then ride the toss. Catch weight with arms on bases' shoulders.

Spotter: Support at the waist. Help drive partner to prep level and then support at the ankles. Catch under arms during dismount.

Common Problems	Corrections
Bases step out as extension prep hits.	Partner should squeeze thighs together as she stands up to extension prep.
Extension prep is standing up slowly.	Bases should stand up faster with their legs.
Partner can't get her weight over the base's shoulders.	Check the bases' grips. Make sure they're not anticipating the dip and raising the partner's feet prematurely.

Bases: Side base grabs toe and heel and leads partner's foot to the shoulders of the main base. Main base grabs partner's foot in a hamburger grip (one hand over the top and one hand under bottom of the partner's foot). After a dip, main base leads partner overhead and catches the other foot with left hand as partner stands on bases' shoulders.

Partner: Start with hands on bases' shoulders. Dip, step, lock, and tighten, shifting weight onto the other foot as the main base grabs it (see figure).

Spotter: Put right hand on ankle and left hand underneath partner's seat. Drive through the top until it's possible to grab both partners' ankles to stabilize stunt as it rests on main bases' shoulders.

Common Problems	Corrections
Partner is stepping over early when standing up.	Make the partner emphasize the "step, lock, tighten" positioning until she stands tall enough to clear the main base's head.
Partner isn't getting any power when driving up to hands.	Spotter should push harder on seat of the partner to help assist in getting her weight into the air.
The side base's grip is getting in the way of the main base.	The side base should grab less toe and heel than normal to allow for the main base a solid grip underneath the foot.

Running Man to Extension Prep

Bases: Main base starts with hands underneath partner's foot (see figure a). Drive up until partner steps onto shoulder. Take another dip and grab extension prep grip. Secondary base grabs foot at shoulder level while the partner stands up to an extension prep.

Partner: Step onto main base's hands and lock out leg; place other foot on main base's shoulder, then stand up to an extension prep.

Spotter: Grab underneath seat of partner as she steps up. Help control ankles on the way to the prep. Drive up until partner steps onto shoulder (see figure b). Take another dip and grab extension prep grip. Secondary base grabs foot at shoulder level and stands up to an extension prep.

a

b

Common Problems	Corrections
Partner keeps falling off of the back of stunt.	Make sure spotter is grabbing underneath the seat and supporting as much weight as possible.
Timing of the load-in is not allowing the partner to stand up to an extension prep.	Take the partner out of the stunt and have the bases go over the counts many times until everyone knows their role and timing.
Partner keeps falling to the side.	During the second bounce, when the partner places her second foot on the base's shoulder, her body weight should also distribute to that foot instead of favoring the first foot.

Bases: Start in a cradle position and pop partner to shoulder level, putting one hand underneath the back and the outside hand underneath partner's toe. During the pop, bring partner to load-in position, and then drive partner to an extension prep.

Partner: Start in a cradle position (see figure a). Stay tight as bases pop to shoulder level. On dip, sit forward, pulling feet down and grab shoulders of bases in a load-in position. Stand to an extension prep (see figure b).

Spotter: Positioned in a comfortable spot to grab partner's waist or underneath seat. From there, toss partner into an extension prep.

a

b

Common Problems	Corrections
Cradle to flat back is loose and not under control.	Have partner squeeze abs to allow body to be maneuvered by the bases and back spotter.
During the flatback to load-in position, the partner's knees are too high for her to carry her body weight.	The bases are not dropping the outside hand low enough to allow the partner to pull her weight up.
The dip after the flatback isn't going anywhere.	Have bases mark their part without the partner. After they dip, their outside hands should drop, and the hands holding the back of the partner should drive up.

Straddle to Extension Prep

Bases: Start in a double lunge (see figure a). Put hands on toe and heel of partner. On given counts, dip and drive partner to straddle position, keeping outside hand on toe of partner and inside hand underneath hips of partner. On given counts, dip with legs, driving partner up to an extension prep.

Partner: Place right foot in first base's hand. Put weight on bases' shoulders during dip, and place other foot in empty hands of second base. Squeeze feet together and land in straddle. From straddle, pull thighs together and stand up to an extension prep (see figure b).

Spotter: Start behind partner with hands on waist. On given counts, assist the load-in position, helping support the partner's waist as partner lands in a straddle. On given counts, help guide partner to an extension prep position.

a

b

Common Problems	Corrections
Partner isn't making it to straddle.	Partner should squeeze legs together until bases pull her out to straddle position.
Partner is falling off the back of the straddle.	Back spotter should hold as much weight underneath seat as possible. Partner should lean slightly forward in straddle to keep weight in line with bases and spotters.
Partner can't stand up to extension prep from straddle.	Partner should squeeze legs together on the way to prep as bases step in.

Bases: Start with right hand over left (cross at wrists). On given counts, partner loads in, and the bases dip with legs, rotating hands until they have toe and heel, and catch partner in an extension prep.

Partner: Start facing the back. Cross right foot and place it into the opposite base's hand (see figure a). On the given count, dip and place left foot in the other base's hand, holding weight on bases' shoulders. Stand up to an extension prep (see figure b).

Spotter: Grab under shins of partner. On set counts, partner dips and spotter guides the twisting load-in up to the extension prep.

a b

Common Problems	Corrections
Partner can't place second foot into the base's hand.	Have partner *flex* her second foot so the secondary base can grab a solid grip. Instead of "giving" her second foot to the base, she should place her second foot close to her first, so the secondary base can gauge where it will land.
Bases' hands slide off of the foot as partner stands up.	Recheck the original grip of the bases. Grip should be *right hand over left hand*, not left hand over right hand.
Twist-up is turning too early.	Have partner drill her role in the stunt. She should be pushing off the shoulders of the bases and then turning over her shoulder. If she turns over her shoulder too early, the stunt will never get to the top.

Extension Prep to Full-Down

Bases: From the prep, dip with legs, extending arms all the way to the top. Follow the partner's body and catch in a cradle.

Partner: Wait for the bases' pop and wrap arms across body, reaching with shoulders and head. When rotation is complete, open up for a typical cradle (see figure).

Spotter: Extend through partner's ankles during the initial toss and catch at shoulder blades. In some cases, helping initiate spin with hands is appropriate to ensure a full rotation. A second spotter is optional. If used, second spotter grabs partner's ankles: left hand to left ankle, right hand to right ankle. If partner twists left, put left hand under; if partner twists right, put right hand under. As partner twists, maintain contact and twist arms over each other to control partner into the cradle.

Common Problems	Corrections
Partner is landing on belly.	Head and neck should continue looking over her shoulder until partner lands in the cradle.
Partner is twisting over bases' heads.	The partner is anticipating the pop and needs to wait until the dip is complete before starting to twist.
Bases are catching too low in the cradle.	Bases need to leave their arms up during the cradle and not anticipate catching low to allow for the partner to complete the twist.

Bases: First base, grab toe and heel as it comes in; hold during second dip and stand up to prep. Second base, wait for first dip and grab underneath foot and shin when partner places back leg (see figure a). Drive up to an extension prep.

Partner: Put right foot into base's hand. During first dip, place back leg behind for other base to catch. Push off shoulders and squeeze legs together for extension prep (see figure b).

Spotter: Guide the thighs as partner places feet in base's hands. Follow partner up to extension prep.

a

b

Common Problems	Corrections
Second base can't catch the back foot of the partner.	Have partner go over the timing. The first dip needs to be controlled and slow to allow for the second base to have time to grab the foot.
Stunt is not making it up to the extension prep.	Partner is anticipating the extension prep and pushing off the main base prematurely.
Bases are stepping away from the stunt as it moves to the extension prep.	Partner should squeeze feet together. Partner often concentrates so much on the timing and pushing off the shoulders that she forgets to squeeze feet and thighs at all times.

Side to Side to Extension Prep

This stunt is a progression from the step-in presto to extension prep. The step-in presto should be mastered before attempting this one.

Bases: First base grabs under toe and heel of partner and lifts (see figure a). As partner swings around, move one hand to the shin. Drive partner up to extension prep. Partner comes down, and second base grabs under her heel and shin (see figure b). As partner swings around, shift grip to toe and heel. Both bases drive partner up to extension prep (see figure c).

Partner: Grab shoulders of main base. Put right foot in main base's hands. Dip and place the other foot in second base's hands. Drive up and come down on the second base, putting weight on his or her shoulders. From there, drive up to the extension prep.

Spotter: Grab at hips of partner and hold weight up as partner goes through transitions. Stabilize the stunt as it goes to the extension prep.

a b c

Common Problems	Corrections
Second base can't catch the back foot of the partner.	Have partner go over the timing. The first dip needs to be controlled and slow to allow for the second base to have time to grab the foot.
Stunt is not making it up to the extension prep.	Partner is anticipating the extension prep and pushing off the main base prematurely.
Bases are stepping away from the stunt as it moves to the extension prep.	Partner should squeeze feet together. Partner often concentrates so much on the timing and pushing off the shoulders that she forgets to squeeze feet and thighs at all times.

Bases: First base puts right hand under partner's right foot. Left hand catches partner's other foot, and partner stands up to a coed-style hands grip. Second base starts in a right-over-left grip with the right foot. As the partner twists into the stunt, slide hands around so hands are under partner's toe and heel.

Partner: Start facing back. Place right foot in first base's hands and put hands on bases' shoulders (see figure a). Dip and drive up to hands (see figure b).

Spotter: Start by grabbing the thighs and ankles of the partner. As partner loads in, twist her up to hands, grabbing ankles to support.

a

b

Common Problems	Corrections
Partner can't place her second foot into the base's hand. Second base's hands slide off foot as partner stands up.	Have partner *flex* her second foot so second base can get a solid grip. Instead of "giving" her second foot to second base, partner should place her second foot close to her first so second base can gauge where it will land.
Twist-up is turning too early.	Have partner drill her role in the stunt. She should be pushing off the shoulders of the bases and then turning over her shoulder. If she turns over her shoulder too early, the stunt can't get to the top.

High Star

Bases: First base grabs left foot in an extension prep grip (see figure a). On the dip, rise to a star position, grabbing underneath foot and at shin (see figure b). Go to sponge and drive to extension prep. As foot comes around, second base grabs foot and underneath shin. Go to sponge and drive to an extension prep (see figures c and d).

Partner: Grab front spotter in handshake grip. Lift left leg to main base. Dip and shift weight forward into hands while landing in a star. On sponge, try to put weight in arms of front spotter and stand up to extension prep.

Spotters: As partner swings around, first spotter grabs legs and holds partner in a star. On sponge, get underneath the hips and drive to an extension prep. Second spotter (front spotter) grabs partner in handshake grip. Hold weight as partner stands up to the star. On sponge, support weight in partner's hands during the dip back up to extension.

Common Problems	Corrections
The star is collapsing before making it to the top.	Tell partner to go over the "step, lock, tighten" technique (page 66) to ensure she is locking out her legs aggressively.
The star is falling off the front.	Front spotter needs to stay underneath partner and use her body weight to push her up to the star position.
Stunt collapses forward on the way to the sponge.	Partner needs to redistribute her weight when the bases dip for the sponge and make sure weight shifts from the front spotter to her two bases.

a

b

c

d

Pretty Sit to Extension Prep

Bases: First base starts off to the side and grab partner's left foot. From the sit, dip and stand up with a half-turn to the extension prep. Second base dips and puts partner in a chair sit over left shoulder while gripping the bottom of partner's foot. Dip to an extension prep.

Partner: Grab shoulders of base and spotter and jump to a chair sit, pulling one leg over the other (see figure a). After turning, dip to an extension prep (see figure b).

Spotter: Put partner on the right shoulder, gripping foot for an extension. Do a half-turn and stand up to an extension prep.

a

b

Common Problems	Corrections
Partner is falling off the back of the chair sit.	Partner needs to hold body weight in the chair sit and not rely on back spotters to hold the weight by themselves.
Partner is having a difficult time standing up to the extension prep.	Bases need to take a bigger dip with their legs to give partner momentum to stand up strong.
In chair sit, partner's knees are too high, and she is falling off the back.	Bases need to drop the feet of the partner down so she can easily hold her own weight up.

Bases: First base grabs partner's hitched leg as she steps into pocket of second base. Hold grip as partner stands to an extension prep. Second base holds a thigh stand (see figure a). As partner stands up, grab with an extension prep grip.

Partner: Step in for a thigh stand, giving right leg to the second base in a hitch position. Step up, putting weight on the right foot. Stand up in an extension prep (see figure b).

Spotter: Grab under hips of partner. On given counts, dip and grab ankles, helping the stunt stand up to an extension prep.

a

b

Common Problems	Corrections
Partner can't stand up on the hitched leg.	Base needs to secure a solid foundation before initiating the transition.
Once the dip occurs to extension prep, partner falls back to the original hitch position.	Partner needs to be aggressive when she stands up and "step, lock, and tighten" onto the main base.
The stunt falls to a split on the way to extension.	Partner needs to squeeze feet and thighs together to keep the bases in.

Stretch to Extension Prep

Bases: First base starts with hands under the toe and heel of partner. On set counts, drive the foot up to shoulder level (see figure a). Second base starts with right hand on partner's thigh and left hand on the toe of partner's extended leg. On set counts, drive thigh up and move right hand to partner's heel in an extension prep position (see figure b).

Partner: Settle right foot in hands of main base. Kick left leg to heel stretch position, holding on to foot with left hand. Grab wrists of back spotter with right hand. On set count, jump off ground, keeping legs straight, standing up to an extension prep position.

Spotter: Grab partner's waist. On set counts, drive partner's waist up, releasing and regrabbing at partner's ankles or bases' wrists.

a

b

Common Problems	Corrections
Base can't lift partner above head on the way to extension prep.	Main base needs to swing partner's foot in a J motion to get her hips up over her feet before the stunt can reach the extension prep.
Stunt is moving too slowly to the extension prep.	Partner needs to snap stretched leg downward to initiate the movement to the extension prep.
Partner is falling off the back on the way to extension prep.	Back spotter needs to aggressively toss the partner to give her enough power to make it to extension prep.

Bases: Main base grabs partner's heel with left hand and partner's toe with right hand (left over right). On set counts, first base dips with legs and drives partner up, settling in an extension prep. Second base puts right hand on partner's ankle and left hand under partner's seat (see figure a). On set counts, bases drive partner up and catch partner's left foot as it comes around in an extension prep grip.

Partner: Place right foot forward and hands on bases' shoulders. On set counts, stand up tall, turning over left shoulder at the very top (see figure b). Land in extension prep.

Spotters: First spotter grabs partner's ankle with both hands. On set counts, release one hand off the ankle and regrab in an extension prep position. Second spotter (front spotter) grabs partner's waist. On set counts, help toss partner into air, recatching the stunt in an extension prep.

a   b

Common Problems	Corrections
Partner is not getting over the heads of the bases.	Partner needs to review the "step, lock, tighten" technique (page 66) and make sure she is giving solid leverage for the bases to push against.
Partner is not making it around to the front.	Partner is initiating the twist too early. The twist needs to happen at the top of the drive upward.
Stunt is kicking out on the way to extension prep.	Partner is trying to "give" the secondary base her foot rather than squeezing her feet together.

T-Carrier

Bases: Both bases wait in a double lunge. When partner flies into sponge, dip and drive up to extension prep.

Partner: Grab extra post and spotter with an overhand grip and hit a T motion (see figure a). While being carried forward, lift feet, placing them in bases' hands, keeping chest forward (see figure b). Push through arms and stand up to an extension prep (see figure c).

Spotter: Grab partner's hand and under the arm (with the additional post) and carry partner forward. When partner reaches bases (and additional post), push through partner's arms to help partner stand up on the stunt.

a

b

c

Common Problems	Corrections
Partner's weight is in her seat when she moves to the load-in position.	Bases roll the partner's shoulders forward so she can distribute her weight evenly during the sponge.
Spotter cannot assist in pushing the partner up to the extension prep.	Partner needs to keep her arms locked out during the transition so the spotters have leverage to push against until the stunt reaches the top.
The stunt is favoring one side (right or left) on the way to the extension prep.	Spotters need to review their timing to ensure they're working on the same counts. Also, the height of the spotters could be affecting the stunt.

Summary

The stunts explained in this chapter provide a balance of basic technique with innovative flair. While it is not essential to your team's success to attempt and master every single stunt listed in the intermediate category, the material offered should provide challenging and exciting goals for your team. These skills are great for those teams with background and experience in cheerleading and should make cheering on the sideline that much more fun.

eight

Advanced Stunts

© Photosport

Advanced stunts are for teams with a lot of familiarity with stunting technique. It's not necessary that every team member has done stunts, but most members should have experience in stunting before a team takes on advanced stunts. Most advanced stunts progress to an extended level at which the arms of the bases are above their heads. Advanced stunts also include one-legged stunts, in which the difficulty of the skill is multiplied by the partner's ability to balance weight on one leg. These stunts are considered the most difficult set of stunts covered in this book, so using them in conjunction with other skill-specific stunts (basic and intermediate) is a good idea. Many times, even the most advanced cheerleaders can grow tired during a game or performance. With fatigue comes a higher risk of injury when performing advanced stunts. As with any new stunt, proper safety and technique should be emphasized when learning these advanced stunts.

Extension to Cradle

Bases: Bases are in double-lunge positions, facing each other. First base grabs under foot. On sponge, second base grabs under second foot. Driving through the legs, bases lift and extend arms (see figure). During dismount, bases dip with legs. Bases should not bend their arms as they drive through the legs, nor should they throw the feet. Bases catch partner high and absorb weight into legs.

Partner: Place first foot into first base's hands. With weight on the first base's shoulders, sponge second foot into second base's hands. Push off the shoulder and straighten legs for lift. Keep legs locked during cradle and land in pike position.

Spotter: Support at waist. Help drive partner to extension level, then support at ankles or wrists.

Common Problems	Corrections
Bases step out as extension hits.	Partner should squeeze thighs together while standing up to extension prep.
Extension is standing up slow.	Bases should stand up faster with their legs.
Partner can't get body weight over the bases' shoulders.	Check the bases' grips. Make sure bases are not anticipating the dip and raising the partner's feet prematurely.

Bases: Side base grabs partner's toe and heel and leads partner's foot to shoulders of main base. Main base uses hamburger grip (over the top and bottom of partner's foot). After a dip, main base leads partner overhead and catches other foot with left hand as partner stands in an extension (see figure).

Partner: Starts with hands on bases' shoulders. Dip, step, lock, and tighten, shifting weight onto the other foot as the main base grabs the foot. Stand tall in an extension.

Spotter: Put right hand on ankle and left hand underneath seat of partner. Drive through the top until it's possible to grab both ankles of partner to stabilize stunt as it moves to an extension.

Common Problems	Corrections
Partner is stepping over early when standing up.	Ask partner to emphasize the "step, lock, tighten" technique until partner stands tall enough to clear the main base's head.
Partner isn't getting any power when driving up to hands.	Spotter should push harder on partner's seat to help get her weight into the air.
Side base's grip is getting in the way of main base.	Side base should grab less toe and heel than normal to allow for main base to have a solid grip underneath the foot.

Running Man to Extension

Bases: First base starts with hands underneath partner's foot (see figure a). Drive up until partner steps onto shoulder (see figure b). Take another dip and grab with an extension grip. Second base catches foot at shoulder level and stands up to an extension.

Partner: Step onto main base's hands and lock out leg; place other foot on base's shoulder and stand up to an extension.

Spotter: Grab underneath seat of partner as partner steps up. Help control ankles on the way to the extension (see figure c).

a

b

c

Common Problems	Corrections
Partner keeps falling off the back of stunt.	Make sure spotter is grabbing underneath the seat and supporting as much weight as possible. Partner should also center weight by keeping her chest, hips, knees, and feet in line.
Timing of the load-in is not allowing the partner to stand up to an extension.	Take the partner out of the stunt and ask bases to go over the counts several times until everyone is aware of his or her role and timing.
Partner keeps falling to the side.	During the second bounce, when partner places her second foot on base's shoulder, weight should also be distributed to that foot instead of favoring the first foot.

Bases: Start in a double lunge. Put hands on toe and heel of partner. On set counts, dip and drive partner to straddle position, keeping outside hand on partner's toe and inside hand underneath partner's hips. On given counts, dip with legs, driving partner up to an extension prep.

Partner: Place right foot in one base's hand. Put weight on bases' shoulders during dip and place other foot in empty hands of other base. Squeeze feet together and land in straddle. From straddle, pull thighs together and stand up to an extension prep.

Spotter: Start behind partner with hands on waist. On set counts, assist the load-in position and help support the partner's waist as she lands in a straddle. On set counts, help guide partner to an extension prep position.

Common Problems	Corrections
Partner isn't making it to straddle.	Partner should squeeze legs together until bases pull partner out to straddle position.
Partner is falling off the back of the straddle.	Back spotter should hold as much weight as possible under partner's seat. Partner should lean slightly forward in straddle to keep body weight in line with bases and spotters.
Partner can't stand up to extension from straddle.	Partner should squeeze legs together on the way to prep as bases step in.

Twist-Up to Extension

Bases: Both bases start with right hand over left. On set counts, partner loads in, and bases dip with legs, rotating hands until they have partner's toe and heel. Bases then catch partner in an extension.

Partner: Start facing the back. Cross right foot and place it in the opposite base's hand (see figure a). On set counts, dip and place left foot into the other base's hand, holding body weight on bases' shoulders. Stand up to an extension, squeezing feet together (see figure b).

Spotter: Grab under the shins of the partner. On set counts, partner dips and spotter guides the twisting load-in up to the extension.

a   b

Common Problems	Corrections
Partner can't place her second foot into the base's hand.	Have partner *flex* her second foot so the second base can grab a solid grip. Instead of "giving" her second foot to the base, she should place her second foot close to her first, so the second base can gauge where it will land.
Bases step out as stunt hits the extension.	Partner should squeeze her feet together until the stunt is completely executed.
Twist-up is turning too early.	Have partner practice her role in the stunt. She should be pushing off the bases' shoulders and then turning over her shoulder. If she turns over her shoulder too early, the stunt can't get to the top.

Bases: From extension, dip with legs, extending arms all the way to top (see figure). Follow partner's body and catch in a cradle.

Partner: Wait for the bases' pop, then wrap arms across body, reaching with shoulders and head. When rotation is complete, open up for a typical cradle.

Spotter: First spotter extends through partner's ankles during initial toss and catches at shoulder blades. Front spotter (optional), grabs ankles—left hand to left ankle, right hand to right ankle. If partner twists left, move left hand under; if partner twists right, move right hand under. As partner twists, maintain contact and twist arms over each other to control partner into the cradle.

Common Problems	Corrections
Partner is landing on her belly.	Head and neck should continue looking over her shoulder until she lands in the cradle.
Partner is twisting over the bases' heads.	The partner is anticipating the pop and needs to wait until the dip is complete before beginning to twist.
There is no air time before the partner lands in the cradle.	Bases need to emphasize dipping with their legs; the partner needs to wait for their pop.
Partner is not completing rotation.	Partner should keep her right hip and shoulder in line with each other during rotation.

Step-In Presto to Awesome

Bases: First base grabs toe and heel as they come in; hold during second dip and stand up to prep. Second base waits for first dip and grabs underneath foot and shin when partner moves left leg back. J-stunt up to an awesome.

Partner: Put right foot into first base's hand. During first dip, move left leg back for second base to catch (see figure a). Push off shoulders and squeeze legs together for an awesome (see figure b).

Spotter: Guide partner's thighs as partner places feet in bases' hands. Drive the stunt up to an awesome and squeeze ankles together to stabilize stunt.

a

b

Common Problems	Corrections
Second base is not able to catch the partner's back foot.	Ask partner to review timing. The first dip needs to be controlled and slow to allow second base time to grab the foot.
Stunt is not making it up to the awesome.	Partner should squeeze her legs together until her feet touch.
Bases are stepping away from the stunt as it moves to the awesome.	Partner should squeeze feet together. Cheerleaders sometimes concentrate so much on timing and pushing off the shoulders that they forget to squeeze their feet and thighs at all times.

This stunt is a progression from the step-in presto to extension prep. The step-in presto should be mastered before attempting the side to side to awesome.

Bases: First base grabs under toe and heel of partner and lifts. As partner swings around, move one hand to the shin (see figure a). Drive partner up to an awesome (see figure b). Partner comes down, and second base grabs under heel and shin of partner. As partner swings around, shift grip to toe and heel (see figure c). Drive partner up to an awesome (see figure d).

Partner: Grab first base's shoulders and put right foot in his or her hands. Dip and place left foot in second base's hands. Drive up and come down on the second base, putting weight on his or her shoulders. From there, drive up to the awesome.

Spotter: Grab at hips of partner and hold her weight up as she goes through transitions. Stabilize the stunt as it goes to the awesome.

a   b   c   d

Common Problems	Corrections
Second base is not able to catch the partner's back foot.	Ask partner to review timing. The first dip needs to be controlled and slow to allow second base time to grab the foot.
Stunt is not making it up to the awesome.	Check for partner anticipating the awesome and pushing off the main base prematurely.
Bases are stepping away from the stunt as it moves to the awesome.	Partner should squeeze feet together. Cheerleaders sometimes concentrate so much on timing and pushing off the shoulders that they forget to squeeze their feet and thighs at all times.
Partner is standing up too quickly.	Bases, partner, and spotters should review their timing together.

Single Base Style: Twist-Up to Extension

Primary base: Put right hand under the right foot of partner. Left hand catches partner's other foot. She stands up to a coed-style hands, continuing the movement all the way to the extension.

Secondary base: Start in a right-over-left grip with the right foot. As partner twists into the stunt, slide hands around so they're under partner's toe and heel (see figure a). Press to extension.

Partner: Start facing the back. Place right foot in bases' hands and put hands on bases' shoulders. Dip and drive up to hands and follow through to an extension.

Spotter: Start by grabbing the thighs and ankles of the partner. As she loads in, twist her up to extension, grabbing ankles to support (see figure b).

a

b

Common Problems	Corrections
Partner can't place her second foot into the base's hand.	Ask partner to review timing. The first dip needs to be controlled and slow to allow second base time to grab the foot.
Bases' hands slide off of the foot as partner stands up.	Recheck bases' initial grip. Grip should be *right hand over left hand*, not left hand over right hand.
Twist-up is turning too early.	Have partner drill her role in the stunt. Partner should be pushing off the shoulders of the bases and then turning over her shoulder. If she turns over her shoulder too early, the stunt will never get to the top.
Stunt is shaky and unstable.	Partner needs to be aggressive and lock out her legs.

Primary base: Grab left foot in an extension prep grip. On the dip, rise to a star position, grabbing underneath foot and at shin. Go to sponge and drive to extension.

Secondary base: As foot comes around, grab foot and underneath shin. Go to sponge and drive to extension.

Partner: Grab front spotter in handshake grip. Lift left leg to the main base (see figure a). Dip and shift weight forward into hands while landing in a star (see figure b). On sponge, try to put weight in arms of the front spotter and stand up to an extension.

Spotter: As partner swings around, grab legs and hold in a star. On sponge, get underneath hips and drive to extension.

Front spotter: Grab partner in handshake grip. Hold weight as partner stands up to the star. On sponge, support weight in hands as bases dip back up to extension (see figure c).

a

b

c

Common Problems	Corrections
The star is collapsing before making it to the top.	Have partner review the "step, lock, tighten" technique (page 66) to ensure she is locking out her legs aggressively.
The star is falling off the front.	Front spotter needs to stay underneath the partner and use body weight to push the partner up to the star position.
Stunt collapses forward on the way to the sponge.	Partner needs to redistribute her weight when the bases dip for the sponge and make sure it shifts from the front spotter to her two bases.

Pretty Sit to Extension

Primary base: Start off to the side and grab partner's left foot. From the sit, dip and stand up with a half-turn to the extension.

Secondary base: Dip and put partner in a chair sit over left shoulder, while gripping the bottom of her foot (see figure a). Dip to an extension.

Partner: Grab shoulders of base and spotter and jump to a chair sit, pulling one leg over the other. After turning, ride the dip and stand up in an extension, giving other leg to the bases (see figure b).

Spotter: Put partner on the right shoulder, gripping her foot for an extension. Do a half-turn and stand up to an extension.

a

b

Common Problems	Corrections
Partner is falling off the back of the chair sit.	Partner needs to hold her own weight in the chair sit and not rely on the back spotters to support the weight themselves.
Partner is having a difficult time standing up to the extension.	Bases need to take a bigger dip with the legs to allow partner the energy to stand up strong.
In the chair sit, partner's knees are too high, causing her to fall off the back.	Bases need to drop the feet of the partner down so she can easily hold her own weight up.
Bases can't get a strong grip on partner's feet.	Make sure bases have a solid grip on the toe and heel of the partner.

Bases: First base grabs partner's hitched leg as she steps into pocket of second base (see figure a). Hold grip as partner stands to an extension. Second base holds a thigh stand. As partner stands up, grab with an extension grip.

Partner: Step in for a thigh stand, giving right leg to second base in a hitch position. Step up, putting weight on the right foot. Stand up in an extension.

Spotter: Grab under hips of partner. On set counts, dip and grab ankles, helping stunt stand up to an extension (see figure b).

a

b

Common Problems	Corrections
Partner can't stand up on the hitched leg.	Second base needs to take a little dip to help maneuver the partner into the extension. Partner needs to shift her weight and center it over the bases.
Once the dip to extension occurs, partner falls back to the original hitch position.	Partner needs to be aggressive when she stands up and step, lock, and tighten onto the first base.
The stunt falls to a split on the way to extension.	Partner needs to squeeze feet and thighs together to keep the bases in.

Stretch to Extension

Bases: First base starts with hands under partner's toe and heel. On set counts, drive the foot up to an extension. Second base starts with right hand on partner's thigh and left hand on partner's toe of extended leg (see figure a). On set counts, drive the thigh up and move right hand to the heel of the partner in an extension position.

Partner: Settle right foot on hands of first base and kick left leg to a heel stretch position, holding on to foot with left hand. Grab back spotter's wrists with right hand. On set counts, jump off floor, keeping legs straight, standing to extension position (see figure b).

Spotter: Spotter grabs partner's waist. On set counts, drive partner's waist up, releasing and regrabbing at partner's ankles or bases' wrists.

a   b

Common Problems	Corrections
Base can't lift partner above head on the way to extension.	First base needs to swing partner's foot in a J motion to get partner's hips up over her feet before the stunt can reach extension.
The stunt is moving too slowly to the extension.	Partner needs to snap her stretched leg downward to initiate the movement to the extension.
Partner is falling off the back on the way to extension.	Back spotter needs to aggressively toss partner to give her enough power to make it to extension.
Stunt can't get off the ground.	Partner needs to jump with her right leg and push off the wrist of the back spotter.

Bases: First base grabs partner's heel with left hand and partner's toe with right hand (left over right). On set counts, dip with legs and drive partner up, settling in an extension. Second base puts right hand on partner's ankle and left hand under partner's seat (see figure a). On set counts, help drive partner up and catch partner's left foot in an extension grip as it comes around (see figure b).

Partner: Place right foot forward and hands on bases' shoulders. On set counts, stand up tall, turning over left shoulder at the very top. Land in extension.

Spotters: Back spotter grabs partner's ankle with both hands. On set counts, release one hand from the ankle and regrab in an extension. Front spotter grabs partner's waist. On set counts, help toss the partner into the air, recatching the stunt in an extension.

a

b

Common Problems	Corrections
Partner is not getting over the heads of the bases.	Partner needs to review the "step, lock, tighten" technique (page 66) and make sure she's giving solid leverage for the bases to push against.
Partner is not making it around to the front.	Partner is initiating the twist too early. It needs to happen at the top of the drive upward.
Stunt is kicking out on the way to extension.	Partner is trying to "give" the secondary base her foot rather than squeezing her feet together.
Stunt is not getting off the ground.	Second base needs to follow through all the way when pushing the seat of the partner.

T-Carrier

Bases: Wait in a double lunge (see figure a). When partner flies into the sponge (see figure b), dip and drive up to extension (see figure c).

Partner: Grab spotter and extra post in an overhand grip and hit a T motion. After being carried forward, lift feet—placing them in the hands of the bases—while keeping chest forward. Push through arms and stand up to an extension.

Spotter: Grab at the hand and under the arm (with the additional post) and carry partner forward. When partner reaches the bases, push through partner's arms to help her stand up on the stunt.

a

b

c

Common Problems	Corrections
Partner's weight is in her seat when she moves to the load-in position.	Bases should roll the partner's shoulders forward so she can distribute her weight evenly during the sponge.
Spotter can't assist in pushing the partner up to the extension.	Partner needs to keep her arms locked out during the transition so spotters have leverage to push against until the stunt reaches the top.
Stunt is favoring one side (right or left) on the way to the extension.	Spotters need to review their timing to ensure they're working on the same counts. The height of the spotters could also be affecting the stunt.

Primary base: Begin in a double lunge with hands on toe and heel of partner. On set counts, dip with legs and extend the foot above the head, switching grip at the top. (The primary base position is identical to the position of the base in an extension.)

Secondary base: Begin in a double lunge. Right hand goes under the foot of the partner and left hand goes over the foot in a hamburger grip. On set counts, dip and extend arms. At the top of the stunt, turn left shoulder to stand under the stunt and share partner's weight with the primary base. On set counts, the base dips in and partner lands in a cradle.

Partner: Partner puts her right foot into the hands of the bases. On set counts, the partner pushes off the ground and bases' shoulders to stand up. For the liberty position, partner locks out her right leg and pulls her left leg up until her knee is parallel to the ground (see figure). The left foot will remain tight, resting slightly next to the right knee. On set counts, the partner is cradled and returns to the ground.

Back spotter: Back spotter puts right hand on partner's ankle and left hand under partner's seat. On set counts, spotter dips and pushes seat of partner up to help her get off the ground. As partner stands up, back spotter places both hands on the right ankle of partner. On dismount, back spotter dips in and catches partner at head and shoulders.

Common Problems	Corrections
Bases complain that stunt feels "heavy," and they can't make it over their heads.	The timing between the bases, back spotter and partner should be reviewed. If the stunt group is not dipping in a synchronized manner, it may make the stunt feel very heavy. Drill until the group is synchronized.
Liberty is standing up too slowly.	Bases should push up faster with their legs. Partner should push off bases' shoulders, lifting up with her upper body.
Liberty is continuously falling to the partner's right side.	The partner may be anticipating the movement of pulling her foot in and is overcompensating. When hitting a liberty position, the hip should be pulled upward, not towards the right side.

Liberty Variations

The role of the bases and back spotters for these stunts remain consistent with that of the liberty. However, the partners must master flexibility, balance, and body control before attempting these skills as they require much more coordination. The arabesque (figure a), scale (figure b), scorpion (figure c), heel stretch (figure d), and overstretch (figure e) are some of the most common liberty variations.

a

b

c

d

e

Summary

Advanced stunts should prove to be challenging and exciting for your team. When attempting any advanced sequence, never forget the basic stunt technique described in earlier chapters. While advanced stunts are a lot of fun for the well-practiced team, when they aren't executed correctly, mistakes and injury are likely to occur. If the cheerleaders on your squad are determined, hard working, and willing to put in the practice, they will have the crowd fired up in no time with these innovative advanced skills.

nine

Single-Based Stunts

© Photosport

Single-based stunts typically involve one male, one female, and at least one spotter. These stunts are great for impressing a crowd and have lured many males into cheerleading. Fans look on with envy at what appears to be an impossible task of a single person lifting another person over his head.

Many of the technical drills useful in group stunting also apply to single-based stunting, but much more precision, trust, and timing are necessary to get these skills ready to perform on the sideline. As with any new skill, progressions and drills should be employed and safety should be stressed as the skill is learned and mastered. Most cheerleading companies require an additional spotter for most of the stunts, even after the stunts have been mastered. Don't hesitate to assign additional spotters. Obviously, it's better to have too many spotters than too few for a single-based stunt. That said, it's important for the base (almost always a male in single-based stunts) to accept full responsibility for the well-being of the partner in the air. When surrounded by attentive spotters, a base might become lax in his responsibility to catch a falling stunt. Don't let this happen.

Let's focus on the primary role of the base and the partner in single-based stunts. Clearly, the base's role is much more advanced than in group stunts because the entire responsibility of balancing the partner lies on him. There is much more microbalancing involved. Microbalancing is the detailed balancing maneuver necessary to keep the partner's foot steady and secure. For example, if the partner's right toes begin to shift forward, the base would microbalance by pushing the toes in the opposite direction, providing support for the partner wherever she seemed to resist.

The primary role of the partner in single-based stunts is almost simpler than it is in group stunts. The partner needs to stay tight during all transitions and executions. This means maintaining all extremities, hips, and muscles in a locked position. It's easier to lift and balance a tight body than a loose one. The tighter the partner, the better chance of success for the stunt. Any partner in any stunt should remain tight, but the consequences of becoming loose are magnified in single-based stunts because there's only one base to handle any adjustments that must be made.

Now let's look at some stunts as well as some troubleshooting tips in case problems occur.

Walk-In Chair

Base: Start in a front lunge with right leg forward. Grab partner's left ankle with left arm while placing the right arm under the seat of the partner (see figure a). As partner dips, drive right arm up, locking out the right arm before standing up out of the lunge into a shoulder-width stance. With left arm, hold left ankle of the partner close to chest for control. The right arm should be extended above the head and close to the head of the base. For the dismount, dip with the legs, keeping arms locked out. Recatch partner at the waist at the highest point possible and slow down her landing to the floor.

Partner: Start with left foot in the deep pocket of the base. Hips are turned slightly to the side, with shoulders facing the base. On set counts, dip and push over the head of the base. Lock out left leg. Turn to the front and pull right knee up, letting foot rest on the extended arm of the base (see figure b). For dismount, stay tight as the base dips, then drop your right leg and regrab at the wrists of the base.

Common Problems	Corrections
The partner lands correctly in the chair but then falls to the right side.	View the position of the base's right arm. His right arm should be extended over his head, with biceps up against his head. If the arm is too far to the right, the weight of the partner will pull the chair down.
The base has a difficult time getting a grip under the seat of the partner.	The partner might not be pulling her knee high enough to give the base proper room. Instruct her to place her foot on the right arm of the base once the chair is executed.
The timing of the walk-in never seems to be synchronized.	Rather than attempting the chair sit over and over, instruct the base and partner to concentrate on only the timing. Isolate the walk-in process so the base and partner can learn each other's timing and tendencies when building this stunt.

a

b

Ground-Up Chair

Base: Start in a squatting position with partner positioned over right shoulder. Place left hand on partner's left ankle and right hand under her seat (see figure). On set counts, stand up forcefully, driving right arm to an extended level above head. Left hand holds partner's left leg in front of chest.

Partner: Begin standing in front (but slightly to the right) of the base. Raise left leg and put left arm on base's right shoulder. On set counts, jump off right leg and stand on left leg. Jump up again, also moving slightly to the left to get body weight over the base. Stand up to chair position and wait for dismount (see previous stunt).

(continued)

Common Problems	Corrections
Partner falls repeatedly in front of the base.	Drill the climbing aspect of this stunt. The partner might be pushing away from the base instead of pushing down. Ask her if she's looking down the back of the base. If she says she isn't, she's likely not pushing down on the base as instructed.
The partner lands correctly in the chair but then falls to the right side.	Check the position of the base's right arm, which should be extended over his head with biceps up against his head. If his arm is too far to the right, the partner's weight will pull the chair down.
The base has a difficult time getting a grip under the seat of the partner.	The partner might not be pulling her knee high enough to give the base proper room. Instruct her to place her foot on the right arm of the base once the chair is executed.

Walk-In Torch

Base: Start in a walk-in position by squatting to a double lunge (see figure a). Place left hand in front of stomach and right hand underneath (lower than) left hand. On set counts, dip with legs, driving partner up to chest level with hands close to body. As partner turns into a torch position, place your right arm on partner's front right thigh, holding her upright. Left hand remains underneath partner's left foot, providing a solid platform for her to stand on.

Partner: Begin in a walk-in position, placing right foot in base's hands. On set counts, push vigorously off base's shoulders, locking out right leg. Stand up, taking a quarter-turn over your left shoulder, then rise to a torch position (see figure b).

Common Problems	Corrections
The stunt falls off the right side of the base.	The base should apply more pressure with his right hand to keep partner stable.
The stunt falls to the front after execution.	Instruct the partner to drill the torch body position on the ground. She might need to focus on pulling her hips up more when lifting her left knee.

a

b

Toss

Base: Start with knees slightly bent. Hold partner's waist with both hands. On set counts, dip with legs at the same time that partner dips. Drive partner upward and slightly behind and above your head while flicking your wrists at the top of the toss to allow for more height. For dismount, hold partner's waist as she comes down, then ease her landing to the ground.

Partner: Start with one hand around each of the base's wrists. With chest up and elbows back, wait for the set counts. As you dip (at the same time as base dips), apply pressure to the base's wrists and jump vigorously, pushing away the base's wrists at the top of the toss (see figure). Keep feet straight and underneath your body, squeezing legs together. For dismount, regrab the base's wrists, keeping feet underneath you and chest up as you land.

(continued)

Common Problems	Corrections
The partner is not leaving the ground.	Tell her to jump more vigorously. Ask her to demonstrate a jump from the ground so you can assess if her legs are doing enough of the work.
The base's and partner's timing is not synchronized during the flick.	Isolate the problem by drilling the toss and observing who is "flicking" first. The early flicker is likely anticipating the flick and needs to wait for the other.

Toss Chair

Base: Start with knees slightly bent. Grasp partner's waist with both hands. On set counts, dip with the legs at the same time partner dips. Drive partner upward and slightly back and over your head while flicking your wrists at the top of the toss to allow for more height. At the top of the toss, drop your left arm and grab partner's left ankle. Your left arm will stabilize the chair sit and steer partner to where she needs to be. With your right hand, aim to catch under partner's seat, which provides a platform for her to sit on (see figure). For dismount, dip with legs and pop partner off your hands. Regrab her waist as she lands on the ground.

Partner: Start with one hand around each of the base's wrists. With chest up and elbows back, wait for the set counts. As you dip, apply pressure to the base's wrists and jump forcefully, pushing away base's wrists at the top of the toss. Keep feet straight and underneath your body, squeezing legs together. At the top of the toss, pull your right knee slightly up, giving the base a platform to grab. As the base grabs your left leg, keep that leg locked out to give him leverage. For dismount, wait for the set counts, regrab the base's wrists, and land on both feet.

Common Problems	Corrections
The partner is landing correctly in the chair but then falls to the right side.	The partner should wait for the flick and pull the leg up into the chair-sit position later in the toss.
The base's and partner's timing is not synchronized during the flick.	View the position of the base's right arm. It should be extended over his head, with his biceps up against his head. If his arm is too far to the right, the partner's weight will pull the chair down.
The base has a difficult time getting a grip under the partner's seat.	The partner might not be pulling her knee high enough to give the base proper room. Instruct her to place her foot on the base's right arm once the chair is executed.

Toss to Hands

Base: Start with knees slightly bent. Grasp partner's waist with both hands. On set counts, dip with legs at the same time partner dips. Drive partner upward and slightly back and over your head while flicking your wrists at the top of the toss to allow for more height. Once the toss is executed, grab under partner's feet with both hands. Ideally, hold as much of the sole of each foot as you can to provide stability for the partner (see figure). For dismount, regrab partner's waist as she comes back down and then ease her landing to the floor.

Partner: Start with one hand around each of the base's wrists. With chest up and elbows back, wait for the set counts. As you dip, apply pressure to the base's wrists and jump forcefully, pushing away his wrists at the top of the toss. Keep feet straight and underneath your body, squeezing legs together. Once the toss is executed, continue to squeeze feet together and flex them in a way that provides leverage for the base. Once the base grabs your feet, spend little time balancing and adjusting. Remain tight with legs locked out to give base enough support to keep the stunt in the air. For dismount, regrab base's wrists, keeping feet underneath body and chest up for landing.

Common Problems	Corrections
The toss is getting no air time.	Drill the partner's and base's use of legs. Leg strength is crucial in this skill.
The base cannot reach the partner's feet when she lands in a hands position.	Drill the partner on squeezing her thighs together during the toss. Not squeezing her thighs causes her legs to kick out.
The base is catching the hand position with his body extremely bent and standing low to the ground.	Instruct the base to take the time to extend the toss before anticipating catching the partner's feet in a hands position.

Base: From the toss-to-hands position, you might choose to press the stunt to an extended position. On set counts, dip with legs and drive partner overhead. Continue to squeeze shoulders and place partner directly over your head rather than in front of your body (see figure). On set counts, return partner to shoulder-level position and dismount appropriately.

Partner: From the toss-to-hands position, wait for the set counts as the stunt presses to the extended position. While moving into the extension, continue to pull legs together to make the process easier on the base. Hitting a solid motion at the top of the stunt helps to stabilize the extension. On set counts, the stunt is returned to shoulder-level position. Continue to control your body as much as you can.

Common Problems	Corrections
The partner is being lifted to extension very slowly and with strain on the base's back.	Instruct the base to drill the action of dipping quickly with his legs and extending his arms at the same time he extends his legs.
The partner falls in front of the base.	The base needs to extend the partner directly over his head. This might feel unnatural and incorrect at first, but it gets easier and feels better with repetition.
The partner's legs move to a wide stance during the extension.	The partner should focus on her legs during the extension as much as she focuses on squeezing her upper body. When the stunt moves to an extended position, she should continue to pull her legs in—even more than at the hands position.

Cradling a Single-Based Stunt

Base: When choosing to cradle any single-based stunt, dip with the legs, extending arms upward to increase the height of the cradle. Make a 45-degree turn over your right shoulder to turn and face partner. Catch under the partner's back and legs in a cradle position, dipping slightly on impact to soften the catch.

Partner: As the base dips for a cradle, ride the pop upward, hitting a hollowed body position (see figure). As you reach the top of your ride, begin to slightly arch and turn your shoulders to the left, anticipating the base's cradle. As the base makes contact with your seat, reach over his shoulders with your hands and wrap them around his neck. Pike your body.

Base: Once you have partner to hands and have mastered the press extension, the liberty is the next logical progression. On set counts, dip with legs and drive partner overhead. As you reach extended-arm position, bring your hands closer together. At the top of the drive upward, release partner's left foot with left hand and move to grab underneath the toe on her right foot. Squeeze your shoulders and place partner directly over your head, not in front of you (see figure). On set counts, return the partner to shoulder-level position and dismount.

Partner: From the toss-to-hands position, wait for the set counts as the stunt presses to the extended position. While being extended, continue to pull legs together to make things easier on the base. As the base extends his arm, pull your body weight in toward the middle. At the top of the extension, pull your left leg up and lift your hip. The ridge of your left foot will secure itself into the crevice created by the kneecap of your right leg. On set counts, the stunt is returned to shoulder-level position. Continue to control your body as much as possible.

Common Problems	Corrections
The partner is pulling her left foot out of the base's grip before he's ready.	Both the base and partner need to review the timing of their execution. The base might be dipping too slowly and the partner anticipating switching her weight too early.
The partner falls in front of the base.	The base needs to extend the partner directly over his head. This might feel unnatural and incorrect at first, but it gets easier and feels better with repetition.
The partner continuously falls to the right side of the base when trying to execute the liberty.	The partner needs to concentrate on pulling her weight up and toward the middle rather than forcing her left foot over to the right. The hip is moving too quickly, which accounts for the stunt falling off to the right side.

Summary

Single-based stunts are a favorite among cheerleaders and fans alike. Although they are exciting to attempt, they require a high level of precision and communication. All the stunts presented in this chapter require at least one spotter, but many squads use more than one. You should use as many spotters as you feel is necessary to guarantee safety.

Tosses

The skill of basket tossing continues to advance in cheerleading. The basket toss tends to receive more national attention than other skills because of the fantastic eye appeal of the amazing heights. A basket toss can be an incredible tool to get an audience's attention and ignite a response from fans.

Basket tosses are most useful on the sideline during a time-out or when using signs. Timing a basket toss to be executed at the same time as the crowd is instructed to yell a word or letter (e.g., "BHS") can make for excitement. Obviously, you would not want to throw a basket toss at a critical time in a game, when the focus of fans needs to be on the court or field.

Cheerleaders and coaches should take a cautious view of basket tosses because they are as dangerous as they are appealing. They require many, many progressions and should be performed only in a safe environment by trained, attentive athletes. As each progression is described, be mindful that safety is, as always, the top priority.

Basket Toss Basics

As is true of any stunt, the basics are important in the basket toss. Sometimes when first attempting basket tosses, advanced cheerleaders feel their squad is experienced enough to throw them without practicing the basics beforehand. Clearly, this is a mistake. Skipping the basics is inviting trouble. The three primary basics of basket tossing are concentration, timing, and patience.

Concentration. Basket tosses require a higher level of concentration than any other cheerleading skill. All squad members should remain focused. Music should be turned off; any other possible distractions should be minimized.

Timing. Precise timing among the bases and partner is crucial to the success of a toss. If the timing is off by much, a dangerous situation occurs as bases must travel great lengths to catch their partner.

Patience. New skills are seldom mastered overnight. Taking the time to master a new skill reduces stress and decreases risk of injury.

Before attempting to throw basket tosses, consider your team's skill level. Because of the increased safety issues, certain standards must be set in basket tossing. First and foremost, a cheerleading squad must be able to safely execute an extension prep with a high pop cradle (see chapter 7). Being able to safely catch a partner is crucial to the safety of a basket toss. Since the height of a basket tends to be at least twice that of the height created by cradling an extension prep, this progression makes sense.

Bases should stand with legs about shoulder-width apart. They will dip into a lunge with their knees facing forward. Bases must keep their backs upright to avoid too much strain on the back. Turning the knees out (which is popular among cheerleaders) feels more comfortable but tends to cut off the height of the basket toss when it's actually thrown. See figure 10.1 for proper positioning for bases.

The bases' grip in the basket toss is formed by the two bases interlocking arms. This grip is

Figure 10.1   Bases' stance.

unique in cheerleading and is where the term "basket" comes from. To assume the proper grip, each base grasps her own left wrist with her right hand. Then facing each other, the bases reach forward and grasp the other's right wrist. This creates an interlocked "basket" for the partner to stand on (figure 10.2).

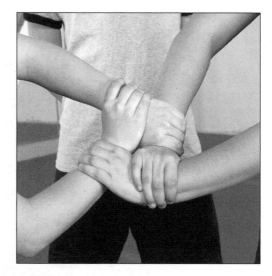

Figure 10.2   Bases' grip.

Preliminary Toss Drills

The following drills should be used for basket tosses. Typically, drills are exercises that a squad executes after learning a new skill to reinforce proper technique. In the case of basket tosses, however, drills can be done before, during, or after skills are mastered. If bases use the correct grip and partners assume the correct body position (see chapter 7), these drills should be safe for your squad as they work toward a perfect basket toss.

Timing Drill

The main objective of the Timing Drill is to get bases accustomed to tossing using the unique interlocking grip of the basket toss.

Bases: To begin, interlock arms with one another, as shown in figure 10.2 on the previous page. In the double lunge, with hands interlocked, await timing from partner. On the first "down, up," take a small dip with legs, following timing of partner's hands. On the second "down, up," explode into a jump from the ground to feel the motion of tossing with an interlocking grip.

Partner: Using your hands, simulate the timing of stepping into the basket (see figure). Start with one hand on the right half of the basket. On set counts, push your hand down to create the feel of an actual foot and place your other hand on the other half of the basket toss. Counts should be spoken out loud: "1, 2, down, up, down, up." On second "up," partner pulls her hands up above the basket as if they were her feet, being thrown.

Points: This drill emphasizes the need for good timing between the two bases. If timing is off in a basket toss, the partner could travel in an unexpected direction, causing a safety hazard.

Load-In Drill

The Load-In Drill is similar to the Hang Drill described in chapter 6. This drill is meant to teach the partner how to load into a basket correctly. Once the Hang Drill has been mastered, and you're confident that the bases and partner have the correct timing and body position down, the Load-In Drill is the next logical progression.

Bases: Interlock arms and get into a double lunge as if preparing to throw a basket toss.

Partner: Start with hands on bases' shoulders. Place right foot into the right side of the basket, making sure toes have a platform to stand on. On set counts "1, 2, down, up," dip with the leg on the ground, using momentum to pull body weight off the ground and over the basket. As your second foot settles on the bases' hands, freeze your body position. The bases should freeze as well (see figure).

Back spotter: Your main job in the Load-In Drill is to support partner's weight as she steps into loading position. Ideally, however, a partner should be holding her own weight in a basket toss position, so you are there not for support but to catch her in case of a mishap.

Points: Once partner is in loading position, a coach or an experienced cheerleader should do a quick check to answer the following questions:

1. Is the partner's weight distributed through her hands onto the bases' shoulders? (The answer should be yes.)

2. Can the bases feel any weight from the partner on their hands? (The answer should be no.)

3. Is the partner's chest over her knees and toes, forming a straight vertical line? (The answer should be yes.)

4. Are the partner's feet placed on the hands, as shown in the photo? (The answer should be yes.)

If everything is correct, cheerleaders can progress to the next drill. If the stunt group does not pass the "quick check," the drill should be repeated until mastered.

The aim of the Trophy Drill is to get the partner accustomed to standing up straight in a basket. Many cheerleaders are too timid when taking off from a basket, which cuts the height of the toss short.

Bases: Begin in starting position for a basket toss. As partner steps in, one foot at a time, dip with your legs and extend arms *without* breaking your grip on each other's hands. Once arms are extended, immediately retract by bringing arms back down and setting the base.

Partner: Start by loading one foot into the basket. On set counts, put both feet into the basket and push off the bases' shoulders. Stand up quickly and position arms in a touchdown motion, as if riding a basket (see figure). Once the drill hits top position, retract by bending legs and placing arms on bases' shoulders.

Back spotter: Help load in partner during initial counts. You should need to do very little to hold up partner's hips as she loads in. As partner stands, grab her ankles and stabilize the stunt as it reaches the top. As partner comes back down, grab under her seat to ensure a safe dismount.

A common misconception about the Trophy Drill is that teams try to stabilize the trophy body position at the top and balance the partner in the extended position. But the sole purpose of this drill is to get the partner accustomed to standing up in the basket. Thus, the extended trophy position should be held only long enough for the partner to become comfortable while standing up.

1-2-3-4 Drill

This drill helps bases become accustomed to catching traveling baskets. To start the drill, all four tossers in the basket (two bases, front spotter, back spotter) are assigned a number (1, 2, 3, or 4) to correspond to a direction in which the basket could easily travel.

Bases: Start with arms in air, extended in a touchdown position, ready to catch. Arms must remain in this up position through the entire drill to reinforce the need to catch high no matter what happens in an actual basket toss. Although baskets hardly ever intentionally move, many times poor timing, communication, or technique can cause a basket to travel unexpectedly. Thus, bases need to be prepared for anything.

When the designated speaker (a coach or a cheerleader not involved in the drill) calls out a number, the foursome moves as a group in the direction corresponding to that number and simulates a traveling basket toss. As each number is randomly called out, the base group should get better and better at moving quickly to catch the imaginary partner. The arms of the bases should remain up at all times.

Points: Once the bases have proven they can handle last-second developments in a basket toss, they can progress to performing actual tosses.

Ready for Tosses

The section that follows contains the first category of progressive tosses to be attempted by a cheerleading squad. These tosses are the easiest among many possibilities. Learning the tosses in order from easiest to more difficult allows a team to progress at its own pace.

Straight Ride

Before attempting a specific skill in a basket toss, the bases—and especially the partner—must become accustomed to throwing a straight ride (also referred to as a "pencil"). Many times, when teams are having problems with some of their more advanced tosses, the problems can be traced back to the straight ride. Some consider the straight ride an actual skill, whereas others see it only as a progression.

Bases: Start in a double lunge with arms interlocked, as described earlier in the chapter. Keep arms relaxed, not locked out. On set counts, dip with partner and load both of her feet. On the second "down, up," dip with legs and explode upward, with elbows leading the way, creating a slingshot effect. At the top of the toss (where the Trophy Drill would end), release grip of the other base and extend hands upward. Arms of both bases should be in an upright position to maximize the height of the basket toss.

For the cradle, leave arms in an extended position above your head, awaiting partner's dismount. As partner comes within reachable distance, grab her and pull her into a safe cradle.

Partner: Begin the load-in process as you would in the Load-In Drill (page 134). On counts "1, 2, down, up," dip and place your second foot into the basket. On the second "down, up," hold body weight in the basket and begin to stand on bases. When standing up for the basket toss, arms should be in a touchdown position, reaching for the sky. As the basket reaches its maximum height, pull arms out and pike torso to help assist in the cradle. A common error during this part of the process is to arch the torso, as if riding a cradle. During this straight ride, you must remain upright, keeping toes under shoulders.

Back spotter: You have three options when it comes to loading in the basket toss. Your role depends heavily on partner's body awareness and her ability to hold her own weight when being tossed. Here are the three options in back spotting:

1. Load in partner around waist (see figure a). This is especially useful when the partner has a difficult time loading her weight in properly. This way, you can ensure her weight is evenly distributed and keep weight off bases' hands. This method is not preferred in throwing the highest basket—only in helping keep the partner in check. Once partner is loaded in and begins to stand, continue lifting through the waist and toss her.

2. Load in partner and grab under seat (see figure b). This method is preferred by intermediate stunt groups. Throwing from under the seat allows you to help hold some of the weight up for the partner but also gives the back spotter some freedom to help with the toss as well. Once partner is loaded in, the back spotter can grab under the seat and extend arms, helping lift the partner in the straight ride.

3. Load partner in and place hands under the bases' interlocked arms (see figure c). This is the best way for a back spotter to throw a basket but should be used only with an advanced partner who's confident in distributing her weight properly in the load-in. What makes this method so advanced is that the back spotter can throw from underneath the basket and help the bases until the final moment when the partner leaves their hands. In options 1 and 2, the back spotter's involvement in the toss ends when partner's hips leave the reach of the back spotter. If you use option 3, you can be a crucial part of completing the bases' toss.

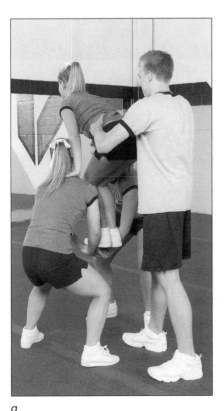  

a b c

(continued)

Front spotter: Your role is crucial in a basket toss. Although many stunts can make do without a front spotter, basket tosses improve in height when a front spotter is used.

Many front spotters try to latch onto the basket grip in hopes that doing so makes the grip more secure. This is a misconception—latching onto the grip might actually *inhibit* the toss.

Start with both hands in blades (palms up), and place them under the bases' interlocked grip (see figure d). As partner loads in, simply follow the timing of the bases. As bases stand up and begin to extend arms, the front spotter can be most useful. Follow along with your hands in blades and deliberately break through the interlocked grip at the top of the toss. This ensures the bases are following through correctly and extending their toss to its highest potential.

For the dismount, the partner can either step aside to get out of the way of the bases or move to one side and assist in the cradle.

d

Toe-Touch Basket

A toe-touch basket is one of the oldest and most commonly used baskets in cheerleading. It's not necessarily the easiest, but it tends to be the first basket cheerleaders try. A common error new cheerleaders make in learning a toe-touch basket is to ride the basket and try to throw a toe touch in the air as they would on the ground. Because of the height, speed, and direction of a basket toss, a different form of technique is required.

Bases, front spotter, and back spotter: As is the case for many of the other baskets we'll describe in this chapter, the roles of the bases, front spotter, and back spotter in a toe-touch basket are identical to their roles in the straight ride.

Partner: Initiate the toss as for a straight ride. Ride toss with hips and toes under shoulders. When beginning to hit top of basket, roll hips forward into toe-touch position. (This is where the basket toss toe touch differs from a toe touch on the ground.) Pull chest forward and put arms in a T motion to complete execution of a good toe touch.

At this point, initiate the following three steps to create a good arch:

1. Snap shoulders and arms back.
2. Pull hips up toward the sky.
3. Drive heels back.

These steps should make for a strong arch. The arch tends to be the most overlooked aspect of any basket. Many people judge the technique and beauty of a well-executed basket on how impressive the arch is.

Points: Remember that high school cheerleading squads are not allowed to snap their heads back in a cradle (from basket or otherwise) to increase the angle of the arch. Almost all major governing bodies (e.g., National Federation, NCA, UCA) do not allow this, even in competition. All-Star Cheerleading tends to follow other guidelines. If you're entering a competition, be sure to check the sponsor's rules beforehand.

Tuck Arch Basket

The tuck arch basket tends to be one of the easier baskets to execute. While the toe-touch basket is more popular, the tuck arch generally requires less flexibility and coordination in the partner. The tuck arch was one of the first "specialty" baskets that began popping up in the mid-1990s.

Bases, front spotter, and back spotter: Please refer to the straight ride (pages 136-138) for all instructions for bases and spotters.

Partner: Ride the basket in a straight ride. As the basket reaches its peak, get into a tuck position by pulling knees in and chest forward simultaneously. Place palms of the hands on knees to exaggerate the tucked position.

As the basket finishes its ride upward, push knees and arms out into an arched position. Drive heels and shoulders downward while lifting with hips. The cradle will be the same as in the previously described baskets.

Specialty Basket Tosses

In this section, we'll look at a series of more advanced basket tosses, commonly called "specialty tosses." These tosses go a step beyond the first series of tosses discussed. They involve complex maneuvering by the partner and also tend to require more coordination between the bases, either in attaining the necessary height or in the quick movement and turning necessary to catch the partner properly.

Kick Arch

Bases, front spotter, and back spotter: Please refer to the straight ride (pages 136-138) for instructions for bases and spotters.

Partner: Ride the basket toss in straight-ride position. At the top of the basket, kick one leg up to face, keeping shoulders and chest upward as back leg remains straight. If the back foot doesn't remain pointing downward, the skill looks more like a front hurdler than a kick arch. Once the basket is executed, arch into a cradle as previously described.

This basket is typically performed to the side so the crowd can witness its execution completely. When determining in which direction to throw the kick arch, a good rule of thumb is to kick with the leg that's furthest from the crowd.

Pretty Girl

Bases, front spotter, and back spotter: Please refer to the straight ride (pages 136-138) for instructions for bases and spotters.

Partner: At the top of the straight ride, turn shoulders toward the crowd and place back hand (the hand farthest from the crowd) behind head and front hand on waist. While doing this, lift knee (the knee closer to the crowd) into a tucked position.

Pretty Girl Kick

The pretty girl kick is an elite basket because it's a combination of two baskets. This kick requires more coordination than the pretty girl and should be performed only after the baskets already described have been mastered.

Bases, front spotter, and back spotter: Please refer to the straight ride (pages 136-138) for instructions for bases and spotters.

Partner: Ride the basket in a straight ride. Moments before reaching the top, turn shoulders toward the crowd and place back hand (hand farthest from the crowd) behind head and front hand on waist. While doing this, lift knee that's closer to the crowd into a tucked position.

As the basket reaches its maximum height, turn shoulders back to the side and kick the tucked leg outward while keeping shoulders and chest up. If you bend the back leg, you lose some of the power in the basket and it resembles a front hurdler. Once the basket is executed, arch into a cradle as previously described.

Twisting Basket Tosses

Full-twisting baskets are becoming increasingly popular in cheerleading. These baskets are traditionally performed only by teams with elite skills and experience. They require trained spotting and quick thinking from the bases.

Full-Twisting Basket

The full-twisting basket is sometimes considered more difficult than a full-twisting cradle because the legs of the partner begin so close together. In a cradle from an extension prep, the partner keeps her legs apart as a reminder to pull her toes, hips, and shoulders together.

Bases, front spotter, and back spotter: Please refer to the straight ride (pages 136-138) for instructions for bases and spotters.

Partner: Lift as if riding a straight ride, but *before* reaching the top, slice arms across left side of chest, pulling right shoulder over chest. While doing this, simultaneously pull right hip over body as well. (Not pulling right hip can cause the basket toss to get stuck, and you'll begin twisting in sections.) You won't need to lay yourself down in this maneuver because the lay down occurs naturally. Once the rotation is complete, open arms to stop rotation and let bases catch you.

Double Full-Twisting Basket

The double full-twisting basket is much more difficult than the single full-twisting basket. This skill requires a high level of body control from the partner. In a double twist, the partner is much more likely to come off her original axis (that is, she might spin out of control, not landing where she's expected to land).

Bases, front spotter, and back spotter: Please refer to the straight ride (pages 136-138) for instructions for bases and spotters.

Partner: Lift as if riding a straight ride, but *before* reaching the top, slice arms across the left side of chest, pulling right shoulder over chest. The initiation of this movement, in comparison to the single full-twisting basket, needs to happen much more aggressively and dramatically in order for the double full twist to be completed properly. While doing this, simultaneously pull your right hip over your body as well. (Not pulling the right hip can cause the basket toss to get stuck, and you'll begin twisting in sections.) You won't need to lay yourself down in this maneuver because the lay down occurs naturally, usually in a much more extreme fashion than in the single full twist.

After completing two rotations, open arms to stop rotation and let bases catch you.

Skills and Twisting Skills Combination Basket Tosses

The next echelon of baskets is among the most advanced being performed by cheerleaders today and are usually done in competitions only. They require maximum coordination of the partners as well as strong timing and communication from the bases. Most of the baskets described in this section require the bases to make a quarter-turn during the execution of the basket.

Kick Full

Bases: Start off facing the back (away from the crowd) in double lunge and begin a toss similar to the toss of a straight ride. As basket begins to take off, step *toward* each other and do a quarter-turn to catch cradle. (A common error is to do a quarter-turn and naturally step away from each other.) At any point during these baskets, bases should be no further than shoulder-width apart from each other.

Back spotter: Your role in this basket is different from that in baskets previously described. Face the back and load in the partner. Rather than moving hands underneath the interlocked grip, you'll position them to help initiate the quarter-turn that makes this basket effective. Place left hand around left side of partner's waist. Right hand cups underneath partner's seat. As basket begins to stand, follow partner up. Lift with left hand and torque partner by pushing on right side of her hips. Helping initiate the spin makes the full twist after the kick much easier.

Partner: You'll perform a combination of a straight ride, kick arch, and full-twisting basket toss. Begin facing the back. Once loaded in the basket toss, begin to stand up as normal. While beginning to lock out legs, turn slightly over left shoulder, keeping hips and legs under shoulders. Pick a spot on the wall to watch to confirm you're making a complete quarter-turn.

At the top of the ride, kick front leg up to face while keeping shoulders and chest up; back leg remains straight.

At this point, roll over into the twist, focusing on three key points:

1. Do *not* arch, which is the typical tendency when first learning this basket. The arch makes it harder to pull into the full-twist position.
2. Wrap ankle of right foot over body.
3. Slice arms across body (as in a full-twisting cradle).

After the twist is completed, let bases catch you.

Bases: Start off facing the back (away from the crowd) in double lunge and begin a toss similar to the toss of a straight ride. As the basket begins to take off, step *toward* each other and do a quarter-turn to catch the cradle. At any point during these baskets, bases should be no further than shoulder-width apart from each other. The partner might inconsistently travel away from the natural axis of the original basket (more so than in the kick single full). Remain under partner at all times, prepared for the unpredictability of this basket.

Back spotter: Face the back and load in partner. You will position your hands to help initiate the quarter-turn that makes this basket effective. Place left hand around left side of partner's waist. Right hand cups under partner's seat. As basket begins to stand, lift with left hand on partner's waist and torque partner by pushing on right side of her hips. Helping initiate the spin makes the double full twist after the kick much easier.

Partner: Perform a combination of a straight ride, kick arch, and double full-twisting basket toss. Begin facing the back. After loading in the basket toss, turn slightly over left shoulder, keeping hips and legs under shoulders. Pick a spot on the wall to watch to confirm you're making a complete quarter-turn. At the top of the ride, kick front leg up to face while keeping shoulders and chest up; back leg remains straight. Now roll over into the twist, focusing on the same three points as you did for the single full twisting basket:

1. Do *not* arch, which is the typical tendency when first learning this basket. The arch makes it harder to pull into the full-twist position.
2. Wrap ankle of right foot over body.
3. Slice arms across body (as in a full-twisting cradle).

Summary

Basket tosses are exciting both for cheerleaders and the fans who get to witness them. Every year, cheerleading squads are creating new and exciting basket tosses to entertain the crowds. The skills and stunts detailed in this chapter are only some of the ways that basket tosses can be used—as your team gains comfort and experience performing these tosses, you might try adding your own creative variations. Just remember, no matter what type of basket tosses your team attempts, the same basics of technique apply, as explained at the beginning of the chapter—they are the keys to success for your tosses, no matter how easy or difficult the stunt might be!

eleven

Pyramids

Once partner stunts have been perfected, these stunts can be connected to form pyramids. Pyramids are a creative and visual form of stunting that squads can use to draw fans' attention and increase crowd involvement. Building pyramids while performing spirited chants is a refreshing change for both cheerleaders and fans, and it allows squads to impress crowds with their stunting ability. Simple partner stunts, when joined together, can form what looks to be a difficult pyramid. Stunts are performed close together with partners touching each other by connecting hands, arms, and feet. For a safe and solid pyramid, each separate stunt must be perfected before putting the stunts together. The rules for building partner stunts apply to building pyramids as well. Partners still need to "step, lock, tighten," and cheerleaders shouldn't progress to more difficult pyramids until they have perfected the easier ones.

Building Pyramids Safely

Once individual stunts are perfected, they can be joined together. When building pyramids, communication is vital because so many people are involved. Everyone needs to focus and know the correct counts so that timing is synchronized during building and dismounting. Pyramids are usually built to certain words of cheers or chants or to beats of music. When practicing, build the stunts to these same words or beats so it's easier to combine the stunts into a pyramid later. When first putting the stunts together, if one person is in charge of counting, he or she is usually a spotter near the middle who can be heard by everyone. If practicing with counts rather than words or beats, the traditional stunting counts of "one, two, down, up," as described in chapter 6, should be used.

Bases, partners, and spotters comprise the cheerleading positions of a pyramid. When learning a new pyramid, each cheerleader must know his or her responsibilities before the pyramid is built. The responsibilities of each position are the same for an individual stunt built by itself or as part of a pyramid (see previous stunt chapters). For example, the responsibilities of the bases, partner, and spotter in a liberty are the same whether the stunt is being performed alone or joined with other stunts as part of a pyramid. When each cheerleader knows his or her individual responsibilities and performs these duties, pyramids are more likely to be safe, clean, and sturdy. There are a few items that cheerleaders in pyramids need to be aware of that are different from individual partner stunts. We'll go over these differences now.

Bases

- Bases need to be positioned close enough for partners to brace but not so close that they trip over each other.
- For a clean visual effect, bases must lift partners in synchronization to the correct words, counts, or beats of music.
- Bases remain the primary catchers of partners in pyramids.

Partners

- Partners need to be strong in their climbing technique so that pyramids are built smoothly.
- Strong partners are less apt to fall onto other stunt groups making up the pyramid.
- Partners at shoulder height can be used as bracers for other partners.

Spotters

- Spotters need to be focused on and in position to catch their partners.
- Spotters must be aware of the other partners in the pyramid in case one of the stunts falls so they can help protect their stunt group or catch the falling stunt.
- Hands-on spotting assists the stability of the stunts involved in the pyramid.
- Some pyramids have spotters both in front of and behind partners to make the pyramid more solid. For a pyramid to be both legal and safe, you need enough cheerleaders spotting.

High school cheerleaders are usually required to follow some basic safety rules when building pyramids. Many high school squads follow the National Federation Spirit Rules, which concern the safety of the participants. Because there's a higher risk involved when building pyramids, safety rules must be understood and followed exactly. Those rules are listed here:

- Squads are limited to building stunts and pyramids only two people high.
- Each extended partner must have a spotter.
- Partners must receive their primary support from bases in direct, weight-bearing contact with the performing surface.
- One of the cheerleaders bracing a stunt must be at shoulder level or below. The stunt exceptions to this bracing rule are chair, double- or triple-based deadman lift,

and double- or triple-based straddle lift as well as extension and awesome, provided partners have both feet in both hands of their bases.

- Stunt participants can't move over or under a stunt or pyramid.
- Partners in a stunt or pyramid can't be inverted, and partners can't drop their heads backward out of alignment with their torsos.

Hanging pyramids have some added rules for safety:

- Bases must remain stationary and maintain constant contact with the suspended cheerleader.
- Spotters must be present for each shoulder stand.
- Suspended cheerleader must not be inverted and must be lower than the shoulder stands.
- Suspended cheerleader's feet must be hanging free.
- Suspended cheerleader cannot rotate on the dismount.

Basics of Pyramid Building

When building pyramids, partners from separate stunts connect with each other by bracing. Bracing occurs when partners connect by touching hands, overlapping arms, or touching a foot to the body, hand, or arm of another partner. Bracing doesn't mean grabbing or pulling on another partner—when this happens, the entire pyramid (or at least one side) can be pulled down, which is both illegal and very dangerous for the participants. To be legal, one of the people bracing must be at shoulder level or below (except for previously cited exceptions). When first building a pyramid, it helps to have the middle stunt build with one side of the pyramid while the other side spots; then switch sides. Once both sides are solid, the entire pyramid can be built. Pyramids should be performed in front of fans only after they have been checked off by coaches (discussed in chapter 15). This also means that pyramids should be built only when a qualified coach is present to supervise.

Dismounting From Pyramids

When dismounting from pyramids, all participants must know the correct counts, and partners must maintain control. This makes for a clean and safe dismount. All bases in a pyramid should sponge and cradle on the same counts. If partners are bracing, they can return to their individual stunts by letting go and then cradling, or just cradling from the braced position. Partners bracing another partner's foot or leg can also sponge and then lightly release the partner's foot or leg during the dismount.

Building Creative Pyramids

Pyramids don't have to be huge, difficult, or complicated to be creative. Timing and the element of surprise are what make pyramids exciting. It looks impressive when individual partner stunts hit at the same time to form a pyramid. The element of surprise occurs when fans don't see a pyramid coming, and squads suddenly hit it. Moving pyramids are also thrilling. Turning pyramids in a circle or moving them toward the crowd can elicit a strong fan response. Cheerleaders involved in moving pyramids need to make sure everyone is moving on the same counts for the pyramid to look clean and remain solid.

Another way to build a creative pyramid is to transition between stunts, having different stunt groups retake down and back up. Each stunt group can retake at the same time and come back up to the same position or change to a new one. For example, outside partners can be in liberties, retake, and come back up in heel stretches. Or the middle can retake down while the outside groups are popping back up (or vice versa). The important thing to remember on retakes is that everyone knows the correct counts and hits them.

Building pyramids during games takes some planning to perform them safely and at appropriate times. Stunting surfaces and the surrounding area need to be examined before building any type of stunts or pyramids. For example, squads should never build pyramids on concrete, wet surfaces, or uneven surfaces. During basketball games, cheerleaders shouldn't stunt under baskets or other low-hanging objects. Used properly, pyramids can be built to shoulder level during a chant, and then extended up for the finale. Pyramids with accompanying signs might be used during exciting moments in a game to gain the crowd's attention. Because cheerleaders are up higher in a pyramid, fans can see them more clearly and yell along with the chant. Pyramids should be used during a game only to lead fans and increase crowd involvement.

Pyramids are also an essential component of a good competition routine. Many score sheets have a separate section for pyramids. For maximum points in a competition, precise timing of pyramids is vital. Timing not only includes the building of the pyramid but also transitioning between stunts in the pyramid and the dismount. Creative pyramids, which distinguish one squad's pyramids from another's, are also desirable during competitions.

Bases: Outside bases start in side lunges (as if setting for a thigh stand), grabbing the toe and heel of the partners before the stand-up. When partner reaches the top of the pyramid, bases pull in slightly, stabilizing the foot of the partner. Inside base stands on the floor, extending arms upward to catch partners' inside legs (see figure). For dismount, outside bases stabilize partner's foot as partner comes off the front. Inside base steers partners' legs gently toward the ground during dismount.

Partners: Place foot into the pocket of the bases. On set counts, push off the bases' shoulders, lock out the supporting leg, and give inside base the inside leg, extending the leg and pointing the toe. For dismount, keep outside leg locked out while inside leg is steered toward the ground.

Spotters: No spotters are required. However, when first learning this stunt, use back spotters who are responsible for the two partners.

Points: This pyramid is one of the more basic ones and should be executed thoroughly and perfectly before moving to more difficult pyramids.

Common Problems	Corrections
Partner continues to fall backward after pyramid is executed.	Inside base might be standing too far to the back. To best stabilize the partner, the inside base should be somewhat in front of the outside bases.
Partner is falling toward the middle of the pyramid.	Outside bases might be standing too far from each other. Have each outside base move in and rebuild the stunt.

Inside Hitch With Center Prep

Bases: Outside base groups get set using liberty grips, grabbing toe and heel of each partner. On set counts, they drive partner up to shoulder level and stabilize the stunt. For dismount, bases dip with legs and catch partner in a cradle. Inside base builds a shoulder sit (Basic Stunt Technique, pages 71-72).

Outside partners: Build liberties, giving bases outside legs. On set counts, step, lock, and tighten to a one-legged stunt at shoulder level. Now hitch inside legs to the inside shoulder sit. For dismount, keep legs locked out as bases dip, and then fall into cradle.

Inside partner: Build a shoulder sit.

Spotters: Stand behind partners and help drive the outside stunts, grabbing at the outside partners' ankles or calves. For the cradle, remain near to protect the head and neck (see figure).

Points: Variations might include the center in a thigh stand or flatback position.

Common Problem	Correction
Outside partners are falling to the inside.	Partner could be placing too much weight on the inside shoulder sit. Partner should rebuild and place no weight on the inside leg. Also, the outside base groups might be standing too far from the inside shoulder sit. Move the base groups in and attempt the stunt again.

Bases: Both outside and inside bases build extension preps (Intermediate Stunts, page 84).

Partners: Both outside and inside partners build extension preps. At the top of the pyramid, reach arms out to connect with other partners (see figure).

Spotters: Follow instructions for spotting extension prep on page 84.

Points: A variation of this pyramid can be performed with a center prep and outside extensions.

Common Problem

Stunt is unstable because extensions are having a difficult time executing.

Correction

Go back to the basics and review the technique involved in extension and extension preps. This pyramid should not be attempted if the individual skills involved can't be performed properly.

Stair Step

First base: Build a shoulder sit (Basic Stunt Technique, pages 71-72)

Second bases: Build an extension prep (Intermediate Stunts, page 84). Angle the stunt toward the shoulder sit as partners execute the pyramid. For dismount, turn the partner a quarter-turn toward the front and cradle.

Third bases: Begin with a liberty grip, facing the front. On set counts, dip and drive the partner up to a liberty hitch. For dismount, dip on set counts and catch partner in a cradle.

First partner: Build a shoulder sit, as described in Basic Stunt Technique.

Second partner: Build an extension prep. As bases turn first partner to face the shoulder sit, lean over and place hands on shoulders of first partner. For dismount, bases turn second partner toward the front and catch in a cradle.

Third partner: Build a liberty (Advanced Stunts, page 115). Hitch inside leg to the back of the second partner. For dismount, cradle on set counts.

Spotters: Both second partner and third partner should have a spotter responsible for the head and neck. Refer to page numbers noted above for individual stunts and follow the corresponding spotting instructions.

Points: This pyramid is most visual when there are enough cheerleaders to perform the same pyramid going in two different directions (see figure). The shoulder sit can be traded out for a thigh stand.

Common Problem	Correction
Second partner is getting pushed down.	Third partner must make sure that her body weight is centered over her bases and not extended through her hitched leg.

Outside bases: Both outside bases build liberties (Advanced Stunts, page 115).

Inside bases: Build an extension prep (Intermediate Stunts, page 84).

Outside partners: Both outside partners build liberties. At the top of the pyramid, reach arms out to connect with other partners.

Inside partner: Build an extension prep. At the top of the pyramid, reach arms out to connect with other partners.

Spotters: Refer to page numbers noted above for individual stunts and follow the corresponding spotting instructions.

Points: This pyramid is valuable at the early stages of learning to build liberties.

Common Problem	Correction
Outside partners are too close to the inside partner at the top of the pyramid.	Outside bases and outside partners might be anticipating the execution of the pyramid and slightly drive the partner closer to the middle. Rebuild while focusing on executing the liberty upward.

Inside Heel Stretch With Center Prep

Outside bases: Both bases build liberties (Advanced Stunts, page 115).

Inside bases: Build an extension prep (Intermediate Stunts, page 84).

Outside partners: Both outside partners build liberty heel stretches (Advanced Stunts, pages 115-117). At the top of the stunt, kick inside leg to inside partner, keeping that leg locked out with toe pointed.

Inside partner: Build an extension prep. At the top of the pyramid, reach arms out to connect hand with ankles of the outside partners (see figure).

Spotters: Refer to page numbers noted above for individual stunts and follow the corresponding spotting instructions.

Points: This pyramid requires much more flexibility and coordination than the previous pyramid. Make sure proper progression is executed.

Common Problem	Correction
Outside partners are bearing too much weight on the inside partner.	Work on the flexibility of the outside partners. Typically, partners with poor flexibility tend to lean toward the inside because their body can't control the movement of the inside leg.

Outside bases: Both outside bases build liberties (Advanced Stunts, page 115).

Inside bases: Buils an extension prep (Intermediate Stunts, page 84).

Outside partners: Both outside partners build liberty heel stretches (Advanced Stunts, pages 115-117). At the top of the stunt, kick outside leg to a heel-stretch position, keeping that leg locked out with the toe pointed. Inside arm reaches for the inside partner to execute pyramid (see figure).

Inside partner: Build an extension prep. At the top of the pyramid, reach arms out to connect with the arms of outside partners.

Spotters: Refer to page numbers noted above for individual stunts and follow the corresponding spotting instructions.

Points: This pyramid is valuable during the early stages of learning how to build heel stretches.

Common Problem	Correction
Outside partners are bearing too much weight on the inside partner.	Work on the flexibility of the outside partners. Typically, partners with poor flexibility tend to lean toward the inside because their body can't control the movement of the inside leg.

First bases: Build a double-based thigh stand (Basic Stunt Technique, page 69).

Second bases: Build an extension prep (Intermediate Stunts, page 84).

Third bases: Build an extension (Advanced Stunts, page 100).

First partner: Build a double-based thigh stand.

Second partner: Build an extension prep. Lean over and rest hands on first partner's shoulders.

Third partner: Build an extension. Lean over and rest hands on second partner's shoulders or raise arms into a high V (see figure).

Spotters: Refer to page numbers noted above for individual stunts and follow the corresponding spotting instructions.

Points: Based on the number of team members and on ability level, more "layers" of this totem pole can be added behind and in front of the pyramid pictured.

Common Problem	Correction
Stunt groups are too far apart.	Move the base groups in closer, keeping in mind the need for a safe amount of distance should an error occur.

Front bases: Build extension preps (Intermediate Stunts, page 84), maintaining an arm's length of distance from each other.

Back bases: Set with liberty grips, holding the outside leg of each partner. On set counts, dip and execute liberties (Advanced Stunts, page 115) while each partner executes the pyramid. For dismount, each back base group takes a slight step back during the dip to ensure a safe distance from the three front base groups.

Front partners: Build extension preps and extend arms to connect at the top of the pyramid.

Back partners: Set for liberties by giving outside legs to base groups. On set counts, each partner stands up and extends the inside leg to a hitch on the shoulders of the inside front partner (see figure). For dismount, be prepared to travel backward as the bases cradle away from the front stunts.

Spotters: Refer to page numbers noted above for individual stunts and follow the corresponding spotting instructions. The two back spotters need to travel slightly backward to catch partners as they travel away from pyramid.

Points: This pyramid can have incredible visual appeal but is more difficult than previous pyramids. Please ensure that all cheerleaders have the prerequisite skills required to attempt this pyramid.

Common Problem	Correction
Pyramid collapses at initiation of the dismount.	Back partners are putting too much weight on their foot and using the front stunts as leverage to push away from the stunt groups. Instruct the partner to put no weight on the inside foot and let the bases do the dipping.

Opposite Straight-Leg Tabletop

Outside bases: Each begin with stunt group facing the inside. Set using liberty grips, holding the back foot of each partner. On set counts, stand up to liberty. For the cradle, move slightly backward to allow for safe dismounts.

Inside bases: Build on an extension prep (Intermediate Stunts, page 184). After building the extension prep, wait as the inside partner leans over to the front post.

Outside partners: Build liberties (Advanced Stunts, page 115), giving back feet to base groups. Place front legs on the back of the inside partner. While keeping hips slightly to the side, turn chests to the crowd and hit the motion (see figure). For the cradle, partners turn back to the side and wait for the bases' dip.

Inside partner: Build an extension prep. Once the extension prep is executed, lean forward and place hands on the hands of the front base, keeping arms locked out. This body position creates the plane that the outside partners will use to place their feet.

Spotters: Refer to page numbers noted above for individual stunts and follow the corresponding spotting instructions. The two outside spotters need to travel slightly backward to catch partners as they travel away from pyramid.

Points: For the partners, this pyramid can be an awkward body position to execute. It should be done on the ground before attempting to build.

Common Problem	Correction
Partners are twisting off the pyramid and unable to secure a solid connection to inside stunt.	Have partners execute the body position on the ground, focusing on keeping hips to the side and shoulders to the front.

Bases: All bases build their individual stunts: extension preps (Intermediate Stunts, page 84) and extensions (Advanced Stunts, page 100)

Partners: All partners build their individual stunts: extension preps and extensions. At the top of the pyramid, partners reach arms out to connect with other partners (see figure).

Spotters: Refer to page numbers noted above for individual stunts and follow the corresponding spotting instructions.

Points: A variation of this stunt is to alternate liberties, rather than extensions, with the extension preps.

Common Problem	Correction
When extensions are executed, arm placement is off, so the pyramid doesn't connect correctly.	Make sure partners at the top of the pyramid are sliding as they brace rather than grabbing the other partners in a specific grip.

Summary

Pyramids add thrills to cheerleading. Building individual partner stunts into pyramids adds creativity and excitement when cheering for a team or during a competition. Pyramids don't need to be difficult to be effective, but they must be clean and visual. There are many pyramids that squads can perform simply by putting a variety of partner stunts together. As long as safety rules are followed, building pyramids is a safe and exciting element of any cheerleading program.

twelve

Choreography and Formations

Many levels and styles of choreography exist in the cheerleading world, and the area is getting more complex all the time. Choreographing a cheerleading routine is a multifaceted process. Knowing how to effectively incorporate formations is one vital part of creating a well-choreographed routine. Creative formations add organization and visual appeal to any sideline performance. The second half of this chapter focuses extensively on the creation and effective use of formations.

The most important point to remember when planning choreography for a pep rally or competition is that the main role of a cheerleader is to *lead* the crowd. Some programs move away from that idea when they choose to devote many hours of practice to prepare for a local competition or spend a lot of time putting together a dance for a pep rally. As long as a cheer squad never loses focus of their main objective—to *lead* a crowd—planning a choreographed routine for competition can be an exciting and rewarding experience.

Choreography

Before developing a routine for a competition, a squad needs to set goals and objectives. The team needs to decide whether its routine should highlight the squad's strongest current skills or include skills that it hopes to attain by competition time.

Choreographing a routine based on current skills can build confidence in a cheerleading squad. Such a routine reduces the stress involved in competing because cheerleaders know from the beginning they can excel in all the elements they'll be performing. The only real challenges in this plan are ensuring that everyone on the squad knows the correct counts and movements and that all members are well conditioned. Typically, a routine designed around a squad's present skills is easier to perfect in time for the competition. Cheerleaders spend their energy performing and perfecting what they already know rather than worrying about learning elements they're not sure they'll be able to handle.

Despite the apparent positives of "working with what you know," many teams choose to choreograph a routine that includes skills they're not capable of performing at the beginning of the season. Taking on this challenge makes for some stress, yes, but it also brings excitement and gives a squad clear goals to work toward. They must not only memorize the counts and movements that are choreographed but also give much time and effort to drilling the new stunting and tumbling skills so they can perfect the routine in time for the first competition. Clearly, challenging your team to learn new elements motivates them to improve and grow in a way that practicing skills they have already perfected does not. For example, when cheerleaders are expected to have a squad standing back handspring ready for their routine, the lurking date of the competition will generally push weaker tumblers to practice that skill much more intensely.

CREATE A TIMELINE FOR THE ROUTINE Once you have determined what you want your routine to contain, create an organizational timeline for the routine that everyone agrees is realistic and reasonable. This timeline should include the following elements:

- Parent meeting
- Finding a choreographer
- Researching competitions
- Finalizing the competition schedule
- Raising funds to pay for the competition
- Choreography date(s)
- Registration deadlines for the competition
- Securing a facility for practice time
- Show-offs prior to competition
- Deadlines for skill check

CREATE A TIMELINE FOR ROUTINE PROGRESSION Also consider creating a timeline for perfecting specific elements of the routine. This prevents progressions from sneaking up on your squad and gives cheerleaders opportunities to achieve success as they work toward their primary goal of perfecting the entire routine. Here are some examples of elements that might appear in such a timeline:

- Words for the routine memorized
- First run-through without music
- First run-through with music
- Tumbling section perfected
- Stunting section perfected
- First full-out performance

CHOOSE A CHOREOGRAPHER Whether you will outsource choreography for your routine or to do it yourself depends on many factors. Basically, there are three options: the coach or another supervisor does the choreography, squad members do the choreography, or an outside choreographer is hired to do the choreography. Obviously, whenever possible, you want to do whatever needs to be done to give your cheerleaders the best opportunity to perform well in competition. However, funding and other issues also come into play. Let's consider the three options separately.

1. The coach (or another supervisor) does choreography. This happens quite frequently and sometimes is even written

into the contract of the coach (or other supervisor), depending on his or her experience with choreography. The coach tends to know the most about a squad's overall strengths and abilities, and because choreography requires so much coordination and organization, he or she might be the natural selection. However, if the coach has little or no choreography experience, looking elsewhere might be a better idea. Sometimes the best choice depends on the reasons for entering the competition. Is your goal to place high in the rankings or simply to give your squad an idea of what competition feels like?

2. The squad does choreography. In many cases, the cheerleaders themselves can choreograph the routine. This is definitely the least expensive method. Cheerleaders are usually proud to take ownership of a routine. Many of them have backgrounds in cheerleading and competing, so they bring a certain level of experience to the table. They know themselves and their skills and can reasonably decide what is practical and realistic for their ability level. Problems occur if teammates argue over who should go where in formations or if differences in opinion arise. Such conflicts can cause tension that eats away at a team's cohesion and might significantly complicate competition plans if not handled properly.

3. The team hires an outside choreographer. This method is the most common of the three. Many choreographers make a living creating cheerleading routines and can put them together quickly and painlessly. When mapping out formations, they are unbiased and not concerned about pleasing certain individuals by putting them at the front of the formation. A good choreographer will do what's best for the squad's success (because a team's success in a competition also means success for the choreographer) and can eliminate any bickering among teammates and coaches. Of course, the main drawback to hiring a choreographer is the cost, which can be quite steep for some choreographers. However, others are surprisingly inexpensive. Generally, the price tag depends on the choreographer's

years of experience in the industry, his or her success at competitions, and his or her reputation among peers. Before investing in a choreographer, do in-depth research to ensure he or she is qualified and will give your team a product you'll have success with.

KNOW THE SCORE SHEET   Before doing any choreographing, squads should study and understand the score sheet to be used by the judges at the competition. Usually, different categories are allotted different points. It's important that your routine touch on each area to avoid receiving a zero in any category. For example, if a squad doesn't include a jump in its routine, the score for that category will be a zero, which can severely drop the team's overall score.

Teams should also be aware if certain areas are favored. For example, on some score sheets, tumbling is worth 10 points, but stunting and pyramids are worth 20 points. If this is the case, a routine should be choreographed to highlight a squad's strengths and earn points in the appropriate categories. If dance is worth only 5 points out of 100, it wouldn't be a good idea to devote half of the routine to dancing. Maximizing strengths based on the categories on the score sheet is how most teams do well in competitions.

Setting Up the Routine

Most routines for high school and junior high programs require a music segment and a cheer segment. The order in which these occur is typically up to the team. Conventionally, most teams open with a music segment, break into the cheer segment, and finish with an exciting musical ending. This format is hardly ever mandatory (though you'll want to check each competition's guidelines), and teams are not penalized for following a different format. However, the high energy level of the music is a great way to kick off a routine and a climatic way to finish it off.

Cheer Section

Although the entire routine should be fun and fast paced, it's a special challenge to make sure the cheer section of a routine is fun to watch.

The cheer section should support the school or program that the cheerleaders represent. The pace and style of the cheer depends heavily on the competition's guidelines. Some cheerleading companies require a crowd-leading cheer that reflects what's practical on the sideline, whereas other organizations prefer a performance-style cheer that's fast paced and highly entertaining. No particular style is considered necessarily right or wrong, but a choreographer should be aware of what's expected before beginning to develop the routine. Ordering videos from previous years' competitions and viewing the winning performances is a great way to get an idea of what judges are looking for.

Music Section

Music is crucial to the success of a routine. Music sets the tone and pace and adds to the creativity of the choreography; music can also motivate cheerleaders to do their best. The selection process for music should be taken seriously and not put off until the last minute. Basically, you can approach the music mixing in one of two ways:

- Mix the music before the routine is choreographed. Often, hearing the final cut of music sparks great ideas for choreography. Certain sections of the music might be suited for tumbling, whereas other parts might be perfect for a pyramid sequence. If a choreographer gets stuck and runs out of ideas, hearing a general draft of the music might help a lot.

- Mix the music after the routine is choreographed to eight-counts. If a choreographer has an idea of what he or she wants to do, he or she can set formations and transitions to eight-counts and then look for music that best suits this design. This way, the choreographer can express exactly what he or she has envisioned for the routine without being influenced by the music. There will always be places in which the music selected doesn't *exactly* match the eight-counts mapped out, but a choreographer can easily adjust the counts to flow with the chosen music.

Musical selections need to cover a variety of needs. Most cheerleading routines now use more than just a few cuts; in fact, most songs aren't used for more than three or four eight-counts each. That being said, using a library of voice-overs, sound effects, eight-count breaks, and other musical choices can really add to the flavor of the music. The music should always be upbeat and at a rather fast tempo (sometimes slower music is used for dramatic effect, but it shouldn't continue for more than a couple of eight-counts). In general, keeping the bpm (beats per minute) consistent throughout the routine makes it easier for the cheerleaders and more pleasing for the judges.

Perfecting the Choreography

The choreography process doesn't occur overnight. For a team to be successful, the process should be continuous; changes, additions, and improvements should be made throughout the season. At some point, changes obviously need to cease so the team can perfect a routine, but this shouldn't happen too early in the process.

Whether the official choreographer of the routine is an active member of the program or visits periodically during the season before the competition, it's up to the coach to ensure that the choreography continues to improve and complements the strengths and needs of the cheer team. It will bring great success to a squad if all members can get into the mindset that the choreography process lasts from the beginning of the season through the day of competition. Perfecting a routine is covered in more detail in chapter 14.

Things for a Choreographer to Avoid

- Unnatural facial expressions. Some cheerleaders perform their facial expressions in an overly dramatic or exaggerated way. Because judges sit so far away from the cheerleaders, some teams overcompensate for the distance by making their performance unusually gaudy or obnoxious. Judges prefer natural, pleasant facial expressions that are pleasing to the eye.

- "In your face" gestures. When some individuals execute certain skills (e.g., a tumbling pass) with success, they get excited and try to work the crowd in a "Ha, ha, I showed you!" manner. The most successful teams are the ones that work together and perform their skills in unison rather than competing for the spotlight. Friendly spiriting is much more favored than anything that might possibly be viewed as poor sportsmanship. Choreographers should take care not to involve too much extra spiriting into the routine. Although spiriting is quite valuable on the sideline, a team doesn't want to overdo it and distract judges from evaluating the skills that score well on the score sheet.

• Low-quality tapes. Today, compact discs are used almost universally in modern cheerleading, and this is a good thing. If using tapes, they should be the highest quality available. Unfortunately, tapes can be noticeably quieter and can prove to be a disadvantage for a team.

• Slow ripples. Teams that do slow ripples across the floor tend to lose the interest of a judge. A ripple should either be fast paced and high energy *or* it should be used to highlight a team's strength. For example, if a team has exceptionally clean double full-twist cradles out of their stunts, a clear ripple of the cradles can really

highlight to the judges how strong their cradles are. Ripples work against a team when they draw attention to poor technique. If a team has weak flexibility when performing heel stretches, rippling them up only draws attention to each individual stunt group's flaws. When using ripples, it makes the most sense for the ripple to happen from left to right because that's the direction in which the human eye reads. There are obviously going to be exceptions to this rule, but left to right should be a choreographer's first choice when putting together a ripple sequence.

• Suggestive dance movements. It's important to the reputation of the cheerleading industry that cheerleading choreography be appropriate for all ages and family viewing. Some programs have moved away from this, and the industry is beginning to become much more strict in enforcing regulations. Cheerleaders are considered role models by many of today's young people and should behave accordingly.

Formations

Formations refer to the spacing between individuals and the overall picture created by the spacing. In a cheerleading routine, formations are crucial to the success of a team's performance. Formations are not nearly as important on the sideline, but they can make or break a team during competition.

Two traditional types of formations are used in cheerleading. The first (and most common) is called the *bowling pin*. This formation is set up much like bowling pins in a bowling alley. One cheerleader is in the front, two are in the second row, three are in the third row, and so on.

Bowling pin formations work great when you have a few members on a team you want to highlight. The nature of the picture created by the bowling pin draws an observer's focus to the individuals in the front. The only downside of a bowling pin is that the individuals in the back corners (who typically have weaker skills) are in plain view of the crowd and judges and need to be strong to help the team's score.

One mistake cheerleaders commonly make with a bowling pin is double stacking the back

end when there are too many cheerleaders in a formation. Double stacking is when the back line consists of one person who stands directly behind the person in the row in front of them (see figure 12.1). The solution is to remove the cheerleader at the front of the bowling pin. By sinking everyone standing in the centerline back one row, the two individuals who were double stacked can be moved and put into windows of the formation. This makes for a much more aesthetically pleasing formation for viewers.

Another type of formation is called a *staggered line*. A staggered line is as simple as having a line of front-row cheerleaders with the second row in the windows. Staggered lines are useful in showcasing a deep pool of talent and consistency among team members. For example, if a team has many strong jumpers, a staggered line will highlight them because it's difficult to hide weak jumpers in this type of formation.

Vertical lines in formations tend to highlight differences in levels rather than suggest squad uniformity (figure 12.2). Keeping cheerleaders in windows is the most consistent method of

Figure 12.1   Double-stacked bowling pin.

Figure 12.2   Example of bad vertical lines in a formation.

setting up formations. A *window* is created when a line of cheerleaders is staggered between two other lines of cheerleaders (figure 12.3). As discussed with the bowling pin formation, double stacking the back of a formation is not a good setup choice.

Dance and music in formations is a fun category for cheerleaders. Often, this area provides the one time during a routine or a pep rally in which cheerleaders can really let loose and have fun. The crowd always seems to enjoy this segment as well. However, cheerleading-style dance tends to be a bit more rigid than what the common pop culture considers as dance. The motions tend to be sharper, and whereas pop-culture dance tends to highlight rhythm, cheerleading-style dance highlights placement, sharpness, and synchronicity. Many cheerleaders who compete aren't quite aware of the differences in the two styles and will arrive at a competition with a dance section that might go over very well at the school prom, but it won't be nearly as effective in the eyes of the judges.

Unfortunately, in recent years, many cheer and dance organizations have pushed the envelope in terms of suggestive and inappropriate choreography and musical selections. Many cheerleading organizations are putting strict guidelines in motion to keep cheerleading viewed in a positive manner by the public. Before performing a cheer or dance routine, it's important to have the material officially approved by the governing body or administration in charge. Dancing is a fun part of cheerleading and is meant to allow some freedom, but cheerleaders need to remain responsible and respectful enough not to cross the line.

Cheerleading squads need to choose their musical selections with care and foresight. Many routines get choreographed up to nine months before competition. Picking music that's popular during the weeks that a routine is choreographed can backfire. After several months, those songs might well have been overplayed; they might be outdated and annoying by the time competition time arrives. It's wise to use a mix of newer songs

Figure 12.3   An example of a window.

and older songs so that an audience and judging panel are equally entertained. Cheerleaders will often request certain music that they feel will motivate them through sections of their routine. Motivation is an important factor to consider, but the choreographer must remember that the group that needs to feel most motivated is the judging panel.

Shifts in songs need to match shifts in a routine. Many times, the music for a stunt sequence will end, and the pace and tone of the music will change as the running tumbling begins. Sometimes these shifts are apparent, and the routine should be choreographed accordingly. When a music change does not match a transition or shift in the routine, the music can stick out and be a distraction rather than a support for the routine.

Sound effects are as popular as ever in cheerleading and can be used effectively during jumps and pyramid transitions. Sound effects can also be used to blend different music cuts together that otherwise wouldn't seem to work. For instance, finishing an eight-count with a loud crash or thud might deter the ear from noticing the music switching gears into another song. But, generally speaking, choreographers and music editors should use sound effects sparingly, mainly to highlight accented areas of a routine. Routines with too many sound effects tend to distract viewers from the skills being performed.

PICKING A MUSIC EDITOR   Considering how important music is to the flow of a routine, a squad needs to choose carefully when selecting a music editor. Many teams edit music themselves. The positives of going this route include the ability to make any changes as they become necessary. Music editing programs available on computers are becoming more and more common and user friendly.

In any situation, a choreographer wants to offer the team he or she is instructing the best opportunity to do well. That said, if a choreographer doesn't feel comfortable with the software or if there's not enough time to train on a music-editing program, outsourcing the music might be the best way to go. There are many music editors who work with choreographers to provide top-notch productions. To find good

music editors, the choreographer should contact locally successful programs for contact information. When communicating with a music editor candidate, talk about the length of music you're looking for along with your timeline. Also discuss the music editor's availability for updates and changes made to the program (sometimes changes are not included in the total price). Good music is key to a successful routine. It's unfortunate when cheerleaders lose points because of poor music selections.

CHARTING THE ROUTINE   The easiest way to understand and organize the flow of a routine is to chart the routine.

Each line of the chart should represent an eight-count of words or music. On each line, the choreographer can make notes on special assignments to counts (e.g., dip for cradle on 3, stand up on 1). He or she can also make special notes about accents in the music. If there's a sound effect on 5 that would make sense for accenting a pyramid structure, the choreographer can make note of that and ensure there are enough eight-counts leading up to that count to build the pyramid. This kind of organization is crucial when developing a routine. Ideas will change, and counts will change as certain skills are brought to life, but having a basic outline of the routine with eight-counts and words mapped out brings much more structure when learning the routine and can be a significant time saver. A choreographer will feel much more prepared if he or she has this template to go by.

ELEMENTS OF A ROUTINE   When putting together a routine, a squad must master the different elements—including all the skills, transitions, and parts of a routine that bring it together. A squad should begin practicing these elements early in the season, before the routine is choreographed, so cheerleaders won't be overwhelmed by the amount of work to do as the competition draws near. If a squad knows they want a particular stunt in a routine, they can incorporate it into a cheer earlier in the season to get familiar with it.

A routine's pace is important to the judges and needs to be set early on. Essentially, deciding how to start a routine comes down to picking one of two options. You either choose to start with a large, visual, high-energy opening with quick transitions to catch the judges' attention, or you choose to begin with a difficult skill that requires a high level of execution. Either way can work. The main thing is to make sure the judges are engaged within the first few seconds.

Note that a need for a fast-paced and dynamic routine should not be confused with a rushed routine that's in too much of a hurry to get through the elements. Although judges like to watch elements occurring at all times, a team that takes its time to perform a skill well gives judges a chance to appreciate what they have just seen. Routines in which teams barely have time to finish their back handspring before they're taking off to their next element and formation might frustrate some judges. Enough time needs to be allowed within the choreography for a squad to perform the back handspring, stand tall as they finish, and then step in unison into the transition. Rushing the elements makes a routine impossible to clean and doesn't allow judges enough time to soak in all the skills to be assessed.

Within its routine, a squad will want to include a balance of the best skills that individuals on a team have to offer and skills that a team performs together. If three cheerleaders on the team excel in standing back tucks, that skill should be showcased. And if the team has a squad standing back handspring in its repertoire, that should be included in the routine as well. One element might earn points for difficulty and the other for squad participation.

Placement of elements within the routine should be strategic. A team's strengths, weaknesses, and stamina should be taken into consideration. The most difficult and elite elements should occur near the beginning. In the middle, a "breather" needs to be included to let cheerleaders catch their breath and regain energy. Toward the end of the routine, the elements are usually less difficult but higher in energy, such as dance. By the end of the routine, cheerleaders are getting tired and need to be performing skills that are easily executed. When choreographing the routine, it sometimes becomes obvious that elements need to be switched around if a team is to perform them all successfully. Choreographers need to be open minded and allow for necessary adjustments.

When putting together a routine, choreographers should give transitions plenty of focus. Transitions—commonly defined as the paths cheerleaders take between elements—are usually allotted a category of their own on the score sheet. They are also the first element that choreographers tend to disregard. The first rule of thumb in transitions is that cheerleaders should not cross the center of the floor to get from one formation to the next. This movement is distracting and makes the flow of the routine seem messy. The best transitions are those that the human eye hardly notices. Ideally, cheerleaders should never be more than three or four steps from each formation. This requires some planning early on.

For example, when putting together stunt groups at the beginning of the season, a coach should think ahead about who he or she would like to be the "point" or middle stunt group. The coach should then try to make sure some of the best jumpers and performers are part of this group. This way, when it comes time to put a routine together, the transition from the stunt to a jump formation can look nearly flawless as all the bases in the middle stunt take just a step or two over to create the jump formation. A problem arises when you have the weakest jumper basing the middle stunt. After the stunt cradles, the weak jumper must take a very long path to get from the front middle of the floor to the back corner. This can hurt a team's transition score. When possible, practice avoiding these situations early in the season.

Symmetrical transitions are when opposites in a formation take the same path from one formation to the next. A choreographer should incorporate as many symmetrical transitions as possible. Symmetry is pleasing to the human eye. A challenge is to have every transition be as symmetrical as possible. This is an unrealistic request, however, because different elements call for different individuals to move to different places on the floor. Thus, a choreographer should prioritize and ensure that at least one transition is perfectly symmetrical. If a squad is to move from a jump formation to a motion formation, set up both formations so the transition between them looks as if there is a mirror down the middle of the floor. Judges appreciate this level of detail and reward a team accordingly.

A choreographer should try to find crowd pleasers or gimmicks to use to entertain the audience. A crowd pleaser might be a visual, innovative choreography trick or a clever reference in the music. It does not necessarily need to showcase any level of difficulty, but it can be a nice break from the stacked elements to provide an entertaining visual for the crowd.

The ending of the routine needs to be choreographed so the team can execute it flawlessly. Many teams will do very basic stunts or an easy formation with level changes. The judges will remember the final few seconds of the routine as they begin recording scores so make sure their last impression is a positive one.

Summary

Choreographing a routine and effectively using formations is challenging, but paying close attention to the details will take the routine to the next level. If the team decides to move forward with a choreographed performance or competitive routine, be sure to follow the planning guidelines outlined in this chapter. If the squad takes the time to plan effectively beforehand, a successful routine will be the reward for both the cheerleaders and the audience!

thirteen

Games and Pep Rallies

© Icon SMI

Leading school spirit is the number one priority for cheerleaders. Unfortunately, the skills needed to lead a crowd are not inherent to all cheerleaders, which is why these skills must be taught and practiced. Cheerleaders are responsible for welcoming visiting cheerleaders, leading and controlling crowds, and encouraging supporters to cheer for teams with good sportsmanship. While cheerleaders can learn crowd leadership skills during practices, pep rallies are the perfect place to teach fans chants and to explain game behavior expectations. The first impression opposing fans have of a school is usually its cheerleaders. How cheerleaders perform at games influences people's opinions about cheerleaders' skills and priorities and the school's athletic program in general. It will be obvious to fans and administration if cheerleaders pride themselves on leading school spirit with enthusiasm as opposed to just attending games to fill time between competitions.

Cheering at Games

Cheerleaders need to arrive early enough to take care of pregame needs so they're ready to cheer on time. Pregame activities include stretching, preparing stunts, greeting visiting cheerleaders, warming up the crowd, and cheering the team onto the court or field. This means all cheerleaders must arrive by the designated time and be focused on their game responsibilities rather than off talking to friends. Stretching and stunt warm-ups should be done away from the fans if possible, which means finding a quiet site, relatively free from distractions, to prepare for the game. Cheerleaders should arrive early enough to complete stretching and stunt warm-ups prior to warming up the crowd and cheering for the team as they run onto the court or field.

Home cheerleaders should make a point of welcoming visiting cheerleaders by greeting them when they arrive at the school. Home cheerleaders can explain to their visitors where they are to cheer, give them directions to the restrooms and concession stands, and answer any of their questions. At halftime, home cheerleaders can check in with the visiting cheerleaders to see how they're doing. It's also thoughtful to talk to the visiting cheerleaders after the game and wish them luck in the future.

Cheerleaders often find it difficult to get crowds motivated to cheer before the game starts. Fans tend to be busy talking, eating, and getting seated; they really aren't too interested in what's happening on the floor or field yet. Cheerleaders often don't cheer during pregame because it's hard work. Organizing before the game and developing traditions, both of which might take some time, can make pregame cheering easier.

Pregame is an ideal time to work with the band to plan ways to get the crowd involved. Whatever crowd participation ideas you come up with can also be used to kick off the second half as soon as the team enters the court or field. The band should play entertaining songs that cheerleaders can use to lead the crowd. Easy words or actions can be added to the songs for the fans to follow. Taped music is appropriate if a band is not available. The school song usually makes for great crowd involvement during the

pregame to get fans on their feet and ready for the game. Cheerleaders should sing the words to the school song and encourage the crowd to sing as well.

A good time to establish a team or season tradition is during player introductions. Certain claps or a short chant can be performed along with stunts as each player is introduced. The cheerleaders or coach can find out ahead of time how starting lineups will be announced in order to prepare for player and coach introductions to the crowd. Another important element of the pregame is the national anthem. Cheerleaders should always stand at attention with their hands on their hearts while singing the anthem. It's important for all cheerleaders, including cheerleaders in the stands, to model appropriate behavior before, during, and after the game.

Game Time

Warm-ups and introductions are over, and the game has begun. This is what cheerleaders have been preparing for in practice. Cheerleaders must be aware of what is happening in the game and cheer accordingly. They should chant throughout the game to avoid dead time and keep the fans involved. Cheerleaders need to be able to read a crowd and be aware of its mood. Are fans lethargic and need a boost? Do they want to yell but need some direction? Are they getting unruly? Being able to predict a crowd's temperament, choose chants wisely, and execute successfully are signs of a good cheerleading squad.

Organization and professionalism are keys to motivating fans to want to follow cheerleaders' directions. Squads should have a stance that all cheerleaders adhere to during games. This stance might be with legs in a cheer stance and hands behind the back (one hand holding the other arm's wrist). Depending on space, squads might stand in a straight line or in staggered lines; either type of line should be spread out to cover the crowd. When cheering, cheerleaders must cooperate with coaches, officials, and administrators at all times, and they should be aware of the movement of officials, especially during basketball games. Cheerleaders need to watch the game, not only to know what's happening so they can choose appropriate chants, but also to stay out of the way of players and officials. Cheerleaders should not be talking to each other or people in the stands, playing with their hair, eating, drinking, or practicing cheers in front of the crowd during the game. If cheerleaders don't show an interest in the game, the fans might not, either. Instead of cheering on the team, fans might talk to each other, eat, become unruly, or even leave.

Crowd Involvement

Cheerleaders need to project confidence when cheering, which means cheering as if they believe fans will cheer with them. To generate crowd participation, cheerleaders should get close to fans and make eye contact. They need to spread out and cover the crowd rather than standing tightly together in front of one section. The main idea is to make everyone in the stands feel important to the outcome of the game. Every fan wants to feel included and wants to support the team, which is usually why he or she is attending the game. When leading chants, it helps if cheerleaders encourage the crowd to join in by yelling, "Let's hear it!" or "Yell with us!" Using easy chants that ask fans to stand, clap, or stomp their feet helps get the crowd involved.

Repetition is very important for crowd involvement. Don't give up easily! Cheerleaders need to repeat a chant more than three times to give fans the chance to understand what to do and time to do it. Many cheerleaders choose to run up into the stands to get the crowd involved (which is easier at basketball games than football games). When finished with a chant, cheerleaders should thank and compliment the crowd for participating by yelling, "Good job!" or "Way to go!" This kind of enthusiasm encourages fans to continue being involved. If the crowd begins an appropriate chant, cheerleaders need to immediately join in and help them. Both groups ought to be working together to support the school's team.

Developing traditions is a good way to get the crowd to participate. Traditions are familiar to fans of all ages, so everyone is more apt to join in. The school song is a tradition for most schools, so it should be played at key times during a game when the team needs support. Other traditions, such as drum chants with the band, can be done after the team has scored a basket or a touchdown. Another idea is for cheerleaders to perform a jump and yell a short phrase, such as, "Mustang Power, Oh, Yes!" after every basket. Following a touchdown, cheerleaders can do a push-up for each point scored while fans shout out the counts. Other cheerleaders (sophomore, freshman, junior varsity) who are in the crowd are a big help when trying to incorporate new ideas. They should be yelling and getting their friends to yell so that new chants catch on. Another tradition can be to have a section reserved for students interested in cheering at the games. These students can wear T-shirts in school colors and encourage support in the stands. All of these ideas can be explained to fans during pep rallies or sports kickoff events.

When cheering, cheerleaders should use big, sharp motions to attract the crowd's attention. Strong, spirited voices and clearly enunciated words are important to stimulate fans. It's best to use chants that are easy, traditional, and popular. Also, answer-back and spell-out chants get fans to participate because cheerleaders are telling the crowd what to yell. Most students enjoy doing the "wave," which is a fun activity to get the crowd physically involved in cheering. Using signs and poms also draws attention to the cheerleaders and helps them lead the crowd. Signs show which words to shout and make it easier for fans to participate. Selling small team-spirit items such as poms and hankies adds visual color and spirit in the stands; these items can also be used in chants to increase crowd involvement. As always, cheerleaders should use positive, natural, smiling facial expressions when cheering. Cheerleaders who maintain enthusiasm set good examples for the fans to follow.

Chant Selection

Game situations and momentum can change quickly in athletic contests, so cheerleaders need to be organized, prepared, and spontaneous. To be most effective at games, cheerleaders must use practice time to prepare. Instead of practicing long, fancy cheers and chants, time should be devoted to easy chants and answer-back chants to get and keep the fans involved. Proper use of signs and poms must also be practiced. Organized game preparation gives cheerleaders confidence, which makes them more successful at leading chants and cheers.

A good way to prepare for crowd involvement chants is to present game situations in practice for cheerleaders to respond to quickly and appropriately. This means that cheerleaders must understand the sport for which they cheer. To be more effective, cheerleaders should know key referee signals, which allows for a quick response to situations. There are crucial times in games when cheerleaders need to urge fans to yell in support and encouragement for the team, such as when a team needs to score or prevent a score in order to win. When these situations occur, cheerleaders should have several chants ready, including some crowd favorites. At such times, cheerleaders' abilities to be spontaneous and to fuel crowd response is very important.

Figure 13.1 details some situations for which practiced chants or routines should be prepared so that cheerleaders can react automatically when the scenario occurs.

Chant Situations

Offensive Situations

- Team is holding the ball to run time off the clock (basketball).
- Team is in possession of the ball (basketball and football).
- Team needs to score to win (basketball and football).
- Team is returning kickoff (football).
- Team gets a first down (football).
- Team is moving the ball to run time off the clock (football).
- Team is going for two (football).
- Team is inside the 10-yard line (football).
- Team needs a first down (football).
- Team is "going for it" on fourth down (football).
- Athlete needs takedown, reversal, or pin to win (wrestling).
- Athlete is in pinning position (wrestling).
- Athlete is going for a takedown or reversal (wrestling).

Defensive Situations

- Opponent has the ball (basketball and football).
- Opponent is trying to score (basketball and football).
- Team needs to steal the ball or cause a turnover (basketball and football).
- Team needs to prevent opponent from scoring near end of a game (basketball and football).
- Team is kicking off (football).
- Opponent is going for a first down (football).
- Opponent is inside the 10-yard line (football).
- Opponent is going for a first down in order to move the ball down the field (football).

(continued)

Figure 13.1   Chant situations.

- Opponent is going for it on fourth down (football).
- Opponent is going for a field goal, extra point, or a two-point conversion (football).
- Opponent is trying for a takedown or reversal (wrestling).
- Opponent is going for a takedown or reversal to win (wrestling).
- Opponent is trying for a pin (wrestling).

Spirit Situations

- During the start of game or meet (basketball, football, wrestling).
- During an unexciting time in the game or meet (basketball, football, wrestling).
- When team or athlete enters or exits floor (or field or mat) (basketball, football, and wrestling).
- When athlete from either team leaves floor (or field or mat) after a great game or match (basketball, football, wrestling).
- When team or athlete is behind (basketball, football, wrestling).
- After a turnover by your own team (basketball and football).
- Following a big play to keep up the momentum (basketball and football).
- When team or athlete is ahead and needs to keep lead (basketball, football, wrestling).

Crowd Control

- When referee makes call against your team.
- When your team is being taunted by opponents.
- During altercations on the court, field, or mat.
- After "missed" calls by referee benefiting opponents.

Figure 13.1 *(continued)*.

Crowd Control

Crowd control is the responsibility of school administrators, but cheerleaders can assist with this task. Cheerleaders and other athletes should understand that they're held to a higher level of ethical behavior than the fans are—cheerleaders and other athletes should be the role models that others follow. Being aware of and ready to handle possible bad sportsmanship by fans is one of the most important skills cheerleaders can have. Unacceptable behavior includes using inappropriate language, booing, whistling, rustling newspapers, throwing items, turning your back during introductions, and demeaning the opposing team or individual athletes. As mentioned earlier, cheerleaders need to be in tune with the game *and* be aware of and understand the crowd's mood. Knowledgeable cheerleaders are proactive and anticipate possible crowd

control situations. They're ready with popular crowd-involvement chants to keep fans positive and to prevent problems. Good chants for these situations include easy answer-backs, crowd favorites, and chants using the team mascot, school colors, or school name.

The school song is great to use during times of inappropriate behavior because it automatically gets people up on their feet and involved. Another strategy is to have leaders—who have been prepped ahead of time—in the stands encouraging those around them to respond appropriately by using positive peer pressure. Some schools even have athletes read sportsmanship messages before each game to remind fans of game expectations. Developing school pride by exhibiting appropriate conduct takes time, but it's well worth the long-term benefits.

If some fans don't respond to the cheerleaders and continue to display bad sportsmanship, it's the responsibility of the administration to deal with the situation. Crowd expectations need to be conveyed to students, parents, athletes, fans, and coaches during kickoff events, parent meetings, and pep rallies. The main concepts of sportsmanship that schools should expect from their coaches, athletes, and fans are respect, ethical behavior, and integrity. Administrators can prevent many inappropriate situations from occurring by being visible and proactive during events. This means having adequate security personnel at every event. A plan should be in effect to deal with unpleasant situations; administrators need to follow through with consequences for these plans to be effective. If inappropriate behavior isn't dealt with quickly, smoothly, and consistently, it can easily escalate.

There are many ways to deal with inappropriate situations. A first step might be for an administrator to talk to the offending fans and possibly sit near them. A second step might be to escort the offending fans from the premises. A law enforcement official comes in very handy at such times. If a fan is escorted from a game, it's a good idea to follow up with a meeting to determine expectations for attendance at future events. A student might be required to sit with his or her parents at subsequent games. A third step might be to prohibit the offending fan from attending any of the remaining games of the season. Cheerleaders can help keep the game atmosphere positive, but ultimately the administrators are responsible for crowd control.

Use of Signs

As mentioned earlier, cheerleaders should practice using signs correctly before they use them in games. They should practice holding signs low, with the front of the sign facing the crowd. When it's time for fans to respond, cheerleaders lift the signs straight up above their heads. Sometimes cheerleaders make the mistake of holding signs low, with the words or letters turned away from the crowd, and then flipping them up when it's time for the fans to respond. This method doesn't give fans time to read and respond on cue. Another common mistake cheerleaders make when using signs is to lift the signs overhead and tilt them backward instead of holding them straight up

A sign held straight and lifted high gets the best crowd response.

so fans can see the words or letters clearly. When outdoors, make sure signs are made of a strong, sturdy material to withstand rain and wind. Signs should be kept close at hand for easy access. In general, signs should be simple, with only one word or letter per sign, printed big and bold to be read easily by the crowd. The use of signs in a cheer is a relatively simple tactic, but practice is still needed to use them effectively.

When to Cheer

As we've already mentioned, to cheer intelligently, cheerleaders must know the game. Crowd involvement is significantly increased when cheerleaders choose appropriate times to cheer. On the flip side, unpleasant situations can arise when cheerleaders cheer at improper times. Cheerleaders should always cheer with good sportsmanship and respect for opponents. The main purpose of cheerleaders and fans is to cheer *for* their team, not against the other team; this means chants should focus on supporting their own team and athletes.

Appropriate Times to Cheer

- During warm-ups and introductions (basketball, football, wrestling)
- After a foul is called but before the free-throws (basketball)
- After a score (basketball and football)
- When the team is in a huddle (basketball and football)
- When the team is coming out onto the floor or getting into formation (basketball and football)
- During time-outs and between quarters (basketball and football)
- To recognize outstanding performances by either team (basketball, football, wrestling)
- To recognize outstanding performances by any athlete (basketball, football, wrestling)
- When an injured athlete leaves the competition (basketball, football, wrestling)
- Between plays and before the action begins (football)

Inappropriate Times to Cheer

- During free-throws (basketball)
- When an athlete is hurt (basketball, football, wrestling)
- When an opponent makes a mistake (basketball, football, wrestling)
- During public address announcements (basketball, football, wrestling)
- When chant is directed at opposing team or athlete (basketball, football, wrestling)
- To gloat after a win (basketball, football, wrestling)
- During the snap of the ball (football)
- When the ball is in play (football)

Time-Outs

Time-outs should be used for crowd participation, not cheer performance. When cheerleaders perform a cheer to show off stunts without involving the crowd, some fans get annoyed.

Time-outs are an important component of the game and must be prepared for to ensure successful crowd leadership. Cheerleaders need to practice not only proper chant selection but also how to use an entire time-out, which includes running on and off the court. During football games, cheerleaders are usually in position already, but basketball cheerleaders typically need to run onto the floor during a time-out to get in front of the crowd. In any case, cheerleaders need to begin crowd involvement chants immediately after a time-out is called to sustain crowd momentum.

Effective use of time-outs should be part of early season practices. During time-out practice, the coach calls a time-out and cheerleaders begin a chant while running quickly in front of an imaginary crowd. They encourage fans to stand and cheer with them. Because fans enjoy the excitement of tumbling and tosses, these skills should be incorporated while practicing time-outs so cheerleaders are ready to use them during games. Cheerleaders should work on sustaining the chant until the "buzzer" (whistle by coach) sounds, then exit the floor quickly with energy and spirit. If more time needs to be filled during a time-out, cheerleaders can perform two different crowd involvement chants. For example, they might use poms to spell out the school's initials in an answer-back chant, then move immediately into a chant using those initials. Cheerleaders should remember to keep pom motions sharp for the best visual effect. A strong finish should also be practiced ahead of time. When the buzzer sounds and the chant is finished, will everyone jump first or just run off with spirit? As always, cheerleaders need to practice all this with big smiles and strong voices. Time-outs should be worked on diligently in practice until time is being used most effectively at games.

We should stress that the reason time-outs need to be practiced is that cheerleaders too often use time-outs inefficiently. As soon as a time-out has ended, cheerleaders should be preparing for the next time-out. If the tempo of the game changes, cheerleaders might need to quickly choose another chant, but they should still be prepared ahead of time. It's a good idea to have a preset list of big-play chants ready to go. Because game or match action has stopped temporarily, fans' attention is on cheerleaders during time-outs. They want instant excitement; they don't want to wait for cheerleaders to decide what do. Cheerleaders shouldn't run out onto the court and then wait until they're all lined up before they start a chant; they should feed crowd momentum by chanting as soon as the time-out is called. One or two cheerleaders might start the chant with claps or punch motions while running onto the floor (or while standing in front of the fans at football games), and other cheerleaders join in immediately. If the chant has motions, these need to be started as soon as cheerleaders stop in front of the crowd. Stunts should be put up quickly and cleanly. Misuses of time-outs occur when cheerleaders do a short chant, run off, and then stand around waiting for the game to resume. The players are still in their huddle, so the crowd is watching the cheerleaders—but the cheerleaders aren't doing anything! Cheerleaders need to be in tune with the crowd and prepared for time-outs.

Coach's Role During the Game

The cheerleading coach's role during a game is a little different from other athletic coaches. The majority of the "coaching" has already been completed in preparation for the game, so the cheer coach is mainly in an advisory position. Some coaches feel the need to call almost every chant, especially during time-outs and breaks in the game. Remember, though, that cheerleaders learn leadership skills by actually leading. During games, cheerleaders shouldn't constantly be looking over at their coach for guidance; instead, they should be tending to the fans. This doesn't mean coaches shouldn't talk to their cheerleaders during games—just that they shouldn't overshadow the squad's leadership of the crowd. Coaches should be available, of course; halftime is a particularly good time to discuss what's working and what isn't. Ask your cheerleaders what they think should be improved, and share your own ideas. At the end of the game, accentuate the positives so that cheerleaders leave feeling upbeat, especially if changes were made after the halftime talk. There will be time at practice to go over elements and

improve. Of course, if cheerleaders aren't doing their job during a game—such as not cheering or talking instead of watching the game—the coach needs to step in immediately and ask for adjustments. This should be done as quickly and unobtrusively as possible.

During warm-ups, the coach can make sure all cheerleaders have arrived on time and are stretching. Signs and poms should be out and ready for use during the game. The coach should check the cheering surface to make sure it's safe for the cheerleaders—look for holes, slippery surfaces, or debris, and make necessary adjustments to ensure safety. The coach can remind cheerleaders of the rules they're to follow, such as school, conference, and state rules. It doesn't hurt to check that all gum has been discarded, hair has been secured away from the face, nails have been cut, and jewelry has been removed. At this same time, the coach can also verify that all cheerleaders are wearing the proper uniform, including shoes and socks. Once the game starts, the coach needs to be available to monitor stunts for safety.

As we've said, once the game is under way, the cheer coach is chiefly a monitor and evaluator. He or she should observe closely, using this opportunity to gather information for practice needs. One method of gathering information is to use an evaluation form (figure 13.2). Writing down information immediately during a game helps a coach plan practices with specific goals in mind before they're forgotten. Cheerleaders can use the evaluation form to assess their performance as well. The form can be given to the captain to complete following a game, rotated between squad members, or filled out as a group. The coach and squad can then compare forms, talk about the game, and develop a plan for practices and the next game. The evaluation form can be modified to meet various needs and goals; one form might be customized for the cheerleaders and another form might be more coach specific.

A coach will be able to spot some things more easily than the cheerleaders simply because of his or her vantage point. For instance, the coach is usually the best judge of whether all cheerleaders are on task during a game and which specific cheerleading skills need to be practiced. Voice projection and facial expressions are easier for

Game Evaluation Form

1. Did everyone arrive on time for warm-ups and after halftime? If not, why not?

   _____

   _____

2. Did everyone wear the correct uniform, including accessories? If not, why not?

   _____

   _____

3. Did everyone know the material and hit all stunts? If not, what needs to be practiced?

   _____

   _____

4. Was material ready for time-outs and quarters? Did everyone get in front of the crowd quickly? Was time used effectively? If not, what needs to be improved or done differently?

   _____

   _____

5. Did everyone participate in throwing stunts, jumping, and tumbling for spirit? If not, why not? What needs to be done differently?

   _____

   _____

6. Which chants or cheers were effective and involved the crowd? What needs to be changed, added, or not used?

   _____

   _____

7. Were signs, stunts, and tumbling used effectively to lead the crowd? Was everyone involved? If not, what needs to be done differently?

   _____

   _____

8. Was the band used effectively to promote school spirit? If not, what should be changed?

   _____

   _____

9. What improvements can be made for the next game or meet?

   _____

   _____

10. What can be done to get the crowd more involved?

    _____

    _____

    _____

Figure 13.2 Game evaluation form.

the coach to observe and assess as well. Another aspect a coach should monitor is whether all cheerleaders are displaying enthusiasm and good sportsmanship or if they're just going through the motions. The effectiveness of chant selection and the crowd's response should also be observed and recorded. A coach should note if cheerleaders from the school's other squads are in the stands yelling along with those cheering the game, helping to promote school spirit, and motivating crowd participation. Videotaping is an effective tool to use when critiquing a game; many people need to see themselves in action to make changes.

Cheering at Pep Rallies

A pep rally is the perfect place to increase school spirit and unity, teach fans chants, and explain sportsmanship expectations. The purpose of pep rallies is to get people excited for a game, season, or special event. Successful rallies are action oriented, fun, and crowd involving. Good planning and organization of the pep rally keeps fans interested and participating. Rallies should run smoothly, without dead time, and usually last 20 to 30 minutes. Each rally should include traditional team or program elements and at least one new element, which might be a skit, contest, relay race, surprise guest, or another idea to help maintain interest.

Planning and Organization

Every pep rally should have a purpose. No matter the purpose, every rally should promote school and community unity. Once the purpose of the rally is determined, the planning begins. Pep rallies should begin and end with a bang; many rallies use the school song for this purpose. The school song gets fans on their feet and immediately involved. Ideally, if logistics allow, pep rallies should include and recognize as many people as possible without going too long. For instance, pep rallies held in the fall should allow every in-season coach to speak, not just the football coach. However, in order to include everyone, it's important to keep the elements of a pep rally short and to the point. Moving quickly helps maintain crowd interest and keep the rally from dragging. The cheer coach should meet with an administrator to plan the pep rally, get the date on the school calendar, and make sure all ideas are acceptable. Using a planning form (figure 13.3) helps organize a pep rally and ensures all elements are included. If a theme is to be used for a rally, mention this on the form.

When using themes, make sure they allow all students to participate. Most students won't take part if a theme requires a lot of creativity or work. Here are some ideas for easy and successful themes:

School Colors Day—grade or class with most students wearing school colors is recognized and wins a prize.

Beach Day—everyone wears Hawaiian shirts, shorts, sandals, and leis; play Beach Boys or Jimmy Buffett music at rally and between classes.

Pajama Day—everyone wears pajamas, slippers, or robes and brings stuffed animals.

Crazy Day—students wear mismatched clothing and dyed hair.

Tie-Dye Day—students wear tie-dyed clothing; play 60s music at rally and between classes.

Hat Day—everyone wears a favorite hat; award a prize for the most creative headpiece.

Toga Day—students wrap in bed sheets (with shirts and shorts on underneath), which serve as togas.

It's great if you can get the entire school involved by soliciting pep rally ideas or themes from students, perhaps through a contest. You can advertise the contest in the school announcements, over the PA system, and on signs posted around the school. Place a suggestion box in a common area for contest submissions. Students with winning theme ideas might win a prize and be recognized at the rally.

There are many elements to consider when planning a pep rally. The five main planning

Planning a Pep Rally

Things to Consider When Planning a Pep Rally

Purpose: Why is the rally being held?

Kick off the season—good time to review behavior expectations and teach chants

Homecoming—traditional chants for alumni and community involvement

Big game—fire up team and fans

State game—teach easy chants to use at the game

Recognition—honor teams, athletes, and students with awards or trophies they have earned

Location: Where will the rally be held?

Gym

Stadium

Auditorium

City park—possibly at homecoming to get community involvement

Mall or other community involvement site

Alternative site—if rally is outdoors, where will it be moved if weather turns bad?

Calendar: When will the rally be held?

Date—add to school calendar

Time—morning, afternoon, evening

Speakers: Who will be speaking at the rally?

Emcee—very important person to contribute flow and atmosphere

Coaches—keep talks short; spread them throughout the rally

Other people—depending on the purpose of the rally

Elements: What will be included in the rally?

Skits—must be clever; a different school club (acting group, honor society, and so on) performs at each rally

Spirit activities and contests—for enjoyable crowd participation

Routine performances—keep short (if used at all)

School song—a traditional element that must be included

Teaching new material—answer-back chants, band chants, and so on

Theme—not necessary, but some schools like to have a theme for each rally

(continued)

Figure 13.3 Planning a pep rally.

Pep Rally Planning Form

Rally purpose: _____

Date: _____ Time: _____

Location: _____

Skit used: _____

Order of events:

    1.

    2.

    3.

    4.

    5.

    6.

    7.

    8.

    9.

   10.

   11.

   12.

People to notify:

_____ _____ _____

_____ _____ _____

_____ _____ _____

Equipment needs:

_____

_____

Signatures of approval:

Cheerleading coach _____

Athletic director or principal _____

Changes for the future:

_____

_____

Figure 13.3 *(continued)*.

questions to consider are who, what, when, where, and why. All of these questions need to be answered to get information you need to plan and organize a pep rally.

After the pep rally is planned, there are organizational details to consider. Some of these come up naturally during planning, but those that don't shouldn't be overlooked. It helps to have several people involved and promoting the rally ahead of time. A checklist works well to ensure all tasks are accomplished.

Things to Consider When Organizing a Pep Rally

1. Reserve site (if site is outdoors, reserve alternative site)
2. Contact people involved
   - Emcee: to keep the rally moving, such as a local radio announcer
   - Coaches: to speak and fire up the crowd
   - Athletic director or principal: to remind everyone that good sportsmanship is expected
   - Custodians: for moving chairs, podium, bleachers, sound system (microphone, music), and so on
   - Band director: to coordinate needs (school song, fun music, crowd involvement)
   - School staff: so they can plan to participate or attend
3. Plan publicity
   - Announce purpose, date, time, and location
   - Excitement factor: popular or locally famous person as emcee, surprise guest or activity, music, sports teams, cheerleaders
   - Promotion: announcements, signs, newspaper, radio, TV
   - Select crowd involvement activity participants:
     — Choose a cross section of the student population
     — All grade levels should be represented
     — Include teachers and coaches in activities
4. Get required equipment
   - Microphone—make sure it works!
   - Podium
   - Sound system—make sure it works!
   - Tapes, CDs—make sure they play!
   - Items needed for skits and contests
   - Signs, poms, megaphones, other spirit items
5. Finalize agenda
   - Get copies to all participants.
   - Get copies to others involved, such as administration, teachers, and so on.

Sample Pep Rally

A sample pep rally is shown in figure 13.4. Depending on the purpose of the pep rally, some other elements might be included, whereas other elements might be discarded. Be sure to check all sound equipment about 30 minutes before the rally. This allows time for any necessary adjustments before the rally begins.

As long as a pep rally is planned in detail and well organized, the emcee is the person most likely to ensure its success. The emcee keeps the rally going and gets the crowd involved. A popular radio announcer, teacher, administrator, or community member with lots of personality is a good choice for this role. If you use a radio announcer, his or her station might even broadcast the rally. If not, at least the school can be sure the rally will get lots of publicity.

The final pep rally agenda should be given to administrators and teachers early in the week so they know what to expect. A more detailed agenda (figure 13.5) can be given to those who are participating. If there's a set amount of time allotted for the rally, there should be an element or two that can be added or deleted in order to fit the time frame. It's especially important to end on time during a school day, when teachers expect students back in class. If an element is to be added or cut, be sure to notify the emcee beforehand.

Fall Pep Rally

Friday, September 5

Band—Plays upbeat music as fans enter

—Plays "Rock and Roll Part 2" (the "Hey!" song)

—Plays school song

Cheerleaders—Crowd involvement chant

Emcee—Welcomes fans, introduces first two head coaches

Head coaches—Talk briefly about teams

Emcee—Introduces cheer coach

Cheerleaders—Crowd involvement chant or cheer

Emcee—Introduces athletic director or principal

Athletic director or principal—Sportsmanship expectations

Emcee—Introduces crowd involvement activity

Cheerleaders—Crowd involvement activity

Band—Plays upbeat music during activity

Emcee—Announces winner of activity and introduces next two head coaches

Head coaches—Talk briefly about teams

Emcee—Introduces cheerleaders for grade-level chant competition

Cheerleaders—Explain and lead grade-level chant competition

Band or taped music—Play theme song from *Jeopardy!* while coaches decide grade winner

Emcee—Announce winner of grade-level chant competition; ends rally

Band—Plays school song

—Plays upbeat music as fans leave rally

Figure 13.4 Sample pep rally.

Cheerleaders should practice their part of the rally ahead of time to keep pep rallies from dragging. Cheerleaders should know which activities they'll be introducing and practice what they'll say at the rally. Tell cheerleaders which activity or speaker they'll be following at the rally so they'll be prepared. It might be helpful to have small signs for each element of the rally, so cheerleaders can see which activity is next. These ideas help cheerleaders prepare and not waste time.

The band plays a significant role in creating and maintaining the mood of the rally; fast-paced music excites fans as they enter the rally site. Cheerleaders should work with the band and add fun songs ("Rock and Roll Part 2," "The Twist," "Chicken Dance," "We Will Rock You," "Get Ready," and others) or spirit words to drum chants to help amuse the crowd. Use pep rallies to teach fans the words and actions to songs used during games. Having students and teachers help lead the songs always provides some entertaining minutes.

Consider involving athletes in the sportsmanship part of the pep rally. They might begin by thanking the crowd for their support. They could then explain that they're trying to win on the court or field and they'd like their fans to win in the stands. Athletes might even suggest some chants that motivate them and remind fans that negative chants bring them down.

Fall Pep Rally—Detailed Sheet for Participants

Friday, September 5

Band—Plays upbeat music as fans enter

— Plays "Rock and Roll Part 2"

— Cheerleaders use signs ("HEY!" "GO" "MUS-TANGS!")

— Plays school song

Cheerleaders—Chant ("We are the best! We are M-C-H-S!"); display signs ("M" "C" "H" "S")

Emcee—Welcomes fans, introduces first two head coaches

Head coaches—Talk briefly about teams, introduce letter winners and seniors; thank fans for support

Emcee—Introduces cheer coach (who introduces cheerleaders)

Cheerleaders—Crowd involvement chant or cheer; explain where crowd is to be involved, what to yell, and that the chant will be repeated; use signs ("GO," "BIG," "RED")

— "If you're yelling for the Mustangs, yell go!" GO

— "If you're yelling for the Mustangs, yell big red!" BIG RED

— "If you're yelling for the Mustangs, everybody go, big, red. Yell it!" GO BIG RED

Emcee—Introduces athletic director or principal

Athletic director or principal—Sportsmanship expectations (introduced in a positive way)

Emcee—Introduces crowd involvement activity (explain activity and call down participants)

Cheerleaders—Hula hoop activity: help get teams organized; give each team a hula hoop

Band—Plays upbeat music during activity

Emcee—Introduces next two head coaches

Head coaches—Talk briefly about teams, introduce letter winners and seniors; thank fans for support

Emcee—Introduces cheerleaders for grade-level chant competition

Cheerleaders—Explain and lead grade-level chant competition (cheerleaders from each grade level lead their grade during the chant)

— GO! (freshmen)

— MUSTANGS! (sophomores)

— BEAT! (juniors)

— THE WILDCATS! (seniors)

Band or taped music—Play theme song from *Jeopardy!*

Coaches—Huddle up during *Jeopardy!* theme song and decide on winner

Emcee—Announce winner of grade-level chant competition; ends rally on strong note; thanks everyone for coming; reminds them of big game that night

Band—Plays school song

— Plays upbeat music as fans leave rally

Figure 13.5 Detailed rally agenda.

The key to a successful rally is to keep it moving. Speakers should be seated on chairs near the podium to delay walking time to the microphone. Inform coaches beforehand that they'll have only a limited time to speak; if necessary, give them suggestions on what to cover. For instance, they might introduce only the letter winners or seniors on the team and have the other members simply stand and wave. Or they might tell the crowd how excited the team is about the season, give the date of the first home game or meet, and enthusiastically invite fans to attend their events. When all coaches and speakers are given the same information and allotment of time to speak, no sport or activity is recognized more than any other, which helps keep everyone happy.

Immediately after the rally, make some notes for ways to improve the next rally. Write down what worked, what didn't work, and what changes should be made. The pep rally agendas and planning forms (with suggestions for improvement) can be put into a pep rally notebook for future reference. It helps to keep a record of past rallies to see what fans enjoyed and to make sure skits aren't repeated too often. A notebook of comments on past rallies makes it much easier to plan future rallies.

Ideas for Crowd Involvement at Pep Rallies

You can find ideas for pep rallies in many places, including other coaches and cheerleaders, state and national organizations, and the Internet. Cheerleaders and coaches should choose activities that have the best chance of succeeding at their schools. What works at one school might not work at another—you need to know your audience. Some schools like to award prizes to contest winners, but students are often satisfied simply to win over their peers at the rally (for instance, by making more noise than any other grade). If you decide to give prizes, you might use gift certificates for pizza, movie passes, tickets to a game or dance, free CDs and DVDs, or T-shirts. If competitions are held among classes, a box of candy might be awarded to the winning class. If competitions are between grades, a traveling trophy might be an appropriate award. The trophy can be engraved with the graduation year of the winning class and kept in a display case.

When selecting people to participate in pep rally competitions, choose a cross section of the student population, not just the athletes. If only one group of students is selected, other students feel left out, which does little to promote school spirit and unity. Also, students always enjoy seeing teachers or coaches competing in activities. The most popular competitions seem to be those involving five groups: seniors, juniors, sophomores, freshmen, and teachers/coaches. If the pep rally is for the community, have athletes' parents involved in a contest or activity as well. Students like watching coaches, teachers, and random students help cheerleaders lead a chant, sing the school song, or perform other fun activities.

© Human Kinetics

Use an exciting cheer to keep the energy level high at a pep rally.

Homecoming might require its own kind of pep rally. The community might be involved, which could require holding the rally in the late afternoon or early evening. For example, a fun pep rally with competitions between grades can be held in the afternoon at the high school. Many of the pep rally ideas described in the following sections work well for a competition among grades. To engage students who usually shun school activities, creative contests might be necessary, such as giving points to the grade that has the boy with the longest hair and girl with the shortest hair. For each activity, points can be awarded for first, second, and third place. Teachers or local celebrities can be the judges and scorers for the event. The winners of the competition might get to lead the homecoming parade or ride a particular float. The parade can start immediately after the school's pep rally and might lead to a larger community pep rally held at a park in a central location in town. The community rally should begin and end with the school song and might include one or two chants from the cheerleaders, a short pep talk from the football coach, and an introduction of the homecoming king and queen candidates.

Some tried and true pep rally ideas are listed in the paragraphs that follow, but these are just a few of the possibilities. As we've mentioned, it's important to know your audience and get people involved who can make your ideas work. Most of the following ideas allow for many groups to participate. Contests might have a variety of team sizes, depending on the total number of people who participate and the time allotted for the activity.

AIRPLANE TOSS   Everyone is given a piece of paper as he or she enters the pep rally. A table with pencils is available for students to write their name on the paper. Students are then told to fold their papers into airplanes. At a designated time during the rally, a trashcan is put into the middle of the floor. Fans try to throw their airplanes into the trashcan. If someone gets a plane in the trashcan, he or she wins a prize. If no one gets an airplane into the can, give the prize for closest to the can. As a fund-raising idea, papers with special markings (such as unique shapes and designs on the paper to distinguish it as a legitimate entry) can be sold for $1.00 each before a game. The contest would be held at halftime, with the winner receiving a prize.

BALLOON SHAVING CONTEST   Each participant is given a razor and a balloon covered in shaving cream. Contestants have 15 seconds to shave their balloon as close as possible without bursting it. The closest shave without a pop wins.

BANANA EATING "CONTEST"   Contestants are told they're participating in a banana eating contest. They are blindfolded, given a banana, and told to begin eating at the word "Go!" The first one to finish the entire banana (no, not the peel) wins. Right before the call of "Go!" all blindfolds are taken off but one. The one person left wearing a blindfold does not know the others have removed theirs. The audience has fun watching this person eat his or her banana as fast as possible while the other contestants just watch. The banana eater realizes what has happened once his or her blindfold is removed.

BUBBLE GUM CONTEST   Each in-season coach lines up in front of a whipped cream pie sitting on a table. Every pie has a piece of bubble gum buried deep within. A garbage bag, with a hole cut out for the head, is slipped over the head and upper body of each coach; coaches can't use their hands during the contest. The first coach to find the gum and blow a bubble wins.

CANDY CANE PASS   This activity is great for a holiday pep rally. Use participants from each grade, plus a team of teachers. Each team stands in a line from one sideline to the other on the gym floor. Participants are each given a candy cane to put in his or her mouth with the curved end hanging out. The first person in the line has another candy cane hanging from the candy cane in his or her mouth. On a call of "Go!" the first person walks to the second person and passes the candy cane onto the second person's candy cane without using his or her hands (hands are kept behind the back). The candy cane passes down the line and back to the first person. The team finished first wins the relay. Have extra candy canes ready to replace those that drop and break.

CATERPILLAR RACES   Participants on each team line up on the end line of the gym floor. They all put their hands on the floor and their legs and feet on the shoulders and backs of the person behind them. The last person in the line has his or her feet on the floor. Each team races to a finish line (half court) to win. Teams must coordinate their arms to move quickly, yet stay close enough to keep legs and feet on the backs of their teammates.

CHEER AND DANCE CONTEST   Groups are made up of students from each grade, plus a team of teachers. Individuals are selected at the beginning of the pep rally and sent to another room to practice. Each group is taught a short cheer or dance by a cheerleader. Midway through the pep rally, the groups are called in to perform. Coaches select the winning group.

CIRCLE CONTEST   Teams are made up of students from each grade, plus a team of teachers. Each team stands in a circle, shoulder to shoulder, facing out. Everyone on the team sits down and joins elbows. When directed to do so, each group tries to stand up and cross the finish line while still joined at the elbows.

FOOTBALL THROW   The quarterback from each grade throws a football through a hoop held a distance away. Participants continue to play as long as they make it through the hoop. If they miss, they drop out. The hoop is moved farther back until all participants have missed but one. This person is the winner.

FREE-THROW SHOOTING CONTEST   Boy and girl basketball players from each grade shoot two free throws while blindfolded. The player who makes a basket, or comes closest, wins.

HACKY SACK CONTEST   Students sign up ahead of time to enter the contest; decide beforehand how many will be on a team. The team that keeps the Hacky Sack off the floor the longest wins.

HOOP CONTEST   Teams are made up of 10 people from each grade, plus a team of teachers. Each team stands in a circle holding hands. A plastic hoop is hanging between two of the people on a team. Each team must pass the hoop around the circle without letting go of each other's hands, forcing people to contort their bodies through the hoops. It's fun to drop out one group at a time and repeat the contest until it's down to two teams. The contest between the final two teams is exciting because they get better each time.

JELL-O EATING CONTEST   Participants must eat a bowl of Jell-O with their hands behind their back. The first one done wins. It's also fun to watch one person feed another person the Jell-O.

LIMBO CONTEST   Participants limbo under a bar to music provided by the band (or play pre-taped music). If a participant falls while going under the bar, he or she is out. The bar is lowered after each contestant has gone underneath it. The last one to go under the bar without falling wins.

MOTHERS KISS SONS   One or two boys from each athletic team are brought down to sit on chairs in front of the crowd. Female cheerleaders are standing behind each chair. The boys are told they will be blindfolded and that a cheerleader will kiss each of them. They must rate the kisses on a scale from 1 to 10. After the boys are blindfolded, their mothers are brought out. The first mom kisses her son (usually on the cheek), who is asked to rate the kiss and explain why he gave the kiss that rating (be sure to have a microphone available so the crowd can hear his response). This continues down the line. When all boys have rated their kisses, their blindfolds are removed and they see who really kissed them.

ORANGE PASS   Each team lines up on the gym floor. An orange is held by the first person in the crook of his or her neck. The first person walks to the second person and passes the orange to his or her neck without using hands. The first team to move the orange all the way down the line wins. If the orange drops during the exchange, the person passing it has to put it back in the crook of his or her neck and try passing it again.

PARENT INVOLVEMENT   During a community pep rally, try to involve the parents of the athletes. The fathers of the cheerleaders can perform a cheer or dance with them. The cheer or dance may or may not be practiced ahead of time—either way, it's funny to watch. Mothers might be asked to mimic their sons or daughters during a mock game introduction. The Booster Club might also organize parents to perform a skit, dance, or cheer.

SIGN-MAKING CONTEST   Each homeroom makes a big sign using the homecoming theme. All rooms are given the same size of paper on which to make the signs. Signs are hung in the hallways and judged on creativity and use of the theme. The winner is announced at the pep rally, and the the winning homeroom receives a prize. The halls get decorated for homecoming week, and the entire school is involved.

TABLE TENNIS BALL RELAY RACE   Participants line up down the length of the gym floor. Each participant has a spoon. The first person in line has a table tennis ball on his or her spoon. He or she walks quickly to the second person and passes the ball to his or her spoon. The first team to pass the ball all the way down the line wins.

VOLLEYBALL RELAY   Each participant has a large, plastic cup. The first participant places a volleyball on top of the bottom of the cup and walks as quickly as possible to center court. He or she flips the ball into the air, catches it on the top of the cup, then walks back to the next person in line. He or she puts the ball on the next participant's cup, and the sequence is repeated. The first line finished wins the relay. Decide ahead of time if participants are to put the ball on the next person's cup using their hands (easy) or not using their hands (much harder).

WHISTLE SCHOOL SONG   Participants eat soda crackers and then whistle the first verse of the school song. The first one to whistle the entire verse wins.

Summary

Organization and practice are key elements to successful game cheering and pep rallies. Arriving early and getting the crowd to cheer during pregame helps set the tone for the rest of the game. Understanding the game, being in tune with the fans, and performing crowd involvement chants are indications of professional, well-coached cheerleaders. Cheerleaders do their job by leading school spirit and controlling the crowd. Proper chant selection and use of signs are important for time-outs, quarter breaks, and key times during games. Pep rallies are perfect opportunities to fire up the fans for a season, big game, or special event. School and community unity and spirit can be amplified at pep rallies, chants can be taught, and sportsmanship expectations can be communicated. Using traditional chants along with some new ideas at each rally keeps fans interested and excited, whereas involving a diverse cross section of students in pep rallies makes more fans feel connected to the school and event. When cheerleaders are doing their job, cultivating enthusiastic fans and tremendous school spirit is easy.

Camps and Competitions

Camps and competitions offer cheerleaders additional opportunities to improve their cheerleading proficiency. Keeping updated on the latest cheerleading trends and learning new skills are as important to cheerleading as raising school spirit. At camps, cheerleaders can learn new chants, cheers, and stunts. They can perfect their skills, meet cheerleaders from other schools, and bond as a team. Competitions are a great opportunity for cheerleading squads to showcase their abilities while contending against other teams. Competitions help push cheerleaders to higher levels of performance while teaching them the values of teamwork, self-discipline, and good sportsmanship. At camps and competitions, cheerleaders can hone skills that will be useful to them throughout their cheerleading careers.

Camps

Many state and national companies offer camps for cheerleaders, and some college cheerleading programs also hold camps at their schools. Most camps are held in the summer when cheerleaders are not in school, and each camp offers varying degrees of experience and instruction. Cheerleaders and coaches wishing to attend a camp for the first time should collect information about the program so an educated decision can be made about whether to attend.

Camp Selection

Cheerleaders will definitely learn new material at a camp. Attending camp allows cheerleaders to bring new material home and helps them stay abreast of new techniques. Besides teaching cheerleading skills, camps offer cheerleaders a chance to bond and work as a team, especially if cheerleaders are away from home. Most teams are made up of diverse individuals who might not be friends outside of cheerleading. At camp, cheerleaders work together during the day and get to know each other. They meet cheerleaders from other schools, share ideas, and perhaps identify older cheerleaders to use as role models. Good news for coaches is that some camps offer coaches' education programs, so coaches also have an opportunity to gain knowledge and improve their skills by attending a camp.

PURPOSE OF ATTENDING When selecting a cheer camp, your first consideration should probably be the purpose of attending. What are the needs of the squad? Once you have established your squad's needs, the next question is which camp best serves these needs? Camps offer a range of material and present it in different ways and at different levels. One camp's strength might be teaching basic cheerleading skills such as motions, jumps, and stunts. Another camp might specialize in stunts. Still another camp might offer leadership training for cheerleaders along with cheerleading skills and techniques. Some camps might also offer instruction in competitions.

If cheerleaders have skills they'd like to learn or improve, look for a camp that teaches these skills at an appropriate level. This means cheerleaders need to find a camp that pushes them hard enough to excel but not so hard that they get discouraged. In making educated decisions, it helps for coaches and cheerleaders to gather specific information from others who have attended the camps in the past. Preparing a list of questions specific to your desires and needs helps you get the information you want. Some areas to consider are discussed in the sections that follow.

DATES AND FEES Major considerations for most schools, coaches, and cheerleaders are camp dates and fees. Obviously, you want to select camp dates that fit the schedules of the majority of your cheerleaders. Cheerleaders are usually involved in many activities, so camp dates should be selected early to give your squad plenty of notice. If you're the coach, you might select two to three camp dates, meet with your cheerleaders, and find out which camp works best for the majority. Once dates are set, cheerleaders and their families can put them on their calendars and plan their other activities around them.

All coaches like to keep camp costs reasonable, but selecting the cheapest camp isn't always the best option. Establish what you want your cheerleaders to achieve by attending camp, then find a camp that offers this instruction. The cost for lodging, meals, and instruction should be commensurate to the services being received and be in line with other camps in the state. The camp's brochure or Web site should specify what the camp fee covers. Coaches should note due dates for deposits and payment in full as well as cutoff dates for refunds. If money is a problem for some squad members, payment plans might be set up with cheerleaders and their families. In this way the benefits of a quality camp can be obtained without causing families undue hardships. Some schools might even allow fund-raising to help cover the costs of a camp, but it's a good idea to check with the administration beforehand.

LOCATION AND FACILITIES   When choosing a camp, it's logical to select a convenient location with at least adequate facilities. Again, gathering information from coaches who have attended the same camp can be helpful. A site easy to reach plus close to home is usually the most convenient, especially if parents need to drive the cheerleaders to camp. If the camp is in a large city, it's wise to make sure it's in a safe part of town.

Make sure you're completely clear on facilities before leaving for camp. Important information includes knowing if sleeping areas are air-conditioned (or if cheerleaders need to bring fans) and if bed linens and towels are provided. Also look into security measures. Are doors locked during the evening? Are people hired to monitor entry into the building at night? Are bed checks conducted? If so, who will be conducting them? What are the rules of the overnight facility? In case of an emergency, who is in charge and must be notified?

Camp attendees should also know whether instruction occurs in an outside area or indoors. If the camp is held inside, is the area air-conditioned? If the camp is held outside, is an inside area available if the weather turns bad? Another important consideration is the proximity of all facilities cheerleaders and coaches will be using, such as sleeping areas, dining areas, and instruction areas. All areas should be within a reasonable walking distance. If they're not, you'll want to know about transportation to these areas. There are also safety questions to look into, such as the type of surface the cheerleaders will be on during instruction, practice, and performance; whether water will be provided during instruction and if water breaks are sufficient; and whether bathroom facilities are located near the instruction area.

MEDICAL ISSUES   An essential part of any camp is the availability of an athletic trainer. An experienced trainer needs to be accessible during camp to handle injuries and emergencies. Camps usually require that all coaches and cheerleaders have medical information and release forms completed before attending the camp. Either the coach or trainer should have these forms in their possession. Camp attend-

ees must know how to contact the trainer if an emergency occurs at a time when instruction is not taking place, such as before or after sessions. Procedures to follow when taking a cheerleader to the hospital ought to be established and communicated ahead of time as well. If the coach goes to the hospital with the cheerleader, who will be available to monitor the cheerleaders while he or she is gone?

REPUTATION   It's smart to select a company that is established in the cheer business and has an honest reputation. Unless you have heard great things about a new camp, it's usually a good idea to select a camp that has been in service for some years. You can get information from other coaches, especially veteran coaches. The reputation of a company is based on their quality of instruction, dependability, and service. It's also nice to know a camp's philosophy to see if it matches the philosophy of your school and squad.

INSTRUCTORS   Camp representatives should be able to tell coaches how many instructors are available for each squad. For more individualized attention, it's better to have a lower number of cheerleaders per instructor. Of course, quality matters as much or more as quantity. It hardly matters how many instructors are available if they aren't good teachers. If possible, find out how experienced the staff is; ask about their training background. Again, previous camp attendees can share their thoughts. Camps generally want instructors with a high level of skill because they'll be demonstrating to camp attendees. However, all skilled cheerleaders aren't always able to teach. It's important to select a camp that hires both skilled and instructive staff.

CAMP PROGRAM   As we mentioned earlier, each camp has its strengths and weaknesses. Probably the best way to learn a camp's points of emphasis is to look at the camp's daily and weekly schedules. You can see how much time is allotted for each cheerleading skill or technique, how many times each one is taught, and how much time is spent on group instruction, one-on-one instruction, practice, and evaluation. The schedule should also show whether other aspects are included in the camp program, such as education for coaches or leadership training and team building for the cheerleaders. Camps should provide a list of awards presented as well. Cheerleaders and coaches should know which skills are being judged each day, including the final day. Awards presented during camp are another indication of the cheerleading areas a camp stresses.

Types of Camps

The two types of camps most common for cheer squads to attend are private or home camps and resident camps, which are usually held on college campuses. When deciding between a private or home camp and a resident camp, compare the advantages of each. Because each type of camp has advantages and disadvantages, the type of camp that best meets the needs of the squad should be selected. The major benefits of private or home camps and resident camps are listed here:

Advantages of Private Home Camps

- They tend to be much less expensive because you don't have to pay for meals and accommodations.
- There's flexibility with dates and times; teams can select dates that the majority of cheerleaders can attend and select the time of day the camp is held.
- There's usually an option of choosing a one- or two-day camp (as opposed to the three- or four-day resident camps).
- There's generally more choice in skills and materials to be focused on during instruction.
- There's greater flexibility in the length of time a squad wishes to work on specific skills.
- Cheerleaders receive more individual instruction because only one school attends the camp.
- Coaches can work more closely with instructors.
- Cheerleaders go home each night, get a break from each other and the coach, and maintain a familiar routine.

Advantages of Resident Camps

- Cheerleaders and coaches are removed from familiar surroundings and are spending time together during meals and in the evenings, so there's a better chance to bond within squads, among squads, and with coaches.
- There's more exposure to a diversity of material because squads don't have the choice of selecting material with which they're familiar; they get introduced to new ideas and skills.
- Because other schools are present, there's more incentive to learn and perfect material and improve skills.
- Daily evaluations develop stronger squads as they work together to perfect material.
- More days of camp gives cheerleaders time to learn additional material and sharpen skills.
- There are opportunities to meet cheerleaders and coaches from other schools. Cheerleaders and coaches can learn from each other, share ideas, and develop new friendships. New coaches can be mentored by more experienced coaches.
- Competitions are held, so cheerleaders gain experience being in front of others and having their material judged by the instructors.
- There are chances to earn team or individual awards and honors. Publicizing camp awards provides recognition for cheerleaders and the program.
- There's a greater variety of instructors, so squads get a mix of teaching styles and ideas for improvement.
- Coaches' education programs are often available with a set curriculum of materials to help coaches improve their skills.

Preparing for Camp

Once the decision has been made to attend a cheerleading camp, there are ways cheerleaders and coaches can prepare to make the experience positive. Of course, camp registrations and down payments must be sent in early to guarantee

© Human Kinetics

Using the skills learned at camp will help raise spirit during games.

space is held at the camp. If a cheerleader decides not to attend camp, the camp usually keeps part of the registration fee to cover processing costs. Again, be aware of the cutoff date (usually two weeks before camp) after which no money will be returned.

Cheerleaders need to be in shape when they attend camp. It's not healthy or wise to walk into a three- or four-day camp without conditioning ahead of time. Camps usually have sessions in the morning, afternoon, and evening—a tough schedule even for a cheerleader who is in shape! You can prepare for camp in many ways. Some coaches practice with their cheerleaders all summer. With the coach monitoring, cheerleaders are assured of getting in shape. Other coaches give their cheerleaders workouts and allow them some flexibility in the summer. This gives the coach and cheerleaders a break and allows for family time, vacations, jobs, and other activities.

These coaches can then meet with the cheerleaders the week before camp for a little more structured conditioning practice.

Along with physical conditioning, there are organizational details to take care of as well. How will cheerleaders get to camp? What do they need to bring? Parents usually carpool cheerleaders to and from camp, and most parents enjoy watching the last day's events when material is reviewed and awards are presented. A coach needs to check with the administration on school policies for parents driving students; sometimes a form needs to be completed for insurance purposes. If you're planning to ride school buses to camp, check with school administrators beforehand. Some states don't allow students to ride buses to camps because camps aren't a school-sponsored activity. Also, a map showing how to get to the camp location is always helpful for parents. Maps are usually provided by the camp organization in their confirmation packet.

Cheerleaders should be told the coach's expectations before they arrive at camp, and these expectations should be reviewed on the first evening of camp. Some items to discuss are behavior in the dorms (especially regarding noise), putting all litter in the trash, and keeping bathrooms clean. Respect for others at the camp follows along these same lines. Cheerleaders should be supporting the other schools, getting to know other cheerleaders, and cheering for them when they're performing. Of course it goes without saying that cheerleaders need to listen to camp instructors, follow their directions, and show them respect. It's also good to remind cheerleaders they're expected to eat three meals a day and get their sleep because of the long, usually hot days for which they'll need lots of energy. Cheerleaders need to be reminded to work together and stay positive on these days. Specific times for lights out are usually determined by the camp, and cheerleaders need to know that bed checks will be strictly enforced. They should also know ahead of time that there's usually a fee (sometimes large) for lost keys and meal tickets, so they need to be responsible for these items. It helps to have one bag per squad for everyone to put their keys and meal tickets in during sessions so they don't get lost.

To make sure cheerleaders don't forget things, send them home with a list of items they will need for camp. Figure 14.1 shows a sample list that can be revised to suit your purposes. Give the camp's emergency number to all parents and guardians as well as an agenda covering the stay at the camp. The agenda should include the time cheerleaders are leaving for camp, session times, last-day activities, and the time cheerleaders will be returning home.

Make sure to bring all required forms to camp. The most important papers are the medical release forms so cheerleaders can get treatment if they're injured. It's also a good idea to bring a small medicine kit, including Band-Aids, bobby pins, hair ties, tampons, nail clippers, gauze pads, and special medications such as glucose tablets and a glucagon kit for cheerleaders with diabetes.

Camps offer a cheerleading squad an opportunity to learn updated, new material and to perfect their skills. Cheerleaders will be excited to cheer at their games with cheers, chants, and stunts they've learned at camp. With research and planning, cheerleading camp can be an enjoyable, rewarding, and educational experience.

Items for Camp

- Uniform—shell(s) and skirt(s)
- Briefs
- Cheerleading shoes
- Socks
- Underwear
- Pajamas
- Sweatshirt and sweatpants (if needed)
- Pompons (if needed)
- Tank/T-shirt, shorts—3 sets
- Signs for cheers (if needed)
- Signs for room doors, tape
- Sunscreen (SPF 15 or higher)
- Water jug
- Bug spray
- Alarm clock (one per room)
- Camera and film

- Hair ties, ribbons, bobby pins
- Hair dryer
- Toiletries (shampoo/conditioner, soap, tampons, deodorant, contact solution, toothbrush, and toothpaste)
- Needed medication (prescriptions, inhalers, etc.)
- Aspirin, bandages
- Facial tissue
- Hangers
- Bedding—sheets, blankets, and pillows (if needed)
- Fan (if needed)
- Money for t-shirts, camp video, pizza, extras—don't bring a lot!!
- Healthy snacks and water—no soda!

All jewelry should remain at home!!

Figure 14.1   Items for camp.

Competitions

Raising school spirit by leading chants and cheers at games and pep rallies is the main function of a cheerleading squad, but many squads also enjoy participating in competitions. Competitions are a great way for squads to learn life lessons, such as working together to meet individual and team goals. Cheerleaders learn how to handle victory and defeat with poise and good sportsmanship; they also learn to accept and rise up to meet challenges.

Deciding to Compete

More cheerleading squads are participating in competitions than ever before, but should all squads compete? Before even mentioning competition to the cheerleaders, the coach needs to obtain the support of the administration. When meeting with the principal or athletic director, the coach should be organized and have all pertinent information. Administrations are always concerned about money, so all expenses need to be explained, as well as a plan for covering them. Information on the benefits of the competition, the reputation of the group holding it, and the prestige of the awards are items to share as well.

Once a coach is given permission to compete, the first question to ask the squad is whether they want to compete. Competing should be something the team desires, not something forced on them. Cheerleaders might wish to compete for a variety of reasons, such as to gain recognition, win a trophy, showcase their skills, or just have fun. If cheerleaders show enthusiasm for the idea of attending a competition, ask them why they want to compete. What do they hope to gain from the competition? It might help for your squad to complete a form such as the one shown in figure 14.2, which helps cheerleaders focus and set goals for a competition. Every cheerleader on the squad must make the commitment, or preparing for the competition will be difficult. If even one cheerleader doesn't want to compete, that attitude can affect the others through lack of desire, effort, or participation. Cheerleaders need to be aware of the individual commitment required to prepare for a competition. Participants need to manage their time to take care of schoolwork, practices, games, other responsibilities, and possibly fund-raising. Cheerleaders must attend every practice with a positive attitude and incredible work ethic. Cheerleaders on the squad need to keep up their cardiovascular endurance and physical strength through conditioning and weightlifting. Cheerleaders should understand the mental demands of competition; they'll have to deal with frustrations and persevere with respect for each other. They also need to be told about the rewards of working together as a team and striving for something that is difficult. Much pride can be gained from working toward a goal, even if the goal is not achieved.

Win or lose, cheerleaders should find competitions to be positive experiences, and the coach is instrumental in making this happen. If you're the coach, make sure to stress the positives of competing and to keep competition preparations organized, goal oriented, and fun. Cheerleaders need to be inspired, so look for opportunities to praise. Recognizing a squad's sharp motion technique or solid stunt building is a great way to motivate and help build confidence. The coach should also be aware of stressful times and make changes before cheerleaders get discouraged. A coach has the enormous job of balancing the work needed to prepare for a competition while making the experience rewarding.

Selecting a Competition

There are many competitions available for cheerleading squads. Some competitions are incredibly reputable and established in the industry; others are younger and still building a name for themselves. Competitions are available to cheerleaders at the local, state, regional, and national level with the majority provided by private and national companies. Many states hold state cheerleading competitions, and sometimes individual schools hold competitions as fund-raisers. As mentioned earlier, some camps also hold competitions. As when choosing a camp, coaches and cheerleaders must research the reputation and reliability of the group hosting the competition. Registration fees can add up to a lot of money that might be wasted on an unpleasant experience. When selecting a competition, the purpose of the competition should match the squad's purpose for attending the competition. For example, if a squad desires recognition for their skills, they should select a competition with prestige, such as a state or national competition, because top

Precompetition Worksheet

1. Team goals for the competition:

   _____

   _____

   _____

   _____

   _____

   _____

2. What positive experiences do we expect to gain from participation in this competition?

   _____

   _____

   _____

   _____

   _____

   _____

3. How will we display good sportsmanship when the results are announced—even if the results are not what we expected?

   _____

   _____

   _____

   _____

   _____

Our signatures verify that we will do our best at the competition, and we are ready to accept all results with good sportsmanship.

_____   _____   _____

_____   _____   _____

_____   _____   _____

Figure 14.2 Precompetition worksheet.

cheer squads will be competing. Doing well at this type of competition is a huge endorsement for a program. Conversely, the prestige won't be as great for a small competition at a local high school, but if a squad is new to competition, attending a small competition to learn and test their skills is an appropriate choice.

There are practical considerations to keep in mind, too. Depending on the competition, the cost of competing can be sizeable. If going to a national competition, coaches and cheerleaders need to be reasonable about the total cost for registration fees, travel, accommodations, food, and other incidentals. Cheerleaders will not only be practicing their routine but will be spending a great deal of time fund-raising as well. On top of this, they still have school commitments, such as homework and cheering at games. Cheerleaders must not shirk their primary responsibility, which is to lead and promote school spirit. Missing school and cheering responsibilities should be seriously considered when making competition decisions; of course, always get advance approval from the administration for any planned absences.

To make a good choice on which competition to attend, a squad should know the details about each competition. Not all competitions have the same time limits, safety guidelines, and other rules (such as use of props). Most groups holding competitions allow squads to send in videos to verify the legality of their stunts. This is a great idea if a team is unsure about a stunt or two. For the safety of the cheerleaders and the liability of the school and coach, it's important for teams to follow their state's cheerleading safety guidelines at competitions, even if the competition is not following them. If a team thinks they won't be able to compete at the level of the other squads because of rule restrictions, then that particular competition is probably not a good fit. Here's a list of some of the details to look into before choosing a competition:

Overall Competition Information

- Is the group holding the competition reputable?
- Is the competition prestigious?

- Does the competition fit with the skill level of your squad?
- What are the divisions?
- Is the competition held at a reasonable time to compete?
- Is videotaping allowed?

Cost

- Is the cost reasonable for the competition? Is it comparable to the cost of other competitions?
- What will the squad receive for their entry fee?

Quality and Number of Judges

- Are the judges experienced and qualified?
- How many judges will be scoring each routine?
- Will all judges' scores count or will the high and low scores be thrown out?

Judging System

- What skills will be judged?
- Can you get a score sheet ahead of time?

Competition Rules

- Are the competition rules reasonable and consistent with other competitions?
- Are safety guidelines being followed?
- If safety guidelines exist, are they consistent with guidelines you already follow?

Time Limits

- What is the time limit for the overall routine?
- What is the time limit for music?
- Is music required to be used for the entire routine? (Often true for all-star divisions.)
- Is the time limit consistent with other competitions?

Facility

- What is the size of the competition performance area?

- Is this size consistent with other competitions?
- What type of performing surface is used?
- Is the performing surface safe?
- Will cheerleaders be allowed to practice on this surface beforehand?
- Are dressing rooms available?
- Is there sufficient seating for spectators and participants?

Warm-Up Area

- Will a warm-up area be available?
- Does the warm-up area have a safe surface and sufficient space to practice?
- Is a suitable amount of time allotted for each team in the warm-up area?
- Will some type of music system be available for use in the warm-up area?
- If a music system isn't available, can the squad bring and use their own music?

Music

- What type of equipment is available for routine music?
- Who will be in charge of running a squad's music?
- Where is the music table located?

Awards

- What type of awards or recognition will squads receive?
- How many awards will be given in each division?
- Is the number of awards given in each division based on the number of teams competing in those divisions?
- Are awards presented for such areas as spirit or choreography?

Trainer

- Will an experienced trainer be available?
- Where will he or she be located?
- Will the trainer be available to tape ankles? If so, must the team provide the tape?

A typical competition involves the entire team. However, some competitions offer the opportunity for individual, stunt group, or partner stunt competitions. A team needs to decide which type of competition best suits their squad's skills. They also need to decide if they want to compete in just one area of a competition or if they want to compete in more. Competitions usually allow teams to compete in just one team division, but members of the team might be able to compete individually or in small groups. When making decisions, coaches need to know the physical and mental abilities of their squad. Will competing in an individual or small-group event take focus away from the entire team competition? Will dividing a cheerleader's focus allow her to compete well in both events? When making these decisions, consider the timing of each event. Is there enough time between the events for proper preparation?

Preparing to Compete

Once a squad has decided to compete, the planning and work begin. First, squads need to be aware of registration deadlines, including when money is due. The earlier a team registers, the earlier they'll receive the competition information, which needs to be read carefully by all squad members. Sometimes schools get penalized for going over a time limit, having too many cheerleaders, or stepping off the mat. It's silly for a team to lose easy points because they haven't read the rules. If a team has any questions after reading the competition information, they should call the group holding the competition to get clarification.

Deciding on a choreographer, practices, and fund-raising (if needed) are the next steps in the competition process (choosing a choreographer was covered in chapter 12). It's a good idea for a coach to be present and observant when a choreographer is teaching a squad the routine. Of course, the choreographer must understand the skill level of the squad, and the routine should be appropriate for the squad's age group. Ideally, the choreographer should have a copy of the competition's score sheet ahead of time so he or she can be sure to incorporate all of the elements. The choreographer should provide the squad with the routine music on a high-quality tape or CD.

PRACTICES   It takes some planning to organize productive practices so that cheerleaders learn and perfect a routine. Cheerleaders and coaches need to make a timeline and be sure everyone has a copy. This timeline provides the short-term goals needed to reach the end goal of a perfected routine. Again, practices shouldn't interfere with the squad's responsibility as spirit leaders. Separate practices can be held for the competition routine, or practice for the competition can be held immediately following regular cheer practice. Administrators should expect cheerleaders to be prepared for games, and if they're not, the squad's option to compete might need to be reexamined. A great way to practice stunts and cheers in a routine is to use them during games. Stunts can be thrown up using the same words or by adding spirit words (if the words from the routine don't fit the game situation). Cheers can be done between quarters (easier to do at football games) or at halftime. If time is short, just parts of a cheer can be performed. In this way the cheerleaders are using their material to lead fans, practicing their routine, and getting experience in front of a crowd. To be effective, however, the material and stunts must fit the timing of the game. If squads just quickly throw together a stunt during a time-out and then run off the floor—that's not cheerleading; the competition material needs to be incorporated in a way that leads the crowd.

It's imperative for coaches and cheerleaders to understand that the way they practice is the way they'll compete. Participants can't expect to go through practices without always jumping to the best of their abilities, hitting all their stunts, and having sharp motions, and then expect to perform the routine perfectly at the competition. If stunts aren't hitting in practice, the confidence won't be there to hit them at the actual competition, especially with nervousness factored in. Along with perfect practice, it helps to have a routine warm-up that will be used on the competition day as well. A familiar routine helps cheerleaders focus while reducing nervousness, and it gets them completely stretched out and ready to compete.

ELEMENTS OF A ROUTINE   Several elements make up a competition routine, and each of these elements can and should be critiqued. These elements, or ones very much like them, will appear on the competition's score sheet and will determine how cheerleaders will be judged. Elements at the top of a score sheet usually involve the technical skills of a routine, such as motion technique, jump technique, tumbling skills, stunts (pyramids and partner stunts), and dance. Points for coaches to look for and critique are listed here:

Motion Technique

- All motions are hit sharply and precisely with correct timing, so the team looks like one unit.
- Motions of all cheerleaders follow the same pathway.
- All motions have correct level placement.
- All fists face the same direction; fists are closed and wrists straight.
- Cheerleaders have thumbs in (a special problem when hands are in blades). Check thumbs when cheerleaders are standing in formation and transitioning.
- Several different motions are used.

Jump Technique

- Timing of all jumps is the same (mistakes are most apparent during jump approach, execution, and landing).
- All cheerleaders use the same approach.
- All cheerleaders land with feet together.
- All cheerleaders clean in the same way after jumps.
- All jumps are executed with correct form—pointed toes, correct arm levels, and height.
- Several different jumps are used to showcase squad diversity.

Tumbling Skills

- All cheerleaders tumble with the same technique.
- All tumbling is clean and done with good form. Don't use if tumbling form is shaky.
- Tumbling is synchronized at all stages of the skill—starting position, number of

steps, hurdle skip, actual skill, landing, and finish. Practice tumbling skills to beats or counts and then progress to words.

- A combination of standing and running tumbling is used.
- Several different tumbling skills are used. Don't rely on one tumbling skill over and over.

Stunts

- All stunt groups use the same building technique.
- Getting set for a stunt and finishing a stunt are executed together by all stunt groups.
- Stunts are built to counts, and then words added to coordinate stunts.
- Stunts are hitting like motions. Each part of the stunt needs to be strong and clean (not shaky). Change a stunt if it's wobbly or not hitting consistently.
- Dismounts are clean and have a finish. Bases wrap tight on dismounts.
- Several different stunts are used to increase the difficulty level of the routine.

Dance

- Dance is synchronized; squad looks like one unit. Both upper and lower body movements are in sync.
- Dance movements are sharp and precise; remember good motion technique.
- Cheerleaders are moving their feet, not just performing motions to music, to increase the difficulty level of the dance.

The bottom of the score sheet is usually more subjective but just as important. These are areas any squad can perfect regardless of skill level. Elements on the bottom of a score sheet might include expression and showmanship; voice; spacing, formations, and use of floor; transitions; timing and flow of routine; creativity and crowd appeal; degree of difficulty; and perfection of routine. These elements might be lumped together or separated, depending on the group holding the competition. Points for coaches to critique in each of these areas are listed here:

Expression and Showmanship

- Facial expressions should be natural and genuine; smile.
- Cheerleaders should stand naturally without bobbing heads while standing in formation.
- Cheerleaders should make eye contact with judges.
- Cheerleaders are having fun and selling the routine to the judges.

Voice

- Voices are natural, clear, and strong.
- Voice projection is consistent throughout the routine. Be aware of voices that drop while building stunts or in the middle of a cheer.

Spacing, Formations, Use of Floor

- Spacing between cheerleaders in formations is symmetrical. Check spacing between lines, too.
- Formations change every three to four eight-counts.
- The same cheerleaders are not always front and center.
- When standing in formation, cheerleaders keep arms tight to their bodies. Individual cheerleaders shouldn't perform random spirit motions that might distract the judges.
- Cheerleaders use most of the performing surface during the routine; they don't just stay in the middle of the floor.

Transitions

- Cheerleaders don't run into each other during transitions. If problems occur, have them rewind from point B back to point A to pinpoint the difficulty.
- Cheerleaders move effortlessly to new formations on direct paths.
- Transitions are creative and are more than just claps. Turns and motions are added to transitions for creativity.
- Individual cheerleaders shouldn't perform random spirit motions during transitions.

- Arms are held tightly to sides unless performing synchronized motions.

Timing and Flow of Routine

- The timing of jumps, stunts, motions, and dance are synchronized. Watch for timing consistency when building stunts.
- The routine transitions are fluid when moving from one element to the next (e.g., from dance to cheer or during formation changes).
- The routine flows smoothly and doesn't noticeably speed up or slow down.

Creativity and Crowd Appeal

- Cheerleaders are spirited throughout the routine.
- The routine is enjoyable to watch and makes the viewer want to cheer with the squad.
- The routine has variety and creative visuals that grab the viewer's attention.

Degree of Difficulty

- The routine displays a good use of squad skills.
- The majority of the squad performs advanced motions, jumps, tumbling skills, stunts, and dances.

Perfection of Routine

- The overall execution of the routine is solid.
- The routine is performed cleanly without falls or bobbles.

PERFECTING A ROUTINE Once a routine is learned, a squad can work on perfecting it. Focusing on specific elements, having others watch the routine, videotaping, holding a mock competition run-through, and performing in front of an audience are all ways to help perfect a routine. Because it takes time to fine-tune all routine components, working on routine perfection should begin as soon as possible, even during the learning phase. It's a good idea to give positive feedback after each routine practice before mentioning items to improve; this way cheerleaders aren't as likely to get discour-

aged. It's also important to time the routine each time it is practiced so any problems with music or overall time can be caught early.

A great way to clean up a routine is to break it into sections so each participant knows every move in that part of the routine. Starting at the beginning, all elements (motions, jumps, dances, tumbling, and stunts) are perfected for a section or to a pause in the routine. Once this part is critiqued, cheerleaders move to the next section. It's important to concentrate on the little details in a section, such as turning heads to follow a motion, specifying exact locations of motions, and synchronizing dance moves before moving on. Each section of the routine should receive the same level of focus so that the end is as strong as the beginning.

Another way to break up the routine for critiquing is to have cheerleaders focus on specific elements such as motions, jumps, tumbling, or stunts to help them clean up problem areas. For example, the direction "hit all stunts this time" allows cheerleaders to concentrate on stunts only. Stunts should be set, executed, cradled, and dismounted in unison. Another good area to critique, which is often forgotten, is formations. The coach should stand to the side of the routine and check out lines and angles, which, when corrected, make the routine look cleaner.

Cheerleaders in the back of the routine can sometimes become complacent with their performance because they think they can't be seen. For critiquing purposes, each stunt group can take their turn performing the routine and being critiqued by the rest of the squad. This makes individual cheerleaders feel more responsible and commit to performing their best for the squad. The coach needs to remember, too, to watch the back row when critiquing the entire squad.

Once the routine can be run through from beginning to end, the coach or choreographer should look for dead spots. These are places in the routine where the momentum begins to die and the routine looks boring. To make sections of a routine more exciting, adding easy, visual motions or movements can detract from dead time. For example, if a team arrives at a stunt formation on count 5 but doesn't set until count 1, the team needs something to do on counts 7 and 8. This might be a good place for clapping in unison or shouting out the name of the school or mascot. Cheerleaders need to be having fun throughout the routine, just as the routine should be fun for those watching it.

A coach can get into a rut by watching the same routine over and over, sometimes focusing on the same mistakes and missing others. To help with this situation, a coach should find at least three things to critique following a run-through. After sharing some positive points, he or she can pinpoint these three weaknesses, and they can be fixed. Once these areas are corrected, the coach can look for three new elements to critique. This way cheerleaders aren't overwhelmed by all corrections coming at once. Another option is to bring in other qualified people to critique the routine and see it from new perspectives. These people usually find other areas to improve. Cheerleaders like having new faces and ideas at their practices as well.

Videotaping is another routine-perfecting technique. Keeping a television and VCR near the practice area helps delay time when using a videotape for immediate feedback. The squad can watch the tape and see how they look when performing. It's so much easier for cheerleaders to improve motions, jumps, and other areas when they see what they look like when doing it wrong. Cheerleaders can take tapes home, too, so they have time to watch them more closely outside of practice. The coach can use tapes to check formations and transitions in fast motion, which helps pinpoint areas needing work. It's also fun to keep tapes of the early practices and compare them to the actual competition, so cheerleaders can see how much they have improved.

For conditioning purposes, cheerleaders need to be able to perform the entire routine three times during any single practice session to ensure that they can perform the routine safely. This makes the "one time only" performance at the competition seem relatively easy. This also allows a coach to recognize any questionable areas of the routine. If it becomes obvious certain skills might not be executed by the time of the competition, changes must be made. If an elite pyramid sequence has yet to begin hitting con-

sistently, having an alternative sequence ready to go will make the weeks before competition less stressful.

Cheerleaders need to see the score sheet so they understand the importance of each area. A coach should watch the routine from the judges' perspective and use the score sheet to critique the squad. This is a good way to find out if all of the elements of the sheet are being met and which areas need to be improved. When judging, the coach should focus on the whole group and not just one individual. However, if individual cheerleaders stand out, this takes away from the timing and perfection of the routine, so it should be noted. If necessary, cheerleaders can be moved to other positions to make the routine stronger.

COMPETITION WEEK   The coach should talk to cheerleaders the week before the competition to remind them they'll be representing the school and community, so their behavior needs to be above reproach. To help remind cheerleaders why they're competing and what they hope to achieve, the squad should revisit the form they completed back when they decided to compete (refer back to figure 14.2). It's wise to talk about how they'll handle the competition results and prepare in advance for both happiness and disappointment. Good sportsmanship and character are the rules, and these rules should be conveyed to parents and fans, also.

The week before the competition, cheerleaders should practice just as they'll be performing on competition day. Cheerleaders should be dressed in their cheer uniforms at every practice. Clean shoes and shoestrings are also important, as are matching socks and matching ribbons in the hair. Nail polish shouldn't be worn unless it's clear. To make a practice feel more like the real event, invite students, fans, and family members to watch one of the final practices. The cheerleaders should warm up for the same amount of time and in the same way as they'll be warming up at the competition. This warm-up includes stretching, stunts, tumbling, jumps, and a run-through of the routine. When this is completed, cheerleaders can be announced to enter the "competition" area. They then perform the routine and walk off. The squad can discuss what to improve, and then perform the routine again. After performing the entire routine three times, cheerleaders work on any parts that need to be fine tuned. The day before the competition, cheerleaders should run through the routine only twice. Again, each time the routine is performed, someone should be timing it to be sure it's under the time limit.

There's a mental aspect to competition that a coach can help cheerleaders work through. It helps to tell them what to expect and to describe the place where they'll be competing. Cheerleaders can then prepare mentally by visualizing the competition area. They should see themselves performing the routine perfectly. Every time cheerleaders visualize themselves performing the routine, they need to see themselves doing their best. Mental imagery helps cheerleaders focus on performing the routine correctly, which helps them gain confidence.

Another area to discuss with cheerleaders is what to eat and drink, not only on the day of the competition but on the day or two before as well. Cheerleaders should eat meals that settle easily in their stomachs and avoid spicy foods and foods that are hard to digest. Many athletes eat a meal high in carbohydrates, such as pasta, a day or two before an athletic event. Cheerleaders need to avoid big meals and junk food, especially on the day of competition. A healthy breakfast is a must! As always, water is the best liquid for cheerleaders to drink. To perform their best, cheerleaders need to stay hydrated.

A few days before the competition, the coach should again read through the competition information to make sure the squad is in compliance with all the rules. Maps and schedules for the day need to be given to cheerleaders and their parents, with extra copies available for fans. The coach should bring the following items to the competition:

- Small medicine kit with adhesive bandages, gauze bandages, bobby pins, hair ties, tampons, nail clippers, gauze pads, and special medications such as glucose tablets and a glucagon kit for cheerleaders with diabetes.
- Medical release forms in case of injury.

- Music tapes or CDs—be sure to have a couple backup tapes or CDs!
- Music system to play music for the routine in the practice area, if necessary.
- Any other forms required by the competition.

Knowing What Judges Look For

It's important to be aware of what judges are looking for in a competition routine. Most competitions have panel judges scoring the technical aspects of a routine and safety judges ensuring that routines adhere to safety rules or guidelines. There are also people timing routines to ensure time limits for music and the overall routine are followed. Much of what judges look for when scoring a squad were listed earlier under Elements of a Routine, but a few other suggestions are given here. The main word to remember is *clean*.

Judges are interested in creative routines. Because they have to sit through a number of routines at a competition, a creative routine that's fun to watch will catch the judges' attention. Creative elements in the routine differentiate it from others. Visual transitions and level changes grab the judging panel's interest. Unique and catchy music will stay with the judges, but the music must fit the choreography to be effective. Cheerleaders who enjoy performing their routine are easily recognized by the judges as well.

Judges do notice the number of squad members performing skills, so those teams with the majority of its members performing difficult skills will receive higher scores. On the other hand, judges want to see routines executed cleanly; they don't want to see a squad try difficult stunts that wobble or drop. Tumbling passes that fall or are executed with poor technique must also be avoided. Routines should flow and look as if they're easy for the cheerleaders to perform. The routine shouldn't be crowded with technical skills. Sometimes when teams think they need to show every stunt and tumbling skill they possess, the routine becomes chaotic and doesn't flow.

As mentioned earlier, random spirit motions, unusual hairdos, and large ribbons can divert the attention of the judges. Squads don't receive higher scores from cheerleading judges for costuming. Uniforms should be flattering to the performers and not detract from the routine. Cheerleaders wearing too much makeup and glitter (which isn't allowed in some states) can also be distracting. Judges shouldn't even notice what cheerleaders are wearing except that the squad has a clean look. After all of their hard work, a squad should want judges to focus only on their routine, not their "unique" appearance.

Overall, judges are looking for a clean and well-balanced routine. This means the routine contains all of the elements on the score sheet, and all elements are performed in a consistent manner. If a team is strong in stunting and doesn't really concentrate on perfecting the other areas of the score sheet, they won't score as high as another team with very good skills across the score sheet.

On the day of the competition, cheerleaders should arrive at least 15 minutes before the scheduled departure time. A last-minute check of all uniform items, including hair ribbons and socks, should be done immediately. Make sure cheerleaders have matching right and left shoes! The coach and cheerleaders should be upbeat and excited to get going. Once the team arrives at the competition area, find a quiet place to relax. Some cheerleaders might want to watch the competition until it's time to stretch, but others might feel the need to focus. Sometimes squads decide in advance if they're going to watch or not; cheerleaders need to do whatever keeps them from getting nervous.

A stretching time and place should be determined ahead of time; cheerleaders need to be

Performing a clean and well-balanced routine is a good way to impress the judges.

Photo by Paul Hoge

ready to go at this time. Bathroom visits, wrist and ankle taping, and hair braiding need to be completed so that everyone is ready to stretch together. If they stretch before they reach the warm-up area, cheerleaders can use their entire warm-up time to go over their routine. They should put up each stunt, warm up tumbling and jumps, and then run through the entire routine using the same warm-up routine they've practiced at school.

Once cheerleaders leave the warm-up area and are on deck to compete, they need to be pumped up and energized. They should be feeling that they can't wait to get in front of the judges and perform! The coach should be telling the cheerleaders to go out and have fun! Everything is positive before going out to perform. Once cheerleaders have performed, again be positive and excited for them. While the squad waits for the results to be announced, have the team sit

together and be united. After results are read, the coach needs to let the cheerleaders know he or she is proud of them and that they should be proud of themselves. If the cheerleaders have won, they should be graceful in their enthusiasm. If they haven't won, cheerleaders and coaches should congratulate the winning coach and team.

Once the squad arrives home, the coach should get competition results sent to the school, local newspaper, and local television and radio stations. About a week after the competition, the squad might have a pizza party and watch the competition video for closure. During this time, cheerleaders can reminisce about the competition and complete a follow-up sheet (similar to the one shown in figure 14.3). A follow-up sheer allows cheerleaders to reflect and grow from their competition experience, which makes them stronger the next time they compete.

Postcompetition Worksheet

1. What happened at the competition that went above our expectations?

_____

_____

_____

_____

_____

_____

2. What happened at the competition that met our expectations?

_____

_____

_____

_____

_____

_____

(continued)

Figure 14.3 Postcompetition worksheet.

3. What happened at the competition that didn't meet our expectations?

_____

_____

_____

_____

_____

_____

4. What can we learn from this competition to help us better prepare in the future?

_____

_____

_____

_____

_____

_____

Figure 14.3 *(continued)*

Summary

Camps and competitions provide additional learning opportunities for cheerleaders. These extra events should complement the cheerleading program's main purpose of raising school spirit. For positive experiences at camps or competitions to occur, coaches and cheerleaders need to identify their reasons for wanting to attend extra events and pinpoint their needs. Using research and common sense, squads can then select a camp or competition that meets these needs. With positive guidance, cheerleaders can grow and improve their skills by attending camps and participating in competitions. These events have the added benefit of teaching cheerleaders such qualities as teamwork, goal setting, and good sportsmanship—skills they'll use throughout their lives.

fifteen

Practicing and Conditioning

One of the most difficult aspects of cheerleading is organizing practices and conditioning programs. Everyone wants to use time as constructively as possible to get the most out of practices while training and preparing cheerleaders for their activity. Cheerleading has so many elements for which to prepare—motions, jumps, stunts, tumbling, dance, cheers, chants, special events, cardiovascular endurance, flexibility, and strength training—just to name a few! Organized practices help participants develop the skills and conditioning they need to become confident and effective cheerleaders. To help the year run smoothly, coaches should hold a meeting for all parents, guardians, and cheerleaders before the fall season begins. Meeting together as a large group allows everyone to hear the same information and expectations. This can make a big difference during the season when parental support is helpful in achieving expectations outlined at the meeting.

Parent–Cheerleader Meeting

A meeting with cheerleaders and their parents or guardians should be planned as early as possible in the new season to inform everyone about the cheerleading program requirements. Give parents, guardians, and cheerleaders as much advance notice as possible to promote good attendance at this important meeting. It's beneficial to have Booster Club representatives or veteran parents organize a pizza party as part of the meeting. Eating creates a relaxed atmosphere and promotes people getting to know each other. While going over the many items on the agenda, keep the tone of the meeting light and positive.

The coach doesn't have to cover every detail of the cheerleading program at this meeting—just the major issues that parents and cheerleaders should know about. After welcoming parents and athletes and introducing the coaches, the head coach can explain the cheerleading program's philosophy, which should include details about skill development as well as information on the lifelong attributes cheerleaders gain through involvement in cheerleading, such as character development and leadership skills. The head coach might also mention that all coaches in the program understand that for cheerleaders to develop these attributes they must be modeled by every member of the coaching staff and any other adults associated with the program.

The next issue the coach needs to discuss is the inherent risks of cheerleading. Parents and cheerleaders must understand the risks involved in cheerleading, which are basically the same as the risks involved in any athletic activity. Inform parents and cheerleaders that before any workouts occur they will be asked to sign a form that states they understand these risks. An example of an inherent risk form is shown in figure 15.1. Along with the inherent risks of the activity, it's reassuring for parents to hear about safety guidelines and program rules. Many states have adopted cheerleading safety guidelines to decrease injuries, and parents should be aware that these rules will be followed. Parents and guardians should also be informed of rules that cheerleaders frequently violate, such as the rule forbidding jewelry and regulating nails, hair, and glitter. Telling parents the rules up front avoids possible problems later. At the very least, the coach might gain parental support when cheerleaders violate the rules because parents know their children were informed of the rules from the start.

Another way for a coach to ensure, and prove, that the cheerleading program has its cheerleaders' best interests in mind is to require each cheerleader to have a record of a physical examination on file. Sometimes the athletic office keeps all records of physical exams, and sometimes the coach holds onto them. Along with the physical exam record, another form that's beneficial to have on hand is a medical release form completed and signed by a parent or guardian. A sample medical release form is shown in figure 15.2. This document informs coaches of existing medical conditions and can be invaluable in case of an injury or ailment. A medical release form contains all the information a hospital or doctor needs to treat a patient, which can save time if parents or guardians can't be reached right away. Parents should be informed that an injured athlete won't be allowed to participate in the program until released by the doctor or trainer. It's also a good idea to share with parents or guardians the program's plan for handling injuries. Letting parents know an emergency plan is in place demonstrates that the coach is being proactive and planning ahead. Remember that all injuries need to be documented in case questions arise in the future. A sample emergency plan and injury report form are shown in figure 15.3.

At the parent–cheerleader meeting, the head coach should also share the coaching staff's expectations for students involved in cheerleading. Rules concerning attendance at practices, games, fund-raisers, and performances must be announced. Parents and cheerleaders need to understand the commitment required to be part of the cheerleading program. This means activities are planned around cheerleading responsibilities, if possible, or else consequences must result in fairness to others in the program.

Inherent Risks of Cheerleading

Cheerleading is reasonably safe as long as certain guidelines are followed, but there is the inherent risk of injury, as in any athletic activity. Cheerleading is an anaerobic/aerobic activity that includes jumping, stunting, motions, and tumbling. All physicals must be on file in the high school office and a medical card completed before you may participate in practices and games. Keep your coach informed of all injuries or chronic conditions.

Although the probability of injury is minimized if you practice correctly, there is always the possibility of an injury occurring. Injuries that can occur in cheerleading include, but are not limited to, blisters, muscle strains, ligament sprains, joint and muscle soreness, abrasions, contusions, stress fractures, broken bones, spinal cord injuries involving paralysis, and even death. However, with certain precautions, the possibility of such injuries can be greatly reduced. Be sure to consistently abide by these guidelines:

1. Never stunt or tumble unless a coach or coach's designee is present.
2. Always practice in the presence of a qualified coach.
3. Always warm up appropriately before cheering (practices and games) by jogging and stretching.
4. Do not attempt a stunt you do not know how to perform safely and which has not been checked off by the coach.
5. Always use attentive spotters when stunting.
6. Always cheer in an area free of obstructions.
7. Always use mats or a flat, grassy area until a stunt is mastered.
8. Do not stunt on uneven ground, wet surfaces, or concrete. Do not stunt in cold or rainy weather.
9. Never talk, laugh, or mess around when performing a stunt.
10. Report all injuries to the coach as soon as they occur.
11. Follow all trainer or doctor recommendations.
12. Lift weights and maintain proper conditioning to increase strength and guard against injuries.
13. Always wear shoes and clothing appropriate for cheerleading (no sweatpants, sweatshirts, or loose clothing).
14. Never wear jewelry of any kind when cheering (practices and games).
15. Never wear chew gum when cheering (practices and games).
16. Always keep hair pulled back from face and off shoulders (practices and games).
17. Keep all nails (including artificial) cut short so they can't be seen when looking at the palm.
18. Eat nutritious meals.
19. Get plenty of rest.
20. Ask for assistance or advice at any time.

I have read the preceding warning and guidelines. I thoroughly appreciate and understand the assumption of risks inherent in cheerleading participation. I acknowledge I am physically fit and am voluntarily participating in this activity.

Student signature _____ Date _____

Parent signature _____ Date _____

Figure 15.1 Inherent risk form.

Medical Release Form

Student's name _____ Grade _____

I certify that _____ is physically capable and able to fulfill requirements as an athlete at Mason City High School. I understand this form legally releases all obligations and responsibilities for the medical treatment of my son/daughter in the event of illness or injury during an athletic-related activity when either parent cannot be reached. If there is any physical or medical reason why he/she should not participate fully, the school requires a doctor's release to return to participation.

Parent/Guardian signature _____ Date _____

Medical Treatment Permission Form

In the event of an emergency occurring while my son/daughter is at a school-sponsored practice, performance, game, meet, or trip, I grant my permission to the school and its employees to take whatever action necessary. In the event I cannot be reached, I hereby authorize the school or its employees to give consent for my son/daughter to receive medical treatment.

Parent/guardian names _____

Address _____

Home phone _____ Cell phone _____

Father's place of work _____ Phone _____

Mother's place of work _____ Phone _____

Person to be notified (other than parent/guardian) in case of emergency:

Name _____ Relationship _____ Phone _____

Name _____ Relationship _____ Phone _____

Family doctor _____ Phone _____

Family dentist _____ Phone _____

If you **do not** grant permission or authorization for consent to medical treatment, what procedure should be followed? _____

_____

Insurance company _____ Policy number _____

Parent/guardian signature _____ Date _____

Medical Information

Heart condition or disease	Yes	No	Allergic to medication Yes	No	
Asthma	Yes	No	Convulsions	Yes	No
Diabetes	Yes	No	Allergic to insect stings	Yes	No

List all allergies _____

Date of last tetanus shot _____

Medications currently receiving _____

Additional medical information that may be helpful: _____

_____

Figure 15.2 Medical release form.

Creating an Emergency Plan

Medical Release Form

A release form is filled out for every participant.

Access to a Phone

911 emergency call sheet is filled out and posted by the phone (see below).

Assignments

Coach stays with injured person; remain calm and confident.

Designated person calls 911.

State name, emergency (what type of injury), specific location, directions.

Designated person calls parent(s).

State name, injury, name of hospital.

Designated person waits for ambulance and directs it to the proper area.

Designated person (if any) rides in the ambulance with injured athlete.

Coach fills out accident report.

Practice Emergency Plan

Determine placement of nearest phone.

Determine who will call 911.

Determine who will contact parents.

Determine who will meet the ambulance.

Determine who will ride in the ambulance.

911 Emergency Call

Hello, this is _____. I am calling because one of our athletes (**state injury**). We are located at (**school name**) at (**address**). We need an ambulance at (**location in school and directions**). We will have someone outside to meet you.

Police department phone _____

Fire department phone _____

Athletic Director phone _____

Injury Report Form

Injured person's name: _____

Date of injury: _____ Time of injury: _____am/pm

Name of supervisor: _____

Nature of injury (specify right or left): _____

_____

Location of accident: _____

_____

Description of accident: _____

_____

Actions taken: _____

_____

Signature: _____ Date: _____

Figure 15.3 Emergency plan and injury report form.

Calendars for the season, which list cheerleading duties, are a great help to parents, athletes, and coaches. By letting everyone know up front when events are scheduled, there are no excuses for other activities to be scheduled at the same time as cheerleading responsibilities. It's also a good idea to have a rules and regulations sheet for each parent and cheerleader to sign, much like the inherent risks form. At the bottom of the sheet they are asked to acknowledge that they have read, understood, and will abide by the rules and regulations of the cheerleading program. If a program has policies on who earns a letter and who doesn't, details about these policies should appear on the rules and regulation form.

Along with cheerleading responsibilities, expectations for the behavior of cheerleaders at practices, school, games, and in the community should be addressed. Remind people that the word "cheerleader" contains the word "leader." Following school rules and state laws is expected of students who have chosen to be leaders. The school's code of conduct policy should be read so that everyone is clear on the policy and the consequences for failing to comply with the code. If a school or program has rules about

grades and participation, these should also be shared with parents.

Parents also need to know about uniform, camp, competition, and other miscellaneous expenses for which cheerleaders and their families are responsible. Parents should have some idea about their payment responsibilities before their children even try out for the squad. Fundraising projects—which help offset expenses—are always appreciated, and this first meeting is a good time to request parental involvement. Having a couple of parents or guardians organize the fund-raising and other program activities frees the coach up for coaching duties.

Finally, coaches should let parents and guardians know they'd like to work together as a team. The coach should keep parents informed and share concerns as they occur, and they should encourage parents to do the same. It's a good idea for a coach to log all communication with parents in case repeated problems occur with the same cheerleader. The coach should answer any questions parents have before closing the meeting. The meeting should end with the coach thanking parents and cheerleaders for their support and attendance and expressing hopes for a great year.

Squad Expectations

Cheerleading squads usually need some guidance to function as a team. It helps to have a meeting just for the cheerleaders to set squad expectations before the season gets underway. This meeting can be held around the same time as the parent–cheerleader meeting. After the meeting, a fun activity can be planned, such as movie night, a sleepover, or another group activity.

Cheerleaders have already learned the coach's expectations for the season at the parent–cheerleader meeting, but they also need to have some intrasquad goals to prevent problems that might otherwise arise in the future. A team worksheet assists cheerleaders in talking about and documenting expectations for the team. A sample team worksheet is shown in figure 15.4. One cheerleader records the answers as each cheerleader answers each question. Once the sheet

is completed, all cheerleaders sign their names to indicate their agreement to follow the commitments listed. Whenever a squad is having problems, the coach can give the team their completed sheet and have them talk about each question again as they try to work through their issues.

Once the team worksheet is completed, the cheerleaders should read and sign a cheerleader's pledge (see figure 15.5). The pledge sheet lists expectations that cheerleaders agree to follow; it is their pledge to their team and coaches. Coaches should explain to the cheerleaders ahead of time what it means to sign their names to the piece of paper. Whether or not a person follows through with a promise is usually a clear indication of the person's character.

At the same meeting, cheerleaders should set individual goals. Give each cheerleader an index

Cheerleading Team Worksheet

1. Things I expect to gain from my experience this year include . . .

   _____

   _____

   _____

2. Things I expect to contribute to the squad include . . .

   _____

   _____

   _____

3. Things that bother me the most about behavior(s) of squad members include . . .

   _____

   _____

   _____

4. When problems arise on our squad we will handle them by . . .

   _____

   _____

   _____

5. Goals we would like to achieve this year include . . .

   _____

   _____

   _____

6. Obstacles we must overcome to achieve these goals include . . .

   _____

   _____

   _____

7. Ways we will overcome these obstacles include . . .

   _____

   _____

   _____

8. Commitments we will make to each other include . . .

   _____

   _____

   _____

Figure 15.4 Team worksheet.

Cheerleader's Pledge

I pledge . . .

To be drug, tobacco, and alcohol free.

To work at improving my cheerleading skills at all practices, games or meets, and performances.

To keep academics as my number one priority.

To be a positive leader and role model for my squad, school, and community.

To be someone others can count on as hardworking, dependable, helpful, and positive.

To keep myself in top physical shape by lifting weights, conditioning, and eating healthy.

To promote school spirit and sportsmanship in my words and actions.

To protect the integrity and reputation of the squad, our coaches, and my fellow cheerleaders.

To follow all rules, safety guidelines, and stunt progressions set up by my coaches.

To be the type of cheerleader I would like to coach.

Signature _____ Date _____

Signature _____ Date _____

Signature _____ Date _____

Signature _____ Date _____

Signature _____ Date _____

Signature _____ Date _____

Signature _____ Date _____

Signature _____ Date _____

Signature _____ Date _____

Signature _____ Date _____

Signature _____ Date _____

Signature _____ Date _____

Signature _____ Date _____

Figure 15.5 Cheerleader's pledge.

card on which to write three goals. Tell them one goal should deal with cheerleading, one with school, and one with their personal life. On the cards they should also specify how they will work to achieve their goals. For example, if the goal is to improve jumps, the cheerleader would explain what he or she is going to do to make this happen. Improving jumps might include working on leg strength by increasing the amount of weight lifted and performing 50 jumps each day. Tell them the index cards are theirs to keep—they can tape them to a mirror at home so they're reminded of their goals every day. At various times during the season, remind them of their goals and ask how close they are to achieving them.

Organizing Practices

To make the best use of practice time, coaches need a written plan. Consider creating a blank form listing elements of a practice. You can use these forms not only to organize practices, but for liability purposes as well. Documentation should show stunt progressions, injury and safety concerns, and dates of absences or nonparticipation. Notes on this form can help refresh memories if questions are asked. For example, if cheerleaders are absent on a day stunt progressions are checked, the next practice should note that these cheerleaders were checked off on this day. Any safety information given to cheerleaders should also be noted. These plans or schedules can be used in future years to better organize practices, especially if changes that should be made for improvement are noted in detail. A sample practice schedule is shown in figure 15.6.

There are many questions a coach ought to ask himself or herself when completing a written practice plan. When and where will practice be held? Ideally, one facility is reserved regularly for cheerleading practice. If not, do arrangements need to be made? What equipment is needed for practice? Some items to consider are mats, music equipment, and CDs or cassettes. A first-aid kit should be brought to every practice, so this wouldn't be considered special equipment. What will be the warm-up sequence? What skills or special events need to be practiced and how much time will be allotted to each? What conditioning will be done at the end of practice? What announcements need to be made? By answering these questions, a coach can develop organized practice plans.

For easy reference at practice, a coach needs only a clipboard, a binder, and a first-aid kit. The clipboard holds the practice plan, attendance roster, warm-up routine, and stunt check-off sheets. In the binder are calendars, past practice plans, cheerleaders' phone numbers, team and pledge sheets, signed rules and regulation sheets, emergency procedure information, medical release forms, injury reports, parent communication logs, and the cheerleading rules book. You can keep a first-aid kit in a small backpack. It's easy to carry and large enough to hold bandages, adhesive strips, wrapping tape, ointments, and so on. By using a clipboard, notebook, and backpack, all materials a coach needs during practice are kept close at hand. This is important since the coach must provide continual supervision for safety and liability purposes.

For practices to have maximum productivity, they must begin on time with everyone ready to practice. Holding practices on the same days and time each week cuts down on tardiness and absences. Well-organized practices need to last only two hours. For the first few practices of a season, practices might last two and a half hours because cheerleaders are just learning warm-up, jump, and overall practice routines. Every practice element should have a purpose and a time limit. Cheerleaders would stunt for an entire practice if you let them, so allotting a set amount of time for each activity helps keep them focused on the task. Cheerleaders learn quickly that if they waste time, stunts won't be practiced before it's time to move on. To make it easier to set time limits, time how long each element takes at an early practice. Plan practices

Practice Schedule

Date: _____

Equipment needed: _____

_____

Announcements

    1.

    2.

    3.

    4.

    5.

    6.

Goals for practice

    1.

    2.

    3.

    4.

Warm-up

    1. Jog/Form Running

    2. Stretches

Jumps

    1.

    2.

    3.

Skill Work

    Special events

    Motions/Poms

    Stunts/Tumbling

    Game/Meet material

Closing reminders

Weights

Absences

    1.

    2.

    3.

    4.

    5.

    6.

Sitting out of practice (reason)

    1.

    2.

    3.

    4.

Injuries/safety concerns

    1.

    2.

    3.

Practice revisions for future

    1.

    2.

    3.

    4.

Figure 15.6 Practice schedule.

with specific improvement goals in mind. Game skills to improve, detailed on the game evaluation form (figure 13.2, page 179), are a good place to find objectives for practices. Some other goals can be to add stunts or jumps to a cheer or chant, get ready for a cheer clinic or pep rally, improve motion technique, or learn a new stunt. Practices need to end on time with cheerleaders feeling that practice was beneficial and that they have accomplished their goals for the day.

A coach must be aware of squad frustration and take steps to revise a skill or change an activity as necessary. Sometimes simply leaving a stunt and coming back to it at a later practice takes care of the problem. To keep motivation high and prevent practices from becoming stagnant during a long season, look for ways to make practices enjoyable while still improving skills and preparing for games or competitions. Sometimes it's fun for squads to participate in a Cheerleading Olympics with events such as the highest toe touch, holding the longest liberty, and performing the most consecutive back handsprings. Old trophies can be awarded to the winners. Depending on the number of cheerleaders and years of experience, this event can be held for all cheerleaders at once or only for cheerleaders on each squad (freshman, sophomore, and so on). Another idea is to have cheerleaders arrive for practice, hear the announcements, and then leave after their jumps. This works particularly well during semester-test week.

Practice Essentials

There are many skills that can be worked on at a cheerleading practice, but all skills don't need to be addressed at each practice. Deciding which elements to practice depends on whether it's the beginning, middle, or end of a season and if there are upcoming special events. Dividing practice time up among elements ensures necessary skills are practiced and that cheerleaders don't run out of time. At the beginning of practice, practice goals should be read aloud, which allows cheerleaders to understand practice expectations.

All practices need to begin with a warm-up that includes an aerobic activity followed by stretching. Some coaches like to vary the stretching routine, but a set routine is faster and helps prevent wasted time. Seniors or varsity cheerleaders can lead stretches as all cheerleaders count out the stretches with them. Specific stretches are discussed later in this chapter under Conditioning.

Following warm-ups, cheerleaders can practice jumps and tumbling. There are several ways to improve jump technique and condition at the same time (refer to chapter 3). Jumps may be practiced using partners, lines, or group jumps to counts. However jumps are practiced, it's important that this time is used for critiquing and improving them, so monitor jumps and keep cheerleaders on task. Add variety to jump practice by one day having cheerleaders perform five side hurdlers on each leg, five pikes, five front hurdlers on each leg, five toe touches, and five combination jumps. The next practice cheerleaders can perform five tuck-toe touches, five pike-front hurdlers, and five combination jumps. One or two of the jump drills from chapter 3 can also be done at this time. After jumps, cheerleaders can move on to tumbling. Cheerleading practices typically don't provide enough time for cheerleaders to learn new tumbling skills, so they should work at perfecting an already learned skill, run through tumbling for timing, or add tumbling incorporations for an upcoming game.

Partner stunts and pyramids are the next skills to practice. Safety and spotting techniques must be taught and reviewed. Teaching of these skills should be documented on the practice plan. As stated earlier, cheerleaders need to begin with basic stunts and progress to more advanced stunts.

The last half of practice can be used for cheers, chants, motions, pom dances, and special events. Learning cheers, chants, and pom dances plus practicing motion technique are all skills that need to be addressed at the beginning of the season. New cheerleaders must learn the material, and veteran cheerleaders need to review. All squads can practice the school song, pom dances (eight-counts performed with the band), motion technique, and chants together. Cheerleaders should split into their individual squads when working on cheers unless they're performing a cheer together. During the middle and end of a season, creativity can be added to practices to keep motivation high. Cheerleaders can concentrate on using signs more often and organizing material to cover time-outs. They can be learning new chants, cheers, stunts, and dismounts. Jumps, stunts, and tumbling can be added to cheers and chants, and variety added to player introductions. If motion technique is slipping, time can be scheduled for motion improvement as well.

Sometimes cheerleaders need to practice for special events. Organizing the practice schedule to allow for this time means taking time away from other elements. Special events might include pep rallies, cheer clinics, local appearances, and team-building activities. As long as practices are organized, these events don't need to take up a lot of time. Many times familiar material is used, and cheerleaders simply need to be organized for the event.

Some conditioning should be included at the end of practice. Weight-training workouts can be alternated with other cardiovascular endurance training. For example, Monday and Wednesday can be weightlifting days, and Tuesday and Thursday can be cardio days with no lifting. Specific weight-training and other cardiovascular workouts are discussed later in this chapter under "Conditioning."

It's necessary for the coach to keep practices moving while providing quick water breaks throughout. Remain optimistic and enthusiastic, always looking for ways to motivate your cheerleaders. When ending practice, touch base with the cheerleaders collectively (as well as individually, if you feel it's necessary). A good time to remind your squad of upcoming events and make announcements is during cool-down stretching. Informing cheerleaders of improvements observed during practice provides positive reinforcement and ends practice on an upbeat note.

Risk Management

Risk management involves coaches anticipating and making changes before injuries occur. All safety rules should be consistently and immediately enforced. If cheerleaders are laughing during stunting, for instance, the coach should stop the squad at once and not allow them to stunt the rest of practice. Cheerleaders need to know the coach is serious about safety expectations. A record should be kept of cheerleaders who are reminded to remove jewelry, pull back hair, remove glitter, and cut nails. Repeated failure to comply with the rules needs to carry consequences if cheerleaders are going to learn to conform to safety regulations. Any communication with parents or guardians about rule breaking needs to be logged in case problems arise.

Practices should be held in an area free of distractions; this area should be checked for wet or slick spots, divots, and uneven ground. Any safety concerns and adaptations should be noted on the practice plan. Stunts must be practiced and performed on safe surfaces. If possible, practice at the location where actual cheering will occur so cheerleaders get accustomed to the surface.

It's important for the coach to know each cheerleader's medical history, which should be included on the physical exam records and medical release forms. Cheerleaders with asthma need to bring inhalers to practices and games. Glucose tablets and a glucagon kit, provided by the cheerleader or parent, should be kept in the first-aid kit for diabetic cheerleaders. Along with medical histories, the coach needs to know individual and squad physical abilities. Cheerleaders should not be asked to perform a skill if they're afraid or not in the proper condition to perform the skill safely. A coach also shouldn't allow squads to perform advanced stunts until they've mastered the lead-up stunts. A form, such as the one shown in figure 15.7, can be used to check off stunts in a progressive format. Mark the stunt responsibility (P for partner, B for base, and S for spotter) and the date the stunt was performed perfectly at least 10 times. Figure 15.8 illustrates a stunt check-off sheet with stunt responsibilities and the dates specific stunts were mastered. This type of sheet provides great documentation of steps taken to ensure cheerleader safety while stunting. When learning stunts, spotters need to be trained to understand their responsibilities. Four-corner spotting (see chapter 5) should be used until a stunt is mastered.

Stunt Check-Off Sheet

Name	Step-up	Date	Thigh stand	Date	Extension prep	Date	Cradle dismount	Date	Extension	Date	Basket toss	Date	Liberty	Date	Full-down dismount	Date

Figure 15.7   Stunt check-off sheet.

Record keeping is very important in athletic activities. Keep logs of injuries, doctor notes, practice plans, and check-off sheets. Store these records in a folder or binder for liability purposes. The statute of limitations for minors does not begin until they reach age 18 and are usually in effect for two years after that. Harassment issues must be dealt with immediately, and written records should be kept on these incidents as well. Most schools have policies covering harassment; a coach should know these policies and enforce them.

Through consistent rule enforcement, thorough documentation, and long-term record keeping, coaches can reduce the risk of cheerleading injuries and their own liability risk as well.

Detailed Stunt Check-Off Sheet

Name	Step-up	Date	Thigh stand	Date	Extension prep	Date	Cradle dismount	Date	Extension	Date	Basket toss	Date	Liberty	Date	Full-down dismount	Date
Alex	P	6/7	P	6/7												
	S	6/7	S	6/7	S	6/7										
	B	6/7	B	6/7	B	6/8										
Ali	P	6/7	P	6/7	P	6/8										
	S	6/7	S	6/7	S	6/7										
	B	6/7	B	6/7												
Anna	P	6/8	P	6/8												
	S	6/8	S	6/8	P	6/8										
	B	6/8	B	6/8	B	6/8										
Beth	P	6/7	P	6/7												
	S	6/7	S	6/7	S	6/8										
	B	6/7	B	6/7	B	6/7										
Bob	P	6/7	P	6/7												
	S	6/7	S	6/7	S	6/7										
	B	6/7	B	6/7	B	6/7	B	6/8								
Courtney	P	6/7	P	6/7	P	6/7										
	S	6/7	S	6/7	S	6/8	S	6/8	S	6/9						
	B	6/7	B	6/7	B	6/7										
Erin	P	6/7	P	6/7	P	6/7										
	S	6/7	S	6/7	S	6/8	P	6/8	P	6/9						
	B	6/7	B	6/7	B	6/8										
Grace	P	6/7	P	6/7	P	6/7										
	S	6/7	S	6/7	S	6/8	S	6/8								
	B	6/7	B	6/7												
Jen	P	6/7	P	6/7												
	S	6/7	S	6/7	S	6/7										
	B	6/7	B	6/7	B	6/7										
John	P	6/7	P	6/7												
	S	6/7	S	6/7	S	6/7										
	B	6/7	B	6/7	B	6/7	B	6/8	B	6/9						
Katie	P	6/7	P	6/7												
	S	6/7	S	6/7	P	6/7	P	6/8								
	B	6/7	B	6/7	B	6/7										

Figure 15.8   Detailed stunt check-off sheet.

Conditioning

As with any athletic activity, cheerleading requires participants to work on flexibility, cardiovascular endurance, and strength training. Improving these three components helps cheerleaders develop stronger skills and decrease their chance of injury. These conditioning components can and should be worked into a comprehensive practice schedule.

Flexibility

Stretching muscles before working out has many benefits. Stretching helps prevent injuries by relaxing muscle tightness, prepares the muscles for exercise, and increases flexibility. Flexibility through the joints allows muscles to move farther while expending less energy. Before any stretching, however, cheerleaders should be involved in some kind of light aerobic activity for at least five minutes to raise muscle temperature by increasing blood flow to the muscles. Once muscles are warmed up, it's time to stretch. Stretches aren't supposed to be painful—they should be held only to the point at which cheerleaders feel a stretch in the muscle. Muscles need to be stretched through their full range of motion to increase flexibility. A stretch should be held without bouncing. Bouncing causes muscles to contract rather than stretch, and it can also cause small tears in muscles. Cheerleaders shouldn't stretch muscles that are cold or tense because this also can result in muscle or tendon tears. Stretching shouldn't be performed on muscles over loose joints or on muscles that are injured.

It's important to stretch out all muscle groups and to stretch correctly. Stretches should be held for a 20- to 30-second count and repeated two to three times for each muscle group. A good rule to follow is the longer the muscle, the longer the stretch. Allow more time for stretching when practicing or performing in cold weather. To increase flexibility, stretches need to be done at least three days a week.

TRICEPS STRETCH

- Lift arms above head.
- Pull right elbow down behind back with left hand (see figure 15.9).
- Hold stretch.
- Change arms and repeat stretch.

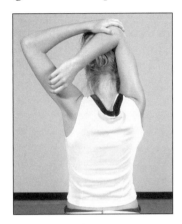

Figure 15.9 Triceps Stretch.

SHOULDER FLEXIBILITY STRETCH

- Clasp hands behind back.
- Lean over and pull arms overhead (see figure 15.10).
- Hold stretch.

Figure 15.10 Shoulder Flexibility Stretch.

CALF STRETCH

- Stand facing a wall with both hands flat on the wall.
- Both feet are a few feet back from the wall.
- Toes are pointing toward the wall.
- Keeping heels on the ground, lean hips forward (see figure 15.11).
- Hold stretch and repeat.

Tip: When repeating the stretch, right foot can be back and stretch held, and then left foot.

Figure 15.11   Calf Stretch.

SHIN STRETCH

- Stand pigeon-toed.
- Lift toes up and down 20 times.

Tip: Use muscles in front of leg to lift toes; don't rock back.

TOE-TOUCH STRETCH

- Stand with feet in a wide, double lunge and hands on thighs.
- Keeping back straight, bend knees, and push hips to the floor.
- Hold stretch.

QUADRICEPS STRETCH

- Place one hand on the wall and grasp right ankle.
- Pull heel and knee toward gluteus (see figure 15.12).
- Hold stretch.
- Change legs and repeat stretch.

Tip: Keep thigh in line with the body.

Figure 15.12   Quadriceps Stretch.

HIPS/GLUTEUS STRETCH

- Sit on floor with right leg straight out in front.
- Bend left knee and place left foot flat on the floor to the right of outstetched leg.
- Push against right leg with outside of left ankle while right leg resists.
- Hold stretch.
- Switch legs and repeat stretch.

FRONT HURDLER STRETCH

- Standing close to a wall, place heel of right leg as high up on the wall as possible.
- Lean body in toward wall and feel stretch in hamstring (see figure 15.13).

Figure 15.13   Front Hurdler Stretch.

- Hold stretch.
- Change legs and repeat stretch.

HIP-FLEXOR STRETCH

- Step forward with right foot and bend right knee.
- Place palms of both hands on floor in front of body.
- Stretch left leg straight out behind body.
- Lean chest toward right knee as hips are pushed toward floor (see figure 15.14).
- Feel stretch in left hip flexor and hold stretch.
- Switch legs and repeat stretch.

WRIST-FLEXION STRETCH

- Hold right arm straight; bend wrist so right palm faces body.
- Use left hand to press back of right hand toward body (see figure 15.15).
- Hold stretch.
- Change hands and repeat stretch.

Figure 15.15   Wrist-Flexion Stretch.

WRIST-EXTENSION STRETCH

- Kneel on the floor.
- Place both hands, palms down, flat on the floor.
- Keeping elbows straight, lean forward (see figure 15.16).
- Hold stretch.

Tip: This position can also be used for wrist-flexion stretches. The only difference is palms are up instead of down.

Figure 15.14   Hip Flexor Stretch.

Figure 15.16   Wrist-Extension Stretch.

TORSO TWIST

- Sit on floor with left leg straight out in front.
- Bend right knee and place right foot flat on the floor to the left of outstretched leg.
- Place right hand on floor behind body.
- Place left arm or elbow on outside of right leg.
- Twist torso while pushing against right leg with left arm or elbow (see figure 15.17).
- Hold stretch.
- Switch legs and arms and repeat stretch.

Figure 15.17   Torso Twist.

PNF Stretching

Proprioceptive neuromuscular facilitation (PNF) involves contracting and stretching specific muscle groups. PNF stretching is a good way to increase flexibility and muscle strength. Cheerleaders need a partner during PNF stretching; partners communicate so that muscles are not overstretched. To avoid injury, range of motion should not be exceeded during the stretch.

The steps for PNF stretching are stretch, hold, relax, and repeat. This same procedure is used each time a muscle group is stretched using PNF techniques:

- The partner holds the limb to be stretched.
- The partner pushes the cheerleader's limb to the point of stretch.

- While the partner pushes, the cheerleader contracts the muscle for a slow 6 to 10 count.
- The cheerleader relaxes the muscle, and the partner pushes the limb to the point of stretch again (which is usually farther than the first time).
- Repeat stretch three times.
- After the last stretch, the cheerleader relaxes the muscle, and the partner pushes the limb a little farther before returning it to the resting position.

PNF HAMSTRING STRETCH

- Cheerleader being stretched lies back on the floor with both legs straight out.
- Cheerleader on floor lifts one leg straight up in the air.
- Partner holds lifted leg around knee (to keep it straight) and on back of ankle (see figure 15.18).
- Partner pushes leg back to point of stretch.
- Cheerleader on floor resists stretch.
- Partner relaxes push, then slowly stretches leg farther back to the point of stretch.
- Repeat two times.
- End with a stretch after last relaxation.
- Repeat stretch with other leg.

Tip: Hips should remain flat on the floor.

Figure 15.18   PNF Hamstring Stretch.

PNF ADDUCTOR/GROIN STRETCH

- Cheerleader being stretched sits on the floor with the soles of feet together.
- Cheerleader being stretched pulls soles of the feet in as close as comfortable to the body.
- Partner puts a hand on the inside of each knee and pushes down while cheerleader resists bringing knees up.

- Partner relaxes push, then slowly stretches knees farther down to the point of stretch.
- Repeat two times.
- End with a stretch after the last relaxation.

Tip: Cheerleader being stretched needs to keep back straight.

Weight Training

One of the most overlooked aspects of conditioning in most cheerleading programs is weight training. Proper weight training has many benefits for cheerleaders, allowing for improvement of skills such as jumps, motions, stunts, and tumbling. Weight training improves the efficiency of a cheerleader's performance by increasing muscle endurance and flexibility, strengthening muscles and bones, and improving balance. Cheerleaders can also decrease their chance of injury by lifting weights. If injuries do occur, the recovery is much faster for a cheerleader who lifts weights and stays in condition. Weightlifting is anaerobic in nature, so it can also help cheerleaders prepare for the short bursts of energy they'll need while cheering. Many times cheerleaders aren't weight training because coaches are unfamiliar with lifting weights themselves. Cheer coaches should find a knowledgeable coach, teacher, or trainer to help design a weight program specifically for cheerleading. During weight training, it's important to focus on muscles used in cheerleading so skills are improved.

To get the maximum benefits from weight training, cheerleaders need to warm up before lifting weights and to lift with correct technique. Cheerleaders can tear muscles if they're not warmed up, if they lift with incorrect technique, or if they lift too much weight. For safety, spotters should always be in position to assist lifts. Cheerleaders won't be as tempted to use poor lifting technique or to return a weight that's too heavy if spotters are assisting. A slow, smooth, controlled movement that works muscles through their full range of motion is the correct form to use when lifting. To keep movements smooth, elbows and knees shouldn't lock out at the top of lifts; doing so can cause injuries. Bouncing or swinging weights into position doesn't increase strength and could cause an injury. Starting with lower weights and gradually increasing weight makes it easier for cheerleaders to use correct form and maintain balance. Another way to balance and focus is by looking straight ahead during lifts. Cheerleaders should exhale during the lift phase (muscle contraction) and inhale during the return phase of a rep (a rep equals one lift). Large muscle groups are worked first during a weight-training session, followed by smaller muscle groups.

To find the correct lifting weight for each muscle group, cheerleaders need to find their "max" at each station. The max (short for "maximum") is the amount of weight a cheerleader can lift a single time only (i.e., further lifts are impossible at the same weight). A thorough weight-training program would use a percentage of the max to calculate the amount of weight to lift at each station. If this is too difficult, cheerleaders who want to increase strength should find a weight at each station that they can lift for only 6 to 10 reps. If the weight can't be lifted six times, the weight is too heavy and should be decreased. On the other hand, if the weight can be lifted more than 10 times, the weight is too light and should be increased. Each weightlifting station should comprise three sets of 6 to 10 reps. Rotating lifting with spotting gives cheerleaders a chance to rest between sets.

Cheerleaders ought to be lifting weights year-round, not just during the season. In fact, the off-season is the most important time to lift weights to gain strength. During the off-season, cheerleaders should lift at least three days a week. During the season, they should lift at least two days a week. There are many weight-training programs available for developing strength and preventing injuries. Coaches should use a routine that meets their cheer-leading program's needs while taking into account the availability of facilities and equipment.

The weight-training program shown in figure 15.19 is intended to be used two days a week. It has exercises designed to work on core strength to improve stability, balance, and twisting move-ments. Core exercises also work leg muscles used in jumps, stunts, and tumbling. Cheerleaders would first record their max at each station. A percentage of the max would then be used to calculate the amount of weight to lift at each station. On one day of the week, cheerleaders would focus on muscles that pull, and on the other day they would focus on muscles that push. Depending on the weight program being used, cheerleaders might lift at 70 percent of their max during the first week, 80 percent of their max during the second week, 85 percent of their max during the third week, 90 percent of their max during the fourth week, and the fifth week they would start the rotation over again. Once the weights are computed, cheerleaders need simply to follow the weights listed on their sheets each day and each week. If the weight at a station becomes too easy to lift, they should lift their max again and refigure their percentages.

Weight-Conditioning Program

Name: _____

Day 1	Max	Week ___ Sets	Weight	Week ___ Sets	Weight	Week ___ Sets	Weight	Week ___ Sets	Weight
Hang clean		3 × 6		3 × 4		3 × 5		3 × 3	
Hang snatch		3 × 6		3 × 4		3 × 5		3 × 3	
Back squat		3 × 10		3 × 6		3 × 8		3 × 4	
Lunges		3 × 10		3 × 6		3 × 8		3 × 6	
Gluteals/hamstrings		3		3		3		3	
Hyperextension		2		2		2		2	
Abdominals		2		2		2		2	

Day 2	Max	Sets	Weight	Sets	Weight	Sets	Weight	Sets	Weight
Snatch squat		3 × 10		3 × 6		3 × 8		3 × 4	
Front squat		3 × 10		3 × 6		3 × 8		3 × 4	
Incline press		3 × 10		3 × 6		3 × 8		3 × 4	
Push jerks		3 × 10		3 × 6		3 × 8		3 × 4	
Dips		3		3		3		3	
Gluteals/hamstrings		3		3		3		3	
Reverse hyperextension		2		2		2		2	

Figure 15.19 Weight-conditioning program.

HANG CLEAN

- Bar is held with a wide overhand grip and straight arms.
- Knees bend so bar touches thighs; shoulders are over the bar (see figure 15.20a).
- To lift, jump up and straighten back while shrugging shoulders and pulling up the bar.
- The body is pulled under the bar; the bar is kept close to the body.
- Elbows rotate up and out.
- The bar is caught at shoulder level as the squat position is hit (see figure 15.20b).

Figure 15.20a Beginning position of Hang Clean.

Figure 15.20b Squat position of Hang Clean.

- Knees go over the feet but not past the toes during the squat.
- Feet are kept flat on the floor with the back straight and chest up.
- Return bar to starting position and repeat lift.

Tip: Bar should be pulled up in a straight path.

HANG SNATCH

- Bar is held with a wide overhand grip and straight arms.
- Knees bend so the bar touches the thigh; shoulders are over the bar.
- To lift, jump up and straighten back.
- Pull bar up by shrugging shoulders and pulling body under the bar.
- The bar is caught overhead with arms locked and extended as the full squat position is hit.
- Squat up to standing position with knees over the feet but not past the toes; heels stay on floor.
- Return bar to starting position and repeat lift.

BACK SQUAT

- Bar is placed high across the upper back and shoulders and held with an overhand grip (see figure 15.21a).

Figure 15.21a Beginning position of Back Squat.

- Feet are shoulder-width apart and angled slightly outward.
- Bend knees and lower hips until thighs are parallel to the floor (see figure 15.21b).
- Knees go over the feet but not past the toes during the squat.
- Feet remain flat on the floor with back straight and chest up.
- Return to starting position by driving the bar upward.
- Repeat lift.

Figure 15.21b Squatting position of Back Squat.

LUNGES

- While standing, hold bar with an overhand grip on the upper back and shoulders; feet are together.
- Take a long step forward with one foot hitting heel to toe until foot is flat.
- Front knee bends until back knee almost hits the ground and the front thigh is parallel to the ground (see figure 15.22).
- Return to starting position by straightening the forward leg and stepping back.
- Repeat by stepping forward with the alternate leg.

Tip: Keep back straight and chest up during lunge. Front knee does not go past the toes.

Figure 15.22 Lunges.

GLUTEALS/HAMSTRINGS

- Begin with knees resting against front pad (see figure 15.23a).
- Lower legs are on the lower pads and ankles under the rollers.

Figure 15.23a Starting position of Gluteals/Hamstrings.

- Bend at the waist and straighten legs to lower body until parallel to the ground (see figure 15.23b).
- Raise body back up by bending knees and keeping hips straight.
- Return to starting position, hold briefly, and repeat.

Tip: Rollers are close to front pad for maximum benefits.

Figure 15.24a   Extended position of Hyperextension.

Figure 15.23b   Parallel position of Gluteals/Hamstrings.

HYPEREXTENSION

- Begin with upper thighs resting against the front pad.
- Lower legs are on lower pads and ankles under rollers.
- With hands across chest, lift upper body until it is extended (see figure 15.24a).
- Bend at the waist and lower body until almost perpendicular to the ground (see figure 15.24b).
- Return to starting position, hold briefly, and repeat.

Tip: Keep head in line with spine.

Figure 15.24b   Perpendicular position of Hyperextension.

ABDOMINALS HANG

- Hang from a bar with legs hanging down and hands shoulder-width apart (see figure 15.25a).
- Slowly lift knees up to chest without swinging up (see figure 15.25b).
- Return to starting position and repeat.

Figure 15.25a Beginning position of Abdominals Hang.

Figure 15.25b Ending position of Abdominals Hang.

SNATCH SQUAT

- Stand with bar lifted overhead using a wide overhand grip.
- Place feet in a wide stance with each foot angled outward.
- Bar is behind head with arms locked out (see figure 15.26a).

- Squat down until thighs are parallel to floor.
- Knees should bend over feet but not past toes during the squat (see figure 15.26b).
- Feet remain flat on floor with back straight and chest up.
- Straighten knees until legs are straight to return to starting position.
- Repeat lift.

Tip: Don't lean forward or push hips back.

Figure 15.26a Beginning position of Snatch Squat.

Figure 15.26b Squatting position of Snatch Squat.

FRONT SQUAT

- Stand with feet shoulder-width apart and angled outward.
- Back is straight and chest up.
- Hold bar with an overhand grip; elbows are bent.
- Bar is held in front of shoulders on upper chest (see figure 15.27).
- Squat until thighs are parallel to ground.
- Knees go over feet but not past toes during the squat.
- Return to starting position and repeat lift.

Tip: Keep feet flat on the floor during the lift.

Figure 15.27 Front Squat.

INCLINE PRESS

- Lie on bench that is inclined at a 30- to 40-degree angle.
- Keeping back flat on the bench, grasp the bar with an overhand grip a little wider than shoulder-width apart (see figure 15.28).
- Bend knees and keep feet flat on the floor.

Figure 15.28 Incline Press.

- Lift bar up and then lower it until it touches the upper chest.
- Slowly push bar back to starting position.
- Repeat lift.

Tip: Don't arch the back or bounce the weight off the chest.

PUSH JERK

- The bar is held in an overhand grip across upper chest and in front of shoulders (see figure 15.29).
- Hands on bar are slightly wider than shoulder-width apart.
- Feet are about shoulder-width apart and angled outward.
- Bend knees and then explode upward, straightening legs and pushing bar (see figure 15.29b).
- Arms are completely locked out above head.

Tip: Push upward from the heels, not from the balls of the feet.

Figure 15.29a   Beginning position of Push Jerk.

Figure 15.29b   Lifting position of Push Jerk.

DIPS

- Facing the machine, grip bar handles with fingers on the outside and palms facing toward the body.
- Jump off the ground and hold body up on bars with straight, locked arms.
- Bend elbows, keeping them close to the sides while slowly lowering body.
- Knees are in front of body and slightly bent.
- Lower body until upper arms are parallel to floor (or until lower chest is at bar level).
- Pause, then straighten arms to push back up to starting position.

Tip: Don't let the body swing when pushing back up. Control the up-and-down motion.

REVERSE HYPEREXTENSION

- Begin in a sitting position with ankles hooked under rollers and gluteus on pad.
- Cross arms across chest and lie back until body is parallel to ground (see figure 15.30).
- Bend at waist pulling body upward until it is perpendicular to ground.

Tip: Lie back as far as possible while still maintaining control.

Figure 15.30   Reverse Hyperextension.

If a weight room isn't available, it's still possible to weight train. Plyometrics (see chapter 3) and walking or jogging up bleacher steps are great ways to increase leg strength. Lunges can be performed by holding dumbbells at the sides or without weights at all. Squats, wall sits, and calf raises can also be performed with or without dumbbells to work the lower body. Push-ups and handstand push-ups can increase arm strength. Triceps can be worked by lowering the body using benches or chairs. Crunches or ab exercises with medicine balls or exercise balls can also be done outside of a weight room.

WALL SITS

- Stand with back against a wall.
- Feet are about two feet from the wall.
- Slowly slide body down to a sitting position with thighs parallel to floor (see figure 15.31).
- Hold for 30 to 60 seconds.
- Repeat four times.

Tip: Move feet as needed to make sure thighs are parallel to floor.

Figure 15.31   Wall Sits.

PUSH-UPS

- Lie face down with palms and toes on floor; hands are shoulder-width apart.
- Lift body to a straight, extended position.
- Slowly bend arms and lower body until almost touching the floor; arms are at a 90-degree angle.
- Straighten arms and push back up.
- Perform 10 to 15 reps for three sets.

Tip: Don't bend at the waist; keep hips in line with rest of body. Keep abdominals tight throughout the push-up.

TRICEPS DIPS

- Sit on a chair or bench with legs extended out in front.
- Place hands with fingers facing backward and palms on edge of chair.
- Lift body slightly off edge of chair.
- Lower body down until elbows are in line with shoulders; don't bounce.
- Straighten arms and push body back up.
- Perform 10 to 15 reps for three sets.

ABS WORKOUT WITH EXERCISE BALL

- Lie back on an exercise ball until back and thighs are parallel to ground.
- Feet are flat on floor and hands behind head or across chest.
- Tuck chin and slowly contract abdominals to lift upper body to about a 45-degree angle.
- Return to starting position and repeat.

Tip: Don't jerk the body up; slowly bring upper body up using abdominal muscles.

ABS WORKOUT WITH MEDICINE BALL

- Lie flat on floor with legs raised straight up.
- Partner places a medicine ball between lifter's legs.
- Slowly drop legs down and then raise them back up while continuing to hold the ball between legs.
- Repeat.

CRUNCHES

- Lie with back and feet flat on floor, knees bent, and arms crossed over chest.
- Curl upper body toward knees without moving lower body.
- Lift shoulder blades as high off the ground as possible by tightening abdominal muscles.
- Slowly lower body to starting position.
- Repeat.

Cardiovascular Endurance

Cardiovascular endurance conditioning can be performed at the end of practice right before cool-down stretches. Although cheerleading is more anaerobic in nature, with its short bursts of activity, cheerleaders still need a solid endurance base to meet normal physical fitness requirements. Cardio conditioning prepares cheerleaders for cheering entire games and assists their performance of chants, cheers, jumps, and stunts. Cheerleaders could do aerobic activities such as jogging (10 minutes or one mile), dancing, jumping rope, swimming, or form running (crossovers, high skips, leaps, seat kicks, back pedals, carioca). After cheerleaders have built up a good cardio base, it might be fun for them to play soccer or volleyball after practice.

Stretching at the end of practice as part of a cool-down reduces muscle soreness. Cooldown stretching allows lactic acid, which causes muscle soreness, to be removed more rapidly. By stretching after workouts, cheerleaders increase flexibility and return to their normal resting state more quickly.

Summary

Organized practices lead to productive and efficient use of participants' time. For this reason, the quality of practices is more important than the quantity of practices. Holding numerous practices without accomplishing much won't make cheerleaders better. Planning ahead with strategies to improve skills helps practices run smoothly and ensures that all goals are achieved. Components need to be infused into practices to improve cheerleaders' physical conditioning, which in turn enhances skill technique. Cardiovascular endurance, flexibility, and strength training are all important aspects that need to be part of a comprehensive cheerleading practice. Conditioning helps cheerleaders increase overall fitness and skill technique and reduces chance of injury. By taking a little extra time to plan, coaches can ensure their cheerleaders are getting maximum benefits from practices and conditioning programs.

index

Note: The italicized *f* and *t* following page numbers refer to figures and tables, respectively.

about the authors

Justin Carrier is director of curriculum for the National Cheerleading Association (NCA). In this role he is responsible for training materials, manuals, books, and curriculum for youth, high school, all-star, and college levels. He has appeared in many of the NCA's training videos and speaks regularly at coaching clinics around the country. Carrier is head instructor for many of the Southern Methodist University and NCA camps, and he personally trains more than 5,000 athletes and 400 high school coaches each summer. In addition, he created and developed the coaches certification program for the NCA from 2000 to 2004 and coauthored the curriculum for the safety programs of both the United States All Star Federation (USASF) and the National Council for Spirit Safety and Education (NCSSE).

Carrier has coached high school and all-star teams to more than 16 NCA national titles. In 2000 he was named NCA Top Head Instructor and won Innovative Choreography Awards each year from 1999 to 2004 for displaying the best choreography at nationals. He is a committee member for the USASF and a former member of the NCSSE.

Carrier resides in Dallas, Texas.

Donna McKay has coached high school cheerleaders for 20 years. She has served on the Spirit Rules Committee of the National Federation of State High School Associations (NFHS), on the Spirit Advisory Board of the National Spirit Group (NSG), and twice as president of the Iowa Cheerleading Coaches' Association. McKay was named the National Federation Section IV Coach of the Year in 1997 and received the NCCC National Outstanding Cheerleading Service of the Year Award in 1995. She compiled a cheerleading handbook, which was distributed to all Iowa high schools, and has twice revised the NCA Coaches Manual.

Her cheer squads and program have earned numerous national distinctions, including recognition as one of the NCA's Best of the Best and an NCA Top 1000 Squad, as well as selection to cheer at the McDonald's All-American Basketball Game on ESPN. Her squads have won two state championships, been awarded four Sportsmanship Trophies at boys' state basketball tournaments, and consistently received Distinguished Academic Achievement Awards. Almost 80 cheerleaders from McKay's squads have been selected to Iowa All-State Squads. She has judged competitions since 1993, speaks at conferences, and coordinates the NCA/NDA National Coaches' and Directors' Conferences. McKay holds an MSE degree in educational administration. She is a teacher and coach in Mason City, Iowa.

*You'll find
other outstanding
cheerleading resources at*

www.HumanKinetics.com

In the U.S. call

1-800-747-4457

Australia..08 8277 1555
Canada...1-800-465-7301
Europe..+44 (0) 113 255 5665
New Zealand.......................................0064 9 448 1207

HUMAN KINETICS
The Premier Publisher for Sports & Fitness
P.O. Box 5076 • Champaign, IL 61825-5076 USA